D1289374

ABOUT THE AUTHOR

DUSTY BUNKER is the author of books on numerology, astrology, and dreams along with a three-book mystery series: The Number Mysteries. She has studied metaphysical subjects for more than 40 years, wrote a dream column for the *Manchester Union Leader* and a numerology column for *Mademoiselle* magazine, and contributed to the bestselling Time-Life book series, *Mysteries of the Unknown*. DUSTY also did some consulting for the American Movie Classics (AMC) six-hour television mini-series, *The Prisoner*. She maintains a busy practice today.

NUMEROLOGY AND YOUR FUTURE

A	B	R	A	C	A	D	A	B	R	A
1	2	9	1	3	1	4	1	2	9	1
3	2	1	4	4	5	5	3	2	1	
5	3	5	8	9	1	8	5	3		
8	8	4	8	1	9	4	8			
7	3	3	9	1	4	3				
1	6	3	1	5	7					
7	9	4	6	3						
7	4	1	9							
2	5	1								
7	6									
13										

THE PREDICTIVE POWER OF NUMBERS

DUSTY BUNKER

REDFeather™

MIND | BODY | SPIRIT

4880 Lower Valley Road, Atglen, PA 19310

This book is for
SKIP *and* **MATT**

Numerology and the Divine Triangle with Faith Javane
ISBN: 978-0-9149-1810-3

Astrology's Hidden Aspects: Quintiles and Sesquiquintiles
ISBN: 978-0-7643-5543-1

The Beginner's Guide to Astrology: Class Is in Session
ISBN: 978-0-7643-5330-7

Birthday Numerology with Victoria Knowles
ISBN: 978-0-9149-1839-4

Numerology, Astrology, and Dreams
ISBN: 978-0-9149-1874-5

Quintiles and Tredeciles
ISBN: 978-0-9149-1869-1

Designed by Danielle D. Farmer
Cover design by Ashley Millhouse

Cover image by Greg Jeanneau on Unsplash
Type set in Neutra Text/Orpheus Pro/Times New Roman

ISBN: 978-0-7643-6035-0
Printed in China

Published by Red Feather Mind, Body, Spirit
An imprint of Schiffer Publishing, Ltd.
4880 Lower Valley Road
Atglen, PA 19310
Phone: (610) 593-1777; Fax: (610) 593-2002
E-mail: Info@schifferbooks.com
Web: www.redfeathermbs.com

For our complete selection of fine books on this and related subjects, please visit our website at www.schifferbooks.com. You may also write for a free catalog.

Schiffer Publishing's titles are available at special discounts for bulk purchases for sales promotions or premiums. Special editions, including personalized covers, corporate imprints, and excerpts, can be created in large quantities for special needs. For more information, contact the publisher.

We are always looking for people to write books on new and related subjects. If you have an idea for a book, please contact us at proposals@schifferbooks.com.

*"The invention of numerals
is perhaps the greatest abstraction the human
mind has ever created."*

—AMIR ACZEL
author of seventeen books
on mathematics and science

CONTENTS

PART II: YOUR TIME MACHINE

CONTENTS

CONTENTS

INTRODUCTION

IT'S JUNE 2019 AS I SUBMIT THIS SECONND EDITION TO MY PUBLISHER. Egads! Forty years have passed since I wrote the original version of this book in 1979. One thing that has definitely changed is the tools with which I write. Can you believe that, way back then, this book was written on my Smith-Corona portable typewriter on my ironing board? I have a hard time believing that!

I can only marvel at my persistence back then because every change that was made in the paper manuscript required an insert such as page 32-A or page 145-A and -B, ad infinitum. I certainly wasn't able to retype the entire book every time a new thought or a change was required halfway through; therefore, page inserts became my lifeline for an entire year. The finished manuscript was then mailed by Return Receipt in a securely wrapped cardboard box with multitudes of inserts. I kept a paper copy at home . . . just in case.

When my publisher called in 2015 asking me to update this book for a new edition, he also asked if I had the disks of the original manuscript that we could use. It was then I was reminded of how old I was. There were no disks in 1979 . . . there were no personal computers in 1979 . . . there was just me and my portable typewriter. The only answer to his request was to sit down at my desk and retype the entire manuscript . . . which I have done. I can now type 90 words a minute! Not without some typos, I must add.

If you're wondering what I was doing between my publishers request in the fall of 2015 and today, the spring of 2019, I wasn't twiddling my thumbs, eating bonbons, and watching the baseball games. Well, I do watch every baseball game. However, during those intervening years, two more books emerged from this desk: in 2017, *The Beginner's Guide to Astrology: Class Is in Session*, and in 2018, *Astrology's Hidden Aspects: Quintiles and Sesquiquintiles*.

Back to this book. During this rewrite, I realized how I have grown through the years, along with my equipment. First, in the early 1980s, I graduated from my ironing board to my first official desk—a proud moment. Although, the ironing board *was* convenient: I could move it from room to room, around the high chairs and toys as the moment demanded, and I could sit or stand depending upon the condition of my body. Raising four children can be tiring. My hackles rise when a woman says, "I don't work. I stay at home with the kids." A sign hangs in my kitchen that says: "A mother is a working woman!" Okay, I'm off that soap box . . . for now.

I eventually bought my first computer in order to write subsequent books—a computer that could store only ten pages of a document, and these documents were stored on floppy disks. Do you remember floppy disks? Writing a 300-page book required many documents and many floppy disks. And the bulbous cube-shaped computer with green lettering on a 10-inch black screen required more desk space.

Time progressed; the computer became slimmer as I became more bulbous. Funny how that happens. Now I work before a 24-inch monitor with a background and lettering any color I choose, and a tower nearby that can store a "gazillion" pages on a thumb drive! And when I'm done with this book, I can attach it to an email and send it over the air waves hundreds of miles away to my publisher. It's magic!

The changes in technology over the past thirty-five years have been truly amazing. In my childhood, I marveled at the comic strip hero, Dick Tracy, who communicated with his chief at headquarters through his wristwatch. That strip was introduced in the *Detroit Mirror* in October 1931 and is still running today. As kids, we all thought this was so cool and sci-fi. Most adults passed it off as fantasy.

But . . . here I am in 2019 updating this book, at a time when Dick Tracy's wristwatch became a reality with the news in 2013 that about 100 product designers at Apple were working on a computer wristwatch. Back then, they said this wristwatch would work like an iPhone and iPad and be able to send messages around the world! Dick Tracy's creator, Chester Gould, was a man way ahead of his time!

The law of physics states the only constant is change . . . which brings me back to this book.

Rewriting this book turned out to be a blessing. I realized revisions and changes and updates needed to be done. So, here I sit at my computer with the ability to insert and move paragraphs around with the touch of a few key strokes (I'm totally in awe). I am rewriting portions of this book in order to streamline, bring clarity to, and update the information, as well as adding new thoughts and—gulp—forecasts for the 2020 decade and the new millennium.

In the midst of my retyping frenzy, I also had the luxury of taking this information to bed with me at night and then waking up in Fitzgerald's "real dark night of the soul" at three o'clock in the morning with "aha!" moments. I am excited to bring back a few of those moments in the form of numerology techniques that I have researched more thoroughly, including your birthday color and your birthday gift. I'm also presenting, in a section titled Let's Call It What It Is, a new way of looking at the sacred history of the vowels and consonants in our language and in your name. All of this is presented here for your consideration.

As I wrote in the Introduction to another one of my books, *Numerology, Astrology, and Dreams*, "The danger of the written word is that ideas freeze in time." So, my first impulse when beginning to rewrite this book was to keep the original Introduction.

However, upon second thought that information reflects who I was at that time in my life. As we grow, we encompass more of life through our daily experiences and our personal methods of education. Therefore, our knowledge increases and hopefully, to paraphrase fiction writer Lawrence Alexander, the depth of understanding accompanies the accumulation of that knowledge. I did find that much of that earlier introduction stands today because of the basic truths therein. However, this new Introduction is enriched with thoughts that have accumulated over the years.

It you've ever wondered about those people who always seem to be in the right place at the right time doing the right thing—enjoying romantic loving relationships, raising happy children, making money, getting ahead in business, and taking yearly vacations—and wonder what it is that makes them different from those less successful people around them, perhaps you should look to the numbers.

We cannot believe that certain people are selected above all others in some mysterious manner to be successful and happy, while others are relegated to less fulfilling lives. If this were true, there would be no purpose to life and we would be merely robots, machines that function according to a set of predetermined instructions, carrying out orders from a higher authority with no will or goals of our own.

Marilyn Ferguson in *The Brain Revolution* (Bantam Books, 1973) stated that the human being is "astonishingly vulnerable to light, to magnetic fields, free electricity, and extraterrestrial forces," and that the human brain "responds to a sea of radiation, and by its [the brain's] responses control [our] every function."

We are indeed subject to the energies around us just as a flower responds to the warmth of the sun and the cool of evening. However, rather than accepting this theory as a denial of free will, I choose to believe that time is not linear but elliptical and if we survive after death then we must have lived before birth. Nature and our solar system and the heavens teach us that life is cyclical.

If this is the case, we may choose our moment to be born, riding in on a frequency that reflects our past and knowing full well the future pattern we have selected for ourselves. Having chosen, once we are born we have to live within a certain framework, which is controlled to a degree by our birth pattern and its ensuing cycles as well as our culture and place of birth. However, I believe we do have free will and we do have choices, and it is by our free will and right to choose that we determine the rewards we receive as the result of our efforts.

Many people succeed admirably because they have, along with determination and a will to achieve, a keen sense of timing. They know what they want to do and why, but most critically, when! The intent of this book is to show you how important timing is, and how you can use your number cycles to succeed in positive ways.

For instance, while you are experiencing a quiet introspective period, your mate may be in an outgoing social cycle. Rather than accuse him of being a social gadfly while you are accused of being a stick-in-the-mud, some understanding of your separate states of mind can help you cooperate with each other more lovingly to avoid unnecessary unhappiness.

Your child may be going through a cycle that requires a quiet space and the room to learn. It would be wonderful if you know when that cycle occurs. You could then help by taking her to the beach or on a hiking trip into the mountains, or by buying more books and allowing her time by herself to read, or perhaps by taking her on a trip to the museum or the theater.

Think of the situations that could arise when knowledge of your personal cycles is invaluable: a business meeting where acceptance of your idea could promote you to a position with better pay and more prestige. Should you be aggressive, assertive, and show your mental independence, or should you be reactive, receptive, and cooperative? There is a time for each, but you need to know when each will be effective, and how each fits into your current cycle for achievement.

Our lives are intricately interwoven and, with a little effort, we can learn to help each other through sensitive periods by an awareness of our own cycles and the cycles of those around us, thus greatly improving our relationships!

I believe this book contains some of the most valuable information you may ever encounter. Spend a few moments learning to follow the simple steps necessary to determine your personal numbers and cycles, and you will be able to foresee what types of energy are available to you on any given day, in any given month, and in any given year of your life.

I have learned that less is more when learning a new subject. Therefore, I have opted for simplicity and clarity throughout this book. I think you will find the instructional chapters fun to work with, especially when you calculate your own personal numbers.

"What's the story on numbers?" you ask. I thought I heard you ask that.

Not that it will change what you will learn in this book, but I want to make two comments about numbers. Once you read these two comments, you can forget them if you want. But they will be buried in those crevices in your mind if you ever need them.

First, 1 through 9 are technically called digits. Beyond the digit 9, they are called numbers. Second, there is a difference between numbers and figures.

Figures are used for counting the quantity of things . . . how much, how far, how heavy, etc. We use figures when counting our money, when determining how many people are coming to a holiday dinner, or how many more minutes before the drill in the dentist's hands is put to rest. We use figures in our times tables and mathematical equations, although we do use the word "number" when describing the aforementioned activities.

Numbers, however, represent qualities and characteristics. If you say there is one person in this room, the word "one" is technically a "figure," indicating a quantity. But if you say the person in this room is number 1 in my book, you're talking about a "number," which indicates a quality or a characteristic.

Each of the digits 1 through 9 represents a specific quality or state of being.

You will discover that numbers also indicate predictable progressive cycles.

You've heard the expression "let's do things by the numbers." This means let's do things in a logical sequence in order to arrive at a desired outcome.

The numbers 1 through 9 represent "doing things by the numbers"; these 9 steps are the laws of the universe, which started with the Big Bang. These nine steps are the only way we manifest our goals.

Just so you know, I will be using the word "numbers" throughout this book; however, I do know the difference. Not that is matters linguistically. Well, maybe a little . . .

So, my friends, hopefully you've read this entire Introduction. It's a shame that so many readers overlook the Introductions in books because important information is often hidden there. Now that you've been a good student and have read all the preceding material, you're off to class. Have fun!

PART I

INTRODUCTION
TO NUMBERS

> "NUMBERS ARE THE HIGHEST DEGREE OF KNOWLEDGE.
> IT IS KNOWLEDGE ITSELF."
>
> —PLATO

WELCOME, DEAR READER.

The first question is: Really now, have you read the Introduction? If not, please go back and do so. Often you will find gems tucked into a book's Introduction. By reading this one, you'll get to know more about the tenor and intent of this book . . . along with experiencing a few chuckles, I hope.

So, let's begin.

Numerology is the universal language.

Numerology is as old as time itself. In the beginning was the Cosmic Egg, the zero you might say, which contained all that is, was, and ever will be. From that Egg, an infinitesimal point of pure energy exploded into Light (the Big Bang) which created the Universe through a prescribed set of nine progressive steps.

The numbers 1 through 9 reveal the structure of the universe, and they are the fundamental laws of nature by which we live.

Schwaller de Lubicz, the twentieth-century student of sacred geometry, an Egyptologist known for his years of studying the art and architecture of the Temple of Luxor, which he described in his book, *The Temple in Man*, wrote: ". . . in the ancient temple civilization of Egypt, numbers, our most ancient form of symbols, did not simply designate quantities but instead were considered to be concrete definitions of energetic formative principles of nature."[1]

The ancients believed that the orderly progression of the nine numbers resulted in time and space and life, and eventually the dissolution of that life, which was then recycled and reborn.

These nine numbers are the irrefutable orderly steps taken in order to achieve a result; this process applies not only to the initial birth and physical structure of the universe as we know it today but also to the birth of a child, to the construction of a house, to the creation of a business, to the forging of a relationship, to the baking of a cake.

In order to complete any goal in life and in our personal lives, these nine steps must be taken in order.

The numbers move through the stages 1, 2, 3, 4, 5, 6, 7, 8, and 9. After the 9, the next cycle begins again with the coupling of the next digit and the zero. For example: 10, 20, 30, 40, etc.

Thus, the numbers were born and have been as close to us as our hands and feet.

The most logical place to learn to count is on our ten fingers; nine of our fingers represent the numbers 1 through 9, and the tenth finger solidifies the system by beginning again at 1. ($10 = 1 + 0 = 1$.) Our tenth finger completes the circle and suggests the cyclical nature of life. The method of using ten as the basis of counting is called the decimal system. It was used widely in ancient cultures as it is today in modern civilization.

Numerology is one of the oldest practices in the world; it is a metaphysical language. Just as the letters of the alphabet form words, then sentences that convey information, numbers also carry information. Once you learn the language, you will be bilingual, not only able to speak the language you were brought up learning, but you'll also be able to speak the language of numbers, truly the universal language.

Life is lived by the numbers! Numbers are the one true language that crosses all cultures and worldly barriers and perhaps even galactic barriers. Number messages are sent into space searching for extraterrestrial intelligence (SETI).

Know your numbers and you'll know yourself, your cycles in life, and how to prepare and work with them. And you'll know the world around you.

So, my friends, let's explore this deceptively simple but profound language whose alphabet consists of just nine "letters," the nine numbers, 1 through 9.

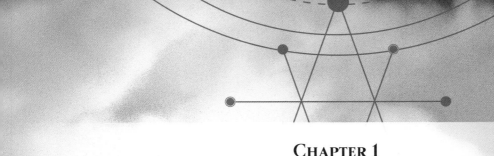

CHAPTER 1

THE FLOOR PLAN OF NUMEROLOGY

NUMBERS AND THE ALPHABET

FOR THOSE OF YOU WHO ARE NEW TO NUMEROLOGY, you will need some background information about this magical process before we delve into the predictive portion. Once we cover these basics, we'll move on to "what the heck is going on in my life?" What fun!

First, in this book, you will discover the five numbers that comprise your birth blueprint; you will then be able to translate these numbers into your spoken language by referring to the number delineations at the back of this book. These number translations will reveal your basic character: your true inner self and how you appear to others, as well as explain the individual path you walk, what you are here to learn, and how it's all put together.

Once you have determined your five basic numbers, you will then discover the invaluable art of timing. Your ability to predict your cycles can lead to the success you desire in your life on many levels.

The key to success in most cases depends upon preparation but, more importantly, success depends on the correct sense of timing. You can plant six healthy tomato plants outdoors in organically balanced soil in the sun and water them faithfully, but if you set them in the ground outdoors in January in Saskatchewan, Canada, for instance, your plants will not survive.

Timing is the key to success, and numbers unlock the door to your bountiful harvest!

At this point, you might want to keep a notebook at hand to record your thoughts and ideas, as well as the information you deem important to remember.

The underlying pattern of life is the numbers 1 through 9. See the following chart:

The first column shows the numbers (1–9)

The second column describes the cosmic process, the pattern behind existence.

The third column lists key words for that number's actions in your daily life.

THE NUMBERS 1-9

NUMBERS 1 *through* 9	COSMIC PROCESS	KEY WORDS
1.	The initial explosion of light, the seed	The beginning, decisions, self-centering, assertive action, standing alone
2.	The incubation of the seed	Partnerships, sex, magic, balance, instincts; behind the scenes activity
3.	The growth of the seed	Expansion, birth, growth, creativity, optimism, generosity
4.	The forming of the physical around the seed	Form, order, structure, work, organization, material possessions
5.	The animation of that physical form	Communication, flexibility, restlessness, awakened senses, the quickening
6.	The balance and perfection of that form	Love, beauty, justice, harmony, home, family, community
7.	The thought that precedes physical manifestation; thought creates reality	Retreat, rest, contemplation, introspection, perfection
8.	The physical manifestation of that thinking process	Karma, rewards, recognition, power, sex, money, responsibility
9.	The breakdown and dissolution of the physical in preparation for recycling	Completions, endings, transitions, letting go, charity

You might want to jot these key words and numbers on a 4" x 6" card so you can refer to them frequently as we proceed. We learn through repetition.

DOUBLE NUMBERS PLUS

When numerologists say "reduce" the numbers, we mean "add" the numbers.

In numerology, all numbers above 9 ultimately reduce to one of the single numbers 1 through 9 by simple addition.

Examples:

10 reduces to 1
$$10 = 1 + 0 = 1$$

41 reduces to 5
$$4 + 1 = 5$$

78 reduces to 6
$$7 + 8 = 15; 15 = 1 + 5 = 6$$

380 reduces to 2
$$3 + 8 + 0 = 11; 11 = 1 + 1 = 2$$

Think of the single numbers as nine separate families. All numbers above 9 reduce to one of the nine families.

For example: You could be one of four children in a family; you all have the same root connection because of your past through your parents, and traditionally you live in the same house and eat the same foods and learn the same language and customs as do your parents and siblings. This is your heritage.

However you and your siblings have different personalities that make you unique within your family unit; your uniqueness sets you somewhat apart from the family dynamic, but you are still part of your original family. The double numbers add shades of personality to each family member.

For example: In the number 5, we have the family members 14 (1 + 4 = 5) and 23 (2 + 3 = 5) and 41 (4 + 1 = 5) and so on. Each of these numbers belongs to the 5 family, and, therefore, they carry the 5 family's signature. And like *Godfather* aficionados know, you don't go against family. The 5 family dynamic is communication.

The 5 represents the principles of curiosity and communication and freedom.

Let's look at 14 and 23, both of which add to a 5. Even though these two numbers are members of the 5 family, the 14 and 23 have slightly different nuances within that family which are shown by the blending of their double numbers.

In reading the following examples, you could use your 4" x 6" card with descriptions of the 1–9 numbers to help you more easily understand the actions taken.

A 14/5 takes charge (1). Her communication skills (5) are organized and well planned (4). She may be a copy editor, checking the spelling and content of written material before it is printed. Or she might be a teacher (5) who takes charge and stands out from the crowd (1), making sure the study plan is well prepared and provides solid foundational material for her students (4).

A 23/5 relies more on instinct (2) to creatively express (3) the magic (2) of communication (5). She may be an artist (3) who illustrates children's books or an actor (3) who can play many roles instinctively (2) or a mother who knows instinctively (2) how to nurture her children through creative and positive (3) activities, which allow them their personal expression (5).

These two different expressions, the 14 and the 23, still relate to the base number 5 which is about the freedom of communication.

An introductory note here: When a number is repeated, such as 22 or 33 or 66, etc., it is called a master number because the energy effect of the number is doubled and intensified.

You can work out similar scenarios as you calculate your number patterns. Try it with family member and friends. Take time to play with the numbers; get a feel for them. The more familiar you are with this language, the more easily you will be able to interpret your own number patterns and the number patterns of others.

Let's move on to the alphabet.

THE NUMBER-LETTER CODE

In order to apply the numbers to your name, you need to work with the following number-letter code which numbers the letters of the English alphabet in order from 1 to 26. See the illustration below.

1	2	3	4	5	6	7	8	9
A	B	C	D	E	F	G	H	I

10	11	12	13	14	15	16	17	18
J	K	L	M	N	O	P	Q	R

19	20	21	22	23	24	25	26	
S	T	U	V	W	X	Y	Z	

In the chart on the previous page, notice that if you reduce the double numbers, they will add to the single number directly above them.

For example, in the first column:

A is 1
J is 10: 10 is 1 + 0 = 1.
S is 19: 19 is 1 + 9 = 10: 10 is 1 + 0 = 1:

Therefore, the letters AJS reduce to a 1. The same holds true for the rest of the letters in the alphabet.

Below is the number-letter code set up in a way that, I think, is much simpler to work with.

NUMBER LETTER CODE

1	A J S
2	B K T
3	C L U
4	D M V
5	E N W
6	F O X
7	G P Y
8	H Q Z
9	I R

You could copy this number-letter code on a 4" x 6" card to use along with your key words for the numbers 1 through 9 card in the next chapters.

When I first started studying numerology, I made memory pegs for the letters that are attached to each number so that I could easily work out the number patterns of names. For instance:

1	AJS	A just student
2	BKT	Booklet, student studying
3	CLU	Clue, looking for clues to life questions
4	DMV	Department of motor vehicles, 4 is a square like your car
5	ENW	New information
6	FOX	Fox, small furry creatures with same loyalty as dogs
7	GPY	Gypsy, the number of the mysteries of the mind
8	HQZ	Headquarters, 8 is the material power world
9	IR	I are, rather I AM, the completion of one cycle

I know these memory pegs may seem awkward to you at first, but they sure worked for me. I can whiz through numbering names with these simple memory pegs rather than laboriously referring to the list for every letter. It did take me time to familiarize myself with them, but it was worth it. You might want to make up your own memory pegs.

We learn through repetition. So, try it. Believe me, you'll be glad you did.

At this point, you have two cards, right? One card is titled *key words for the numbers 1–9*, and the second card is titled the *number-letter code*. Using these cards, you will find the examples in the following chapters much easier to work with.

Chapter 2

YOUR PERSONAL NUMBERS

YOU WERE BORN WITH FIVE SPECIAL NUMBERS THAT are uniquely your own. They were determined by the day you were born and the full name you were given at birth plus the combination of both. These personal numbers describe your character and qualities: the inner most private you, how you appear to others, the path you walk, what you are here to learn in this lifetime, and the whole you. These numbers are the foundation of your life; it is upon this foundation that your life cycles are based.

Before you can discover the power of your cycles and what they mean, as well as the predictive information that can help you plan for the future, you need to calculate your basic numbers.

So, let's figure out your five personal numbers, which come from your name and your birthday, and the sum of your parts.

A NOTE ABOUT YOUR FULL NAME AT BIRTH

Always use your full name that is recorded on your birth certificate at the time of your birth. Any name changes during your life do result in an added dimension to your consciousness from that point forward, but they don't change your basic name vibration at birth.

Your birth name is like the foundation of your home; you can remodel, put on a new roof and siding, and add rooms thereby changing the way you live in your home as well as the way the public views it, but you seldom move the foundation.

If there is confusion about your name at birth then, in order to perform your calculations, use the earliest record you have that states your full name.

The first three numbers in your birth pattern are based upon your full name at birth. First, we will work with the vowel number.

The vowel number indicates the true you inside, not what the public sees of you. The vowels are your home inside—your comfort zone, the natural you. Your innermost secrets are kept here: what you desire and what your want from life. Everything that has ever happened to you in this life, and your past-life times, if that is part of your belief system, is stored here. You might say the Akashic Records are shelved here in that great library in the sky that contains every thought, word, deed, and event that you have experienced as far back as time goes. You draw from this experience especially when you act spontaneously or when a sudden event arises and you don't have time to think about how to respond. This is also a place to which you retreat when you want to nurture yourself.

The first step is to add the number values of the vowels in a name. The vowels are A, E, I, O, and U. Sometimes the Y is considered a vowel if there are no other vowels in the name.

Example 1: Jodi Ann Lee

To find Jodi's Vowel Number, place the number value of the vowels above her full name at birth. You might want to use your 4" x 6" card with the number-letter code.

	6		9		1					5	5	=26/8
J	O	D	I		A	N	N		L	E	E	

Add the numbers together.

Reduce the 26: 2 + 6 = 8

Jodi's Vowel Number is 26/8

You might say: In a past lifetime, Jodi was a power person with great responsibilities in the material world (8), reminiscent of the line from Byron, "oh the weight of these splendid chains." She was most likely the power behind the scenes (2) where she could have influenced the legal system in her community through her impartiality and fair judgments (6).

Her comfort zone in this lifetime continues this thread from the past. She easily calms troubled waters (2) through her impartial judgments (6) which strengthens her inner being and draws people to her through her quiet power (8). She may love reading legal novels.

THE CONSONANT NUMBER

The next step in discovering your birth pattern is to work with the consonants in your name. Consonants are the remaining letters in the alphabet when the vowels are removed.

The consonant number indicates how the world sees you; it's your outer shell, if you will. This is the impression you make on people because of how you appear: the way you look physically, the way you dress, your bearing and attitude. When you want to know how people initially respond to you, and maybe even why you are surprised at their response to you, look to your consonant number, for therein lies the answer. We say, "looks are deceiving," and this is most often true. Study your consonant number to see if it works in your favor. If not, and you are so inclined, you can work on parts of that number to smooth down the rough edges, if there are rough edges to begin with.

Chances are you won't know specifically how others see you because your behavior is naturally ingrained. You could ask family members for an honest but respectful opinion about how you appear to them, not only your physical attributes but how you act and what impressions you make on them. Your siblings may have friends who don't know you well, but they have impressions about you. You could also ask your friends and coworkers. Record these impressions. See how they reflect the consonant number in your name.

To find Jodi's Consonant Number, place the number value of the consonants below her name.

J	O	D	I		A	N	N		L	E	E	
1		4				5	5		3			=18/9

Add the numbers together.

Reduce the 18: 1 + 8 = 9

Jodi's Consonant Number is 18/9

You might say: People who know Jodi casually see her as an independent assertive woman (1) who is capable of taking charge of any organization with confidence and skill (8). They automatically choose her for these positions. They know she won't discriminate against others because of their race, background, sexual orientation, or religious beliefs (9). They see her as a wise person who lives her beliefs (9).

Her vowel number indicates she is comfortable with power (8) but from behind the scenes and in a gentler role (2). In this lifetime, people expect her to be out front, assertive, and in the public (18/9), so there is a bit of a conflict here.

The next step in determining your birth pattern is to add the vowels and consonants in your name at birth.

The name number is your full identity in the eyes of the world. It is the sum of who you appear to be through your full name and, therefore, has a bearing on your standing in the outside world. It may affect the path you take, your profession, and sometimes, because of the ethnicity and cultural connections your name carries, it can further influence your identity.

THE NAME NUMBER

To find Jodi's Name Number, add the numbers of the vowels and consonants. This gives you the total of the entire birth name.

	6		9		1					5	5	=26/8
J	O	D	I		A	N	N		L	E	E	
1		4				5	5		3			=18/9

Top Row Vowel Numbers: 6 + 9 + 1 + 5 + 5 = 26/8
Bottom Row Consonant Numbers: 1 + 4 + 5 + 5 + 3 = 18/9
Total: 44/8

Jodi's Name Number is 44/8.

You might say: Jodi is here to wield influence and make a difference in the outside world (8). The master number 44 increases the energy of all things to do with the earth and the physical body and organizational skills (4). For instance, she may be a force in the world of medicine and healing (4), or an environmental leader who spearheads efforts to clean up the world (4) or a master chef who feeds the bodies of others with healthy foods from the Earth (4) or a super mom upon whom everyone calls to support every effort to raise money (4) for the schools and community. She can do it all.

THE BIRTHDAY NUMBER

The next step in calculating your birth pattern is to determine the birthday number.

The birthday number indicates the lessons you are here to learn this lifetime. As you grow up, you will be constantly reminded of this lesson by circumstances you encounter. Regardless of your profession—"the butcher, the baker, or the candlestick maker"*— this number is the summation of what you are here to learn and to incorporate into your Akashic records.

* The previous phrase comes from a nursery rhyme and relates to all trades or businesses. Note: Fairy tales are metaphors for hidden truths.

To find Jodi's Birthday Number, we add her birthday, July 6, 1968.

In this system, we add the year through once before adding the total birthday. We look for the double number of the year because it implies pairing, balance, cooperation, the Yin and Yang. It's also in accordance with the number of the days in a month which don't exceed double numbers (01 through 31) and the number of the months in a year which don't exceed double numbers (01 through 12).

Her birth year: 1968 = 1 + 9 + 6 + 8 = 24

Add her month (7) and day (6) and reduced birth year (24):

7 + 6 + 24 = 37
Reduce 37: 3 + 7 = 10
Reduce 10: 1 + 0 = 1

Jodi's Birthday Number is 37/10/1

You might say: With a base number 1, Jodi is here to learn how to stand on her own two feet, make her own decisions and not be unduly influenced by what others think (1). She needs to learn and experience life for herself. She is here to be independent and decisive and to understand that being alone does not necessarily mean lonely. Others may follow her because they sense her ability to take charge; however, she needs to forge ahead without thought of the opinions of others.

You can expand your analysis by reading the double numbers. For instance: With the 37, she can be social (3), but her strong creative streak (3) is cultivated by quiet time where she can think and contemplate and use her mind (7).

If she carries her innovative ideas to completion and takes action to promote them (10/1), she will be recognized as a unique individual in her field (1). She has then learned the lesson that she should be unafraid to forge ahead on her own.

THE WHOLE NUMBER

The final step in working out your birth pattern is to determine the whole number.

The whole number is the summation of all that you are, the entire package. Each of your birth numbers tells a part of the story of you. You can be distracted by the individual numbers, but they are only pieces of a puzzle that, when fitted together, fill out the complete person you are—and that may surprise even you.

To find Jodi's Whole Number, add her name number and her birthday number.

$$44 + 37 = 81/9$$

Jodi's Whole Number is: 81/9

You might say: The whole number leads Jodi on a journey of wisdom (9) that she should share with others. As a leader (1) who makes her mark in the material world (8), the public will admire that, through her success in the trades or in business (8), she has much to offer. She stands as an example of one who can make it on her own (1) and who then gives back to the world part of what she has gained (9) through her career accomplishments (8).

***

Jodi's five basic numbers from her birth pattern are:

Vowel Number: 26/8
Consonant Number: 18/9
Name Number: 44/8
Birthday Number: 37/10/1
Whole Number: 81/9

Let's work the numbers through one more example. Example 2: Sandra Louise Coby (see chart below)

Because she has vowels in her name, the "y" is considered a consonant.

To find Sandra's Vowel Number, place the corresponding numbers above the vowels in her name and add.

Top Row Vowel Numbers: 1 + 1 + 6 + 3 + 9 + 5 + 6 = 31
3 + 1 = 4
Sandra's Vowel Numbers add to 31/4.

	1			1			6	3	9		5			6			=31/4
S	**A**	**N**	**D**	**R**	**A**	**L**	**O**	**U**	**I**	**S**	**E**	**C**	**O**	**B**	**Y**	
1		5	4	9		3			1		3		2	7		=35/8

To find Sandra's Consonant Number, place the corresponding numbers below the consonants in her name and add.

Bottom Row Consonant Numbers:
1 + 5 + 4 + 9 + 3 + 1 + 3 + 2 + 7 = 35
3 + 5 = 35/8

Sandra's Consonant Number is 35/8.

To find Sandra's Name Number, add the vowel and consonant numbers.

31 + 35 = 66
66 = 6 + 6= 12
12 = 1 + 2= 3
or 66/12/3

Sandra's Name Number adds to 66/12/3.

To find Sandra's Birthday Number, add the numbers in her birthday.

Her birthday is November 6, 1994.

Add the year of her birthday through once:

$$1994 = 1 + 9 + 9 + 4 = 23$$
Add her month (11) and day (6) and reduced birth year (23)
$$11 + 6 + 23 = 40/4$$
Sandra's Birthday Number is a 40/4.

To find Sandra's Whole Number: add her name number (which is the total of her vowels and consonants) to her birth number.

$$66 + 40 = 106/7$$
Sandra's Whole Number is 106/7.

***

Sandra Louise Coby's birth blueprint is as follows:

Vowel Number = 31/4
Consonant Number = 35/8
Name Number = 66/12/3
Birth Number = 40/4
Whole Number = 106/7

***

There is a story about Pythagoras, the father of mathematics and numerology, a mystic, and a philosopher. It is said he felt there was a mystery contained within the letter Y. To experience the vibration of this letter personally, he used a special name containing the Y sound for some years. He felt that the letter Y indicated a dual path and perhaps choices because of this duality. Even the visual, the way the Y is drawn, suggests a path that eventually forks.

Many numerology books have explicit rules for the use of the letter Y, which, in the English language, is sometimes used as a vowel and sometimes as a consonant. The duality of the letter's usage seems to indicate its double role in a person's life.

It may be that the letter Y works as both a vowel and a consonant within the same name thus offering the individual more variety of expression and experience. It can also indicate a person who had lived and still lives two separate lives, each one independent of the other.

THE MYSTERIOUS LETTER Y

For instance: If you have a Y or Y's in your name, one group of people may describe you one way because of the use of the Y as a vowel. Another group of people may describe you in an entirely different way reflecting the use of the Y in your name as a consonant. And the two groups of people don't know each other, because you have drawn each group to you through your different sets of numbers and, therefore, you interact with them under different circumstances.

With Y's in your name, you might have led a double life in your past, and you might still do so today. In this lifetime, you may live a very public life and career while behind closed doors you live a completely private life with a career that is far removed from what the public sees.

If you have Y's in your birth name, use this letter as both vowels and consonants. You will arrive at two vowel numbers and two consonant numbers. This combination does not change the sum of your total name.

Why not try it out. Perhaps this could reveal why you are described and seen differently by particular segments of your community.

Let's use our earlier example which contains a Y: Sandra Louise Coby

In the following exercise, use the Y as a vowel. If you have more than one Y, use all of them as vowels.

	1			1		6	3	9		5			6		7	=38/11/2
S	A	N	D	R	A	L	O	U	I	S	E		C	O	B	Y
1		5	4	9		3			1		3		2			=28/10/1

Top Row
Vowel Number: 1 + 1 + 6 + 3 + 9 + 5 + 6 + 7 = 38/11/2
Bottom Row
Consonant Number: 1 + 5 + 4 + 9 + 3 + 1 + 3 + 2 = 28/10/1

Now, use the Y as a consonant. If you have more than one Y in your full name at birth, use them all as consonants here.

	1			1		6	3	9		5			6		=31/4
S	A	N	D	R	A	L	O	U	I	S	E	C	O	B	Y
1		5	4	9		3			1		3		2	7	=35/8

Top Row
Vowel Number: 1 + 1 + 6 + 3 + 9 + 5 + 6 = 31/4
Bottom Row
Consonant Number: 1 + 5 + 4 + 9 + 3 + 1 + 3 + 2 + 7 = 35/8

Regardless of using the Y as both a vowel and as a consonant, the name number, the total of the entire name, does not change. Both sets add to 66/12/3.

Using this method, Sandra is viewed two different ways, as if she leads two different unconnected lives.

1. With the Y as a vowel, the 38/11/2 and 28/10/1 set of numbers is in effect.

Through her 28/10/1 consonant number, one group sees her as a quiet private (2) yet powerful (8) woman who knows how to turn things around (10) and reinvent or start things anew that will lead them in a new direction (1). In a group setting, she is not the first one to speak up but waits until the time is right (2), then steps in to help iron out the twists and turns (10).

This group does not know Sandra's 38/11/2 inner vowel comfort zone. She feels more comfortable behind the scenes. She might have lived a secret life as an alchemist who used the hidden (2) magic (11) of her creativity (3) to manifest something tangible (8). Like the alchemists of old seeking to transmit lead to gold, she knows she has worked in private (2) exploring the mysteries of life (11) in order to leave behind a visible record of her efforts (8).

. . . .

2. With the "Y" as a consonant, the 31/4 and 35/8 set of numbers is in effect.

Another group sees her through her consonant number 35/8 as a creative and generous (3), versatile and communicative (5) individual. They expect her to take a significant role because they see her as an experienced leader (8). For instance, she could be picked for the leading role in a play or selected as the leader of a committee in a corporate setting that seeks an artistic advertising plan. She doesn't necessarily see herself this way and may be surprised when she is expected to step up and take charge.

This group of people does not know Sandra's 31/4 inner vowel feelings and comfort zone. She has a generous spirit (3) and will stand up (1) for what is right. Organization (4) is her key asset; she knows how to accomplish goals in the physical world (4) while adding a bit of fun and creative playfulness (3). If she wishes, these are the innate abilities she can use to adjust to the expectations of others.

If you have Y's in you name, you have two sets of numbers:

Your vowel and consonant numbers from using the Y as a vowel, and

Your vowel and consonant numbers from using the Y as a consonant.

Depending upon which group you are with, you will use that specific set of numbers under which to operate. You eventually realize how other people see you and what they expect from you (the consonant number); then you have the option of going to that inner place to find the past experiences (the vowel number) that will allow you to, depending upon the circumstances, work with each specific group or retreat to your vowel number comfort zone when you want to get away.

**

By now, you have calculated your five basic numbers that comprise your birth blueprint. To learn more about the meaning of your five special numbers, turn to page 238. Remember to translate those temporary definitions into the permanent qualities in your life.

Learn how to blend the numbers to tell a story; try it with you own numbers. You might snuggle down in bed each night with your notebook, when the house is quiet and in shadow, and start with your vowel number. Weave imaginary stories about who you were and where you came from and what your inner self desires. And, on one of those nights . . . you never know . . . you might meet your previous self. Who knows what magic awakens in the dark of the night! Work with all your numbers in this way.

Know thyself. That pithy message was said to have been inscribed on the Temple of Apollo at Delphi. The philosopher Socrates taught that "the unexamined life was not worth living."

A note for my astrological colleagues: You might equate the vowel number with the Moon sign, the consonant number with the Ascendant or Rising Sign, the name number with Saturn in its sign, the birthday number with the Sun sign, and the whole number with the entire birth chart.

LET'S CALL IT WHAT IT IS:

THE NEW DESIGNATIONS FOR THE FIVE BASIC NUMBERS EXPLAINED

If you're the least bit familiar with numerology, you may wonder why I haven't called the numbers you just calculated in the previous section the life path, the heart's desire, the personality, the life expression, the path of destiny, or any of the many other names they have been assigned over the years. There are also the ones I was taught and that were used in *Numerology and the Divine Triangle*, the book I cowrote with Faith Javane: soul number, outer personality number, path of destiny number, and life lesson number.

There is much confusion among numerologists about what to call the numbers in the birth blueprint. These overlapping names used by various numerological systems cause confusion for new students who want to learn numerology.

This confusion makes it more difficult for me as well. Recently I have been looking over numerological texts from the past. Because of designations such as destiny, heart's desire, and personality, I had to read further on to be sure what part of the birth pattern they were writing about.

To simplify and make it easier to remember these designations and to welcome new students to this sacred language, I suggest we get together and call these numbers what they are. I know it's hard to change what is familiar to us who have been in this field a long time but, for the benefit of those newcomers, let's end the confusion. The new designations I propose are easy to remember because we will call them exactly what they are.

That's why this section is titled: "Let's Call It What It Is."

So, let's explore the history and metaphysics of why the following designations for your birth pattern numbers make sense.

LET'S CALL IT THE VOWEL NUMBER AND WHY

The vowels are A, E, I, O, U, and sometimes the letter Y.

As stated earlier, the vowels in your name represent who you really are inside, those things that are closest to your heart and, if you happen to believe, what you brought in with you from past lifetimes. The vowel number is your comfort zone and harbor of safety because it is so familiar to you. You instinctively go here for sustenance when you need to retreat from the stresses of the world.

You act instinctively from this source because it contains familiar memories, those memories stored in what is called your Akashic Records, where everything that you have ever thought or done or that has ever happened to you is stored. Others do not recognize this hidden aspect of you.

The vowels represent your inner self, that hallowed place where you commune privately with personal memories and where the vowel sounds connect you with higher levels of consciousness.

The vowel sounds were once considered sacred by many cultures.

Tracing back to 4000 BCE, the Egyptians considered the vowel sounds so sacred that their written language, called hieroglyphics, contained no vowels. Demetrius, a Greek traveler around 200 BCE, wrote about the Egyptian priests: ". . . when priests sing hymns to the Gods, they sing the seven vowels in due succession . . ."[2] Obviously, the Egyptians believed the vowel sounds were the language only their gods should hear.

Ancient Hebrew, a forgotten language, had no written vowels. The Mesha Stele, commonly known as the Moabite Stone, was found in 1868 in Moab. Inscribed on the stone is a message from King Mesha (830 BCE). The message contains an estimated 1,100 consonants; there are no vowels.

Hebrew is the language of the Hebrew Bible and the Old Testament of the Christian Bible. The English word "God" in Hebrew is Elohim; it is plural. So the first sentence in the Bible should read: "In the beginning the gods created the heavens and the Earth." Notice the plural word "gods."

The ancient Hebrew language was the most difficult to translate because of the missing vowels. The vowel sounds were most likely chanted in the temples, hidden from the outside world, where the priests could attune their spiritual bodies to prepare for communication with their god.

The Tibetan Monks are among many cultures that have, for at least a thousand years, traditionally used vowels in chanting to induce spiritual uplifting and healing. The vowel sounds put one in a serene state of mind and can affect something deep within the soul, stimulating visual imagery.

"Om" chanting is considered one of the most sacred sounds on earth. Om has no meaning; it is a sound. Om is the sound that connects to our highest consciousness, to Spirit, the Cosmic Mother. Chanting the vowel "O" in long breaths sets up an inner vibration that resonates throughout our bodies.

The "M" sound that closes the long chanted "O" brings the spiritual vibration down to Earth and into the body. M is the 13th letter in the English alphabet, reducing to a 4. The number 13 is the number of transformation; 4 is the number of the Earth. Many believed, and still do, that sound vibrations can heal the Earthly body down to the cellular level.

Sound healing has been rediscovered in modern times with ultrasound treatments; it has been used for sports injuries over the last fifty years. Ultrasound therapy, although disputed by some, is thought to hasten the normal healing time at the site on the body to which it is applied.

We know that the sound of a violin bow drawn over the edge of a glass sprinkled with sand creates beautiful patterns. Why wouldn't ultrasound create beautiful patterns within the body? Good question; who knows what can happen when the sound is harmonious? After all, the first sentence of the Christian Bible reads that God spoke and the sound vibration went forth to create the world.

When you connect with your vowel number, you find that emotional resonance with your inner being, your soul, and perhaps your past lifetimes that are inscribed in the halls of your Akashic Records.

The vowels in the word "vowels" add to 11; 11 is a master number.

This master number connects to the inner self and indicates flashes of insight and intuition beyond the senses. Those flashes of intuition could come from the knowledge gained in your past lives.

The vowel sound is pronounced flowingly with no occlusion. The definition of occlusion is: "the obstruction of the breath passage in the articulation of a speech sound."

When we pronounce vowels, they flow easily from the throat and mouth. Say a – e – i – o – u, and notice how the mouth stays open. There is no restriction, no occlusion in the throat. The sound moves freely through space.

Chanting the vowels connects you to higher consciousnesses through sound vibrations. That is why vowels are considered sacred.

So, I say, let's call it what it is: the vowel number.

As suggested, in your notebook you could work out your vowel number. Then write a thumbnail sketch about who you might have been in a past lifetime. Your subconscious will direct you so give this process some time . . . meditate on your vowel number . . . you might even sing the vowels sounds to allow insights to flow . . . and as time goes by, write more histories that you might have experienced in your past lifetimes.

At night, keep paper and a pen by your bed. When you rest your head on the pillow, ask for a dream about your past. When you wake in the morning, lie very still; movement chases dreams away. Then record that dream. If you don't remember a dream the first night, try again. The magic number seems to be three. By the third night, most likely you will remember a dream. And it's sweet dreams from thereon in.

This process can apply when you're dozing in your easy chair or daydreaming at the beach or meditating in the forest. Ask for a message from your vowel number and welcome what comes.

You might want to pick up a copy of my book, *Dream Cycles*, which connects the type of dreams you experience with the numerological cycles you are in at any given time.

LET'S CALL IT THE CONSONANT NUMBER AND WHY

The consonants are the letters in the alphabet minus the vowels.

The consonant number reveals the outside world of form, how the world in general sees you, the physical impression you make on others. It influences how you look physically, which you obviously know by looking in the mirror. But sometimes what we see in the mirror is a reflection of how we feel inside and not how we actually appear on the outside.

This number also indicates how you carry yourself, which you may not be aware of because it is so naturally a part of you. But this carriage is what others see when you walk into a room; you might sweep into a room or you might wander into a room or you could slip into a room undetected; therefore, the way you carry yourself influences the first impression you make on others.

The consonant number reveals your body language and physical habits. It reflects your every day personality and how you move through your daily life in the physical world, interacting with those around you. Your inner feelings may reflect outward through your physical habits which others see: You may bite you bottom lip when you're thinking or jiggle your knee when you're anxious or interrupt conversations when you get nervous.

Your behavior patterns set up the expectations of others—what they see is what they get, so to speak. You may not be aware of these assessments because they are so habitual and because you are focused on the moment . . . your relationships, family, money situations, the workplace dynamics, and so forth, the act of daily living.

The consonant number is not who you are, but rather it is how others see you and the way those who know you casually will describe you.

As stated, some ancient languages were written using only consonants. This was the information provided by those in charge who were using written communications for public consumption whether they were sending messages or writing their histories. As mentioned above, Egyptian hieroglyphics and the ancient Hebrew language were all written in consonants for public viewing; these were the visible messages to their people and to their worlds. The consonants clothed deeper messages.

Imagine today trying to decipher a line of script from an ancient language when you have only two consonants. For example: bt. This could be "bat" or "bet" or "bit"; each word has no connection to the other words.

Hooray for vowels! Those letters that make sense of it all . . . that complete the concept, the image, the thought. Imagine today people trying to interpret these ancient languages. It seems to me a lot of guessing and surmising goes on.

In a sense, your consonant number is much like the "bt" example above, that outer description of you that may have little bearing on who you are, but is how the public sees you.

Knowledge of this perception of you in the eyes of others is important and, if you are aware of it, can make for a happier and more fluid life. Often we do judge a book by its cover and often we make lasting impressions based upon that first encounter. Knowing your consonant number can ensure that you make the lasting impressions you desire.

So, I say, let's call it what it is: the consonant number.

The consonants in the word "consonants" add to master number 22 or 22/4.

4 represents the Earth and the physical body, the outside world of form.

As mentioned earlier, the definition of occlusion is: "the obstruction of the breath passage in the articulation of a speech sound." To pronounce a consonant requires a restriction of speech. Pronounce the consonants and feel the occlusion. This restriction suggests closure, or an enclosure, suggesting the world of form in which we live in the material world. In that sense, consonants suggest the "real" world.

Curiously:

The vowels in the word "vowels" add to 11, a master number.

The consonants in the word "consonants" add to 22, a master number.

Together they add to 33, a master number.

Hmmm . . . all master numbers.

The numerical value of vowels and consonants in our alphabet and their sum total are master numbers. The master numbers imbue our alphabet with mystical power because the words can contain hidden messages. Now that you're on your way to becoming a numerologist, you will soon begin to see the magic in your new language.

LET'S CALL IT THE NAME NUMBER AND WHY

In *Romeo and Juliet*, Shakespeare wrote, "What's in a name?" The Romans used the expression *nomen est omen*, or "name is destiny."

Your full name at birth indicates your signature in the world, the totality of who you are. It is the you that is seen on the path you have chosen this lifetime, perhaps indicating your vocation or avocation. Two people may walk the same path, for instance, the field of nursing, but while one person may be developing compassion and understanding, the other individual could be working on discipline and responsibility. Your full name wraps you in your public energy field.

Note an article in the March 16, 2012, issue of *The Week* magazine titled, "What's in a Name?" We don't choose the names we carry, but they have an immense and often hidden effect on our lives.

The article goes on to say that "our names are badges bearing information about our class, education level, and ethnic origin . . . ."

Studies found that resumes bearing an African American name "such as Lakesia Washington gets less attention from potential employers than the identical resume bearing a name like Mary Ann Roberts." Although, hopefully, this type of discrimination is waning.

The article went on to say research shows that we are "unconsciously drawn to things, people, and places that sound like [our] own names . . . a behavior called 'implicit egotism.'"

The Swiss psychiatrist Carl Jung (German for "young") noted that his colleague Sigmund Freud (German for "joy") advocated the pleasure principle, Alfred Adler (German for "eagle") the will to power, and he himself (young) the "idea of rebirth." Sue Yoo of Los Angeles was told growing up that with a name like hers, she should be a lawyer. Today she's an attorney.

So, you see, actually a whole lot is in your name.

Your name has power: The sound of your spoken name sends a vibration into the world that identifies you.

Sound carries vibrations that can destroy or create.

Sound can destroy: Some sonic weapons focus destructive beams of sound. Sound waves above certain decibels can damage or destroy eardrums. Strong enough sound waves can break glass.

Perhaps you recall the song, the "Battle of Jericho." The lines go: "Joshua fit the battle of Jericho . . . and the walls came tumbling down." The Bible tells how, after the people marched around the walls of Jericho shouting and blowing trumpets, the walls fell. The sound vibrations destroyed the walls.

Sound also creates: In the Vedanta-sutra, it is written that sound is the origin of the material world, but it can also dissolve the material world. In the Hebrew Bible, Genesis 1:3 says: "And God said, Let there be light . . ." The act of speaking, the sound, sends out sound waves. And, as noted earlier, the sound of a violin creates beautiful sand patterns when the bow is drawn against the edge of steel, glass, and other such materials upon which sand has been sprinkled.

Sound is the creative force. Think about how many times your name is spoken in your lifetime. This builds up vibrations around you that define your physical presence at different levels.

When your first name is spoken, your attention is drawn in a more casual and perhaps intimate manner. When your first and middle names (if you have a middle name) are spoken, you become a bit more focused. And when your complete name is spoken, you come to attention. Something important is at hand.

You know the power of your name especially when it comes to your mother (or the person who raised you). I can remember when my son was young and resistant to coming in for dinner. I would call, "Matthew, dinner is ready. Come on in." A friendly request. Ten minutes later, I would go to the door and call a second time, "Matthew Reid! Dinner is ready. Get in here." I wanted more of his attention at this point. After another five minutes or so, my weapon came out: "Matthew Reid Bunker . . . now!" A child knows that when his mother uses his full name she wants his full attention and he'd better be listening.

Historically, the naming of a thing had metaphysical implications; it wasn't taken lightly. Some names were not spoken aloud out of respect and sometimes fear.

The different religious ideologies around the world all aim toward a supreme source, the One, The Cosmic Mother, God, the architectural force behind creation. Yet, because there are different names for this source, families are split, wars are fought, and people die.

Three of the world's major religions—Christianity, Judaism, and Islam—have historically fought and still do over the naming of their source and its ideologies. But the aim of these religions is ultimately to reunite with the Source of creation.

There's an old African proverb that tells of their god walking down the road wearing a two-colored cap on his head. I don't recall the exact colors but let's say one side of the cap is red; the other side is green. The people who lived on one side of the road worshipped the god with the red cap while the people who lived on the other side of the road worshipped the god with the green cap. They fought wars over the difference in the color of their god's cap. However, they worshipped the same god.

The naming of a thing carries vibrations and evokes specific energies. In ancient times, the magi, the priestesses and priests, the illuminati, the seekers of truth, knew the power of the name. They knew . . . "what's in a name?"

From the early patriarchal Jewish tradition: ". . . Since the time of Moses when God revealed His sacred name, only the High Priest could whisper this most sacred word while he stood before the Ark of the Covenant in the Holy of Holies of the Temple . . ."[3]

The Tetragrammaton was the four part name of God: JHVH-Jehovah, sometimes written as YHVH-Yahweh. These were the unutterable names of God. These names are thought to be derived from a verb that means "to be" or "to exist." (See page 130 for more of what is illuminating information about the different names of "god.")

Back to you: Your full name demands your attention and is ordinarily used in important and clarifying circumstances: on your birth certificate; signing certain checks or important documents; applying for credit; filling out your income tax forms; researching your family tree; and so on.

Your full name identifies who you are to the world; it influences your profession, your calling, and the path you walk this lifetime. Your name number carries your unique vibration, a sound that moves out and creates your standing in the world. Your name number is your identity badge in the physical world.

So, please join me. Let's call it what it is: the name number

Your most important number this lifetime is your birthday number. Your birthday is a precise day in a precise year in all the trillions plus years that have passed on this planet. In that sense you, and those who have the same birth day as you, are a tiny portion of the world's population since the beginning of time. That day was never before and will never come again.

Just as a wine master can tell, by tasting a wine, the vineyard from which that wine came and the time it was harvested, you are your own wine master, here to drink of your own vintage wine. You must learn to taste its qualities and then to incorporate those qualities into your harvest this lifetime.

Your birthday number is the lesson you have come to learn, your purpose in this life, which will add to the totality of who you are in the Akashic records, that heavenly library that stores the memory of all you have been.

The candles on the birthday cake every year and family and friends gathered around to sing your praises, to recognize that you exist, are an important ritual, one that is a familiar celebration in the West. For everyone on the planet, the birth "day" celebrates the return of the Sun to the same position it was on the day you were born; it's your solar return.

Remembrance of our "birth day" evokes ancient connections to the Cosmic Mother from whose Egg the Universe was born.

"The Cosmic Egg from which the sun, Ra, was hatched was laid by the Nile Goose."[4]

"Mother Goose originated in ancient Egypt where she was Mother Hathor incarnate in the Nile Goose. She laid the golden egg of the sun . . . Some Egyptian writings called the goose the Creatress of the World because she produced the whole universe in a primordial World Egg."[5]

The birth of the universe was a pretty big deal; your birthday is also a pretty big deal; you are a pretty big deal! I expressed this idea in a haiku I wrote some years ago:

> Form, cast out of time,
> Is home for the Sacred Light.
> Kneel. A child is born.

> That child is you.

We pause on our birthdays to remind ourselves of who we are at that moment in time, perhaps to reminisce about events of the past year and what we have learned from those events. At some level, we absorb that past year's experiences into the totality of the person we

LET'S CALL IT THE BIRTHDAY NUMBER AND WHY

are becoming in this lifetime. We stop on our birth day to reflect and to recognize what we have learned over the past twelve months and perhaps even further back.

This is the importance of the number from our birth day. Each solar return, the return of the Sun to our birth day, reminds us of the lessons we are here to learn in our lifetime. Every birth day is a mini-rebirth.

Our life is a journey.

The Tao says: "The journey is the reward."

Buckminster Fuller said the same thing in a poetically profound few lines: "Don't oppose forces; use them. God is a verb; not a noun."

A noun is a word that indicates a static person, place, or thing: It doesn't move; it doesn't change.

A verb is a word that expresses action, an occurrence, or a state of being. Remember our earlier conversation about the root word of the names of god—JHVH-Jehovah and YHVH-Yahweh—is "to be."

The purpose of life is not the noun: a static person, place, or thing.

The purpose of life is the verb: loving, doing, learning, supporting, discovering, experiencing, changing, forgiving, renewing, rising—all verbs that require that we keep living our lives. This is the purpose of life.

As I write this book, I know that the real purpose of this portion of my life is the seemingly endless research, the thoughts I take to bed at night, the hours at the keyboard struggling for the exact words to explain each process, the rewriting of portions of the book over and over looking for perfection—which of course is not possible, yet I still seek it—all this effort I put into writing this book fulfills a portion of my life. The physical purpose of all this energy is this book, the final result bound between these covers that you hold in your hands; the true purpose is the journey, not the destination.

Although I do delight in that first copy that lands in my hands because the baby is born, the victory accomplished. I often experience postpartum blues; the energy has departed and I feel depleted. I find myself looking for the next project.

The purpose of life is living it and learning from it! "God is a verb, not a noun."

Your birthday number represents the living of life and the learning from that living. To absorb this knowledge and learn from it is to become "as wise as Solomon," a common expression in our language.

Speaking of Solomon . . . Solomon is the three-fold spirit of the Sun (sol). In the Hebrew language, the letters of their alphabet of consonants had numerical values. The four letters of the name Solomon, S-L-M-N, are Samekh, Lamed, Mem, and Nun; their numerical values are 60-30-40-50. This adds to 180 or half a circle.

Every day, the Sun travels from sunrise to its highest peak in the sky then to sunset. The movement of the Sun, through this 180° arc during the day when we can see the "Light," carries the hidden message behind the name Solomon: it is with the passage of time and experience and living life every day throughout our lives that we can experience life, see the Light, and grow wise as Solomon.

It is this passage of time embodied in the name Solomon that your birthday number represents.

So many of the ancient names contained hidden messages of terrestrial and celestial movements, and even the stories about the beginning of the universe! Are you intrigued? Be sure to read chapter 6 (pp. 130–134) for more on this subject.

So, back to the subject at hand: your birthday. Let's call it what it is: the birthday number.

But hold on! There is a fifth number you should consider.

We've talked about your parts. Now let's assemble them and talk about your whole. Who is the total you this lifetime?

LET'S CALL IT THE WHOLE NUMBER AND WHY

You've probably heard the expression: The whole is greater than the sum of its parts. This quote is popularly attributed to Aristotle, though he may not have said it quite this way. What this expression means is that the "whole" is better than you would expect from the individual parts because the way the parts fit together adds a different quality to the whole than expected.

We can apply that meaning to the individual numbers in your birth pattern.

The individual parts of your birth pattern—the vowel number, the consonant number, the name number, and the birthday number—make up the whole you. The "whole you" cannot be described by any one of the individual birth numbers. Rather, the individual numbers describe a part of you that cannot paint a picture of the whole you because together they present a greater picture than the individual parts.

For instance, when you meet someone for the first time and don't ever see them again, you leave with them an impression that is only a fragment of who you are. On top of that, you may have had a bad day, and your usually bright and sunny self is hidden under a rainy cloud. And even if you were your normal self at that meeting, you leave just a small part of the person you are, your consonant number, your outer shell, at that meeting.

Because your "whole is greater than the sum of its parts."
So, let's call it what it is: the whole number.

***

So, my friends, I believe that calling the numbers what they are—the vowel number, the consonant number, the name number, the birthday number, and the whole number—gives voice to their long history, spiritual practices, and cosmic roots. And they just make sense. Plus, it will help new students by making this ancient practice more welcoming as well as creating clarity in communications amongst present day numerologists.

***

Now that you've calculated your basic numbers in this chapter, you will want to know what they mean. You can find that information by reading the single number definitions in chapter 12: The Meaning of the Numbers 1 through 9 and the Master Numbers 11 through 99. The single numbers tell the foundational story. With numbers above 9 you can blend their meanings, as we did in the examples in chapter 1, keeping in mind the family to which they belong. It might be wise to use the single numbers first as a learning tool until you feel comfortable with interpreting the double numbers in your numerological blueprint and your cycles.

Keep in mind that the meanings of the numbers in chapter 12 are written to describe the temporary cycles in your life because this is a book about the predictive power of numbers. However, you can translate those temporary vibrations into permanent descriptions of the numbers, and then apply them to the five basic numbers in your birth pattern that are the foundation of your life.

Chapter 12 also contains definitions of what are called the master numbers which, as mentioned earlier, are repetitions of the same number, such as 11, 22, 33, and on up to 99. Because the master numbers repeat the same digit, they increase the intensity of the single number vibration; however, they still belong to one of the basic nine families 1 through 9.

CHAPTER 3

CHAPTER 3
YOUR BIRTHDAY COLOR AND YOUR BIRTHDAY GIFT

I HAVE THOUGHT ABOUT AND WORKED ON THE connections between your birthday number and "colors" and "gifts" for some time; I was reminded of my past research on these subjects when I began to rewrite and update this book for the new millennium.

As I wrote in one of my book's introductions years ago, no ideas should remain frozen in time or bound by iron-clad rules that don't allow room for growth. So it is with this ancient practice of numerology.

Notice the word "practice." Even today we say that a professional is "practicing" her art, be it in the business world, the legal field, the practice of medicine, and so forth. The same applies to the field of metaphysics. The word "practice" allows room for corrections and the addition of new ideas and techniques. We should keep an open mind and entertain new ideas and techniques.

To paraphrase the great poet Robert Browning: "Our reach should exceed our grasp, or what's a heaven for?"

If you've read this far, you know that your birthday number is the most important part of your blueprint because it is the reason you are here; this is what you need to accomplish in this lifetime. Anything that helps you achieve that goal should be examined. I believe your birthday color can be one of those helpers.

In addition, I have included the nine birthday gifts and their connections to the nine numbers as well. It is a suggestion rather than a tried-and-true technique. Play with it and see if it speaks to you. You could also try it on your family, friends, and even notable figures in the world.

When ancient religions and philosophies speak of truths, those truths often come in groups of 7 or 9. These numbers have a strong connection to celestial and terrestrial cycles and, therefore, to our lives. A discussion of the 7 and 9 is not necessary at this point in the book, but a quick online search of these two numbers will reveal this truth.

For now, let's begin by examining the birthday color.

COLOR

Colors are photons of light that emit different amounts of energy. The color you wear or the colors that surround you for any length of time affect your psyche, your feelings and emotions, and other moods.

We are subconsciously aware of the type of energy each color evokes and use their effects in our common expressions: We see red, we're green with envy, we're true blue, to name a few. Culture has something to do with our associations with color but most people react to color in the same manner.

Color can be magical and healing.

Picture the sun's rays streaming through a stained-glass window in a church, flowing over a woman kneeling before an altar in prayer, bathing her in a variety of brilliant colors. Her energy field is uplifted, balanced, and "spiritualized" through the colors that flow over her because these color vibrations are absorbed into her body. The healing effects of colors are part of the serenity and fullness she feels; she also senses the light in her body. The goal of the "seeker of truths" has historically been the "body full of Light."

Light is a metaphor for insight and truth. Ancient religious literature speaks of the moment when a single point, that singularity, the Cosmic Seed, exploded into Light.

Some claim the Hindu Rig Veda is 5,000 years old. This holy book teaches that "in the beginning" a point exploded into Light and the universe was born; the Christian Bible writes: "And God said, 'Let there be Light . . .'" There are ancient beliefs from Egypt, China, and the American Southwest that believe the Light came first, and out of that Light all things emerged.

In modern times, that the universe began from a single point, exploded into Light thus creating matter, was first postulated in 1927. This evolved into the Big Bang theory, a theory accepted by most cosmologists today. Amazing that this theory was already written about thousands of years ago in metaphysical literature!

Speaking of color . . .

Color does have an effect on our psyche. Have you heard of "drunk tank pink"? Pink has a calming effect. This color is painted on the walls of prisons in the United States where violent prisoners are held to calm them down. Prisons in Switzerland have been painted pink to calm aggressive inmates. There are many examples of public places utilizing the psychological effect of this calming color. Pink is the color of love; it is said to lower blood pressure and racing heart beats. One psychologist stated the effects of pink: "Anger levels can reduce in as little as fifteen minutes."

Perhaps that's why little girls are dressed in pink. Patriarchy has tried to mold girls into calm little creatures who don't create disturbances. But I won't go off on that tangent.

Now, with yellow, notice how you feel when you walk into a waiting room with walls painted a sunny yellow. That color tends to lift your spirits. Yellow often bring a smile to your face. Of course, that depends upon what you are waiting for . . . but you see the point.

When you walk into a restaurant or a lounge done in shades of ruby red, this color stimulates the physical appetites—on many levels. I'll leave this last one to your imagination.

Apply these principles to your home or apartment, your work area, and the places where you spend the most time. Especially important is where you sleep; the colors should be soothing and restful if you expect to wake bright-eyed and bushy-tailed. The color themes in your home are the vibrations that you carry out into the world every day.

Color therapy should be used with awareness and an understanding of how color affects your psyche. If someone is very angry, obviously red is not a color that will calm that person down. There are books available on color therapy, also called chromotherapy, which are educational and illuminating.

Back to the point . . .

Everything in the universe, including us, is surrounded by an electromagnetic energy field; it is what holds the universe together. We often call the energy field surrounding humans the "aura." Artists, known for their sensitivity to subtle emanations in their environment, have traditionally painted portraits of saints and holy individuals with a glowing nimbus, a halo, around their heads.

"Sensitive" people can interpret your temperament and mood on any given day by the color of your aura. They know that auras change color according to your moods.

All of us most likely see these auras subconsciously without recognizing them consciously, and that may be why we associate colors with certain mental states: seeing red, having the blues, green with envy, etc.

The famous "sleeping prophet" Edgar Cayce naturally saw people's auras. One particular story is told about the time he was on an upper floor in a department store. He was about to step into an elevator when he suddenly stopped, startled, and stepped back as the elevator door closed. Then, the cable broke and the car crashed to the bottom, killing everyone on board. When asked about the incident later, he said he was stopped in his tracks because when he looked into the elevator, no one had an aura. Their energy fields had already left their bodies.

Each color gives off its own frequency, which differentiates it from the others. At one end of the color spectrum is red, "infrared," and at the other end of the color spectrum is violet, "ultraviolet." These are the first and last colors in the rainbow.

Back to electromagnetic energy . . . I know this may feel like watching a tennis match but we'll put this all together.

As stated above, electromagnetic energy is the attracting force that holds us and the universe together. As physicists have gone deeper into the world of matter, or quantum mechanics, they found a tiny subatomic particle, called a "gluon," the result of the interaction between quarks. As a mediator, the gluon "glues" quarks together.

I have a foggy idea of what that means. I think.

Anyway, the article "The Glue That Holds the World Together" in the July 2000 issue of *Discover Magazine* mentions that the "gluon" generates its own changing color field. This is called "quantum chromo-dynamics." The article did say that the color generated by the gluon has nothing to do with color as we know it; rather, it is the color of the force field. Sounds like the same thing to me; however, it is curious that the term "color field" is used when talking of gluons. And I like the name gluon . . . it sticks in your mind. (Are you chuckling?)

At this point, we have pried into the tiniest subatomic world to find "the color field of the gluon." In contrast, from there we look to the external world for the highest color field that nature treats us to, a field of the perfect alignment of colors . . . the rainbow.

You know the feeling a rainbow inspires. After a rainy period when the sun starts to peek through the clouds, suddenly you spot it. "Look!" you exclaim. "A rainbow!" It evokes awe and lifts our spirits; we point it out to others so they too can enjoy nature's beauty. It is said that this delicate palette of color is a promise that the future will bring fulfillment and happiness, leading to the pot of gold at the end of the rainbow.

Our beliefs and expressions are based on an element of truth.

A rainbow is the reflection and refraction of the sun's light on the rain. Think of that definition . . . a reflection of the sun's light. "Light" is the key word. As mentioned, metaphysically Light represents the Creative force, the Word, the energy behind the manifestation of matter. Neophytes and seekers of truth aspire to a body full of Light.

In *Color Psychology and Color Therapy*, Faber Birren states, "The aura of the superman is filled with iridescent hues . . ."[6] My interpretation of the iridescent hues is the rainbow.

I believe that when we are perfectly balanced, we are wrapped in iridescent hues, a rainbow aura. Our electromagnetic energy field is that which holds us together, the glue of the universe and the colors of the rainbow in perfect balance. We radiate out to all those we encounter, spreading the light, and finally sharing the harmony of life's treasures, sharing our "pot of gold" at the end of the rainbow. This pot of gold at the end of our rainbow-wrapped body is our heads, the pot that contains the true treasure of an elevated awareness.

Our energy field, through continuing cycles of positive thoughts and actions, attract equal treasure into our lives.

THE RAINBOW

How is all this related to the rainbow? I thought you'd never ask.

Well, the rainbow consists of seven colors which always appear in the same order: red, orange, yellow, green, light blue, indigo, and violet. Earlier I mentioned the color spectrum: infrared and ultraviolet, the beginning and the end of the rainbow. We can relate these 7 ordered colors to the cosmic number pattern.

We know there are nine numbers, 1 through 9, the basis of our counting system (and the cosmic pattern of life). These 9 numbers also represent a step-by-step pattern that leads to physical results and then recycling. The 1 plants the seed, then steps 2 through 6 lay out the pattern; in step 7 we mentally plan how to put the pieces together, and then in step 8, we assemble the pattern to create form. Step 9 brings change and transition.

This pattern applies to any endeavor in which you are engaged, whether it be forging a relationship, raising children, getting an education, learning a new job, setting up a new home, writing a book, and so forth. You set yourself a goal, and take the steps to achieve that goal. This pattern is universal and unchangeable!

The first seven numbers are the pieces of a "pattern," similar to the pieces of a pattern for making a dress or a suit. Nothing has been formed yet.

These are the "seven days of creation," the seven preliminary steps necessary to reach our goal. In the Bible, the seven days of creation were the pattern for creation. Nothing had been created on the seventh day; it would be on the 8th "day" that the physical world was formed.

Each color of the rainbow creates the proper electromagnetic field around its corresponding number to ensure its success. The physical world has not yet formed.

As we move through steps 1 through 6, we weave individually colored threads. In the 7th step, we mentally plan how to weave those threads into what will become a complete garment.

1	Red
2	Orange
3	Yellow
4	Green
5	Light blue
6	Indigo
7	Violet

In the 8th step, we create the physical garment in which we wrap ourselves. This garment is made of the seven colors we have previously dyed.

This is our coat of many colors!

This coat of many colors is our aura that is now visible to the world, our rainbow body, our electromagnetic field in living color. We are seen and recognized for that which we have built as a result of the work of the previous 7 steps.

8 is karma, which means we will reap what we have sown.

If, at the 8th step, we find our coat of many colors dull, then our pot at the end of the rainbow will be filled with lumps of coal, our bodies less healthy and our lives unhappy.

And coal is a good item to be left with because of its promise! Under pressure, buried deep in the Earth for millions of years, that lump of coal becomes a diamond!

As a metaphor, we are the lumps of coal, unformed and unpolished, who through years of living our lives in the most positive ways we can, even with all the accompanying pressures, become the polished being, the diamond, the "body full of the light" of understanding, the light body sought after by mystics for thousands of years.

Therefore, if the pot contains coal, we can resolve during the 9th step of endings to let go of the old attitudes and begin to work towards a healthy and happy result beginning in the following 1st step when it's time for a mini-rebirth, a time to begin again.

However, if along the first seven steps toward our goal we have dyed the threads brilliant colors and have woven them into the shining coat of many colors that now surrounds us, then in the 8th step of karma others will recognize us for our solid contributions to the world.

In the 9th step, we then reap the real treasure in the pot of gold at the end of the rainbow, a pot filled with those golden chunks and the glittering jewels of wisdom, which we can then share with others.

That pot, metaphorically, is our heads. Here we discover the true treasure resulting from our efforts of the past 8 steps, which is an elevated consciousness. At this time, we recognize that we have an obligation to share the wisdom and experiences and profits from our past cycle with others. We must give back in some measure that which we have gained.

We can now associate the colors of the rainbow with the cosmic pattern 1 through 9.

1	Red
2	Orange
3	Yellow
4	Green
5	Light blue
6	Indigo
7	Violet
8	Our coat of many colors (our aura now visible to the world, karma)
9	The pot of gold at the end of the rainbow (our head, elevated consciousness, wisdom)

The coat of many colors reminds me of Andrew Lloyd Webber's 1982 Broadway musical, *Joseph and the Amazing Technicolor Dreamcoat*. The musical is based upon the Biblical passage in Genesis where Joseph was given a coat of many colors by his father, thus favoring him above his brothers. The coat of many colors is symbolic of Joseph's natural goodness, his perfect aura, if you will, which his father recognized. The dreamcoat is his rainbow body, the coat of many colors woven by his past goodness and by which he is rewarded in the 8 cycle.

The 9 colored steps just mentioned apply as well to any temporary cycle that you are experiencing. You can use the color associated with its specific cycle to enhance your efforts for success.

See how nicely we fit the disparate pieces—color, color therapy, healing, Light, auras, electromagnetism, the coat of many colors, the rainbow—together to solve this dazzling puzzle that is you!

YOUR BIRTHDAY COLOR

So, we finally arrive at your birthday color. I believe that you have a lifetime color that is attached to your birthday number. Wearing the color of this number or having it around you in some manner, such as in your living space, can enhance the message embedded in your birthday number.

The particular electromagnetic energy of your birthday color can create the right mood and psychological balance so that you can accomplish what you are here to learn in this lifetime. Shades of your birthday color also apply.

Use color, as mentioned earlier, with an awareness of its influence upon your physical and mental well being. Use your birthday color but only if it feels right! Colors do affect us psychologically so use this information wisely. Also be aware that each culture has its own historical associations with color that needs to be taken into consideration.

The following descriptions of the nine basic birthday numbers will round out the picture beautifully! Use the single number to which your birthday reduces to find your color.

Each color has an energy level; red is more aggressive, red-blooded, the warrior spirit, and sexually stimulating whereas light blue is thoughtful and intellectual.

You may love the color associated with your birthday number however . . . you don't have to like the color or even wear it, but that color has something in its energy field that will stimulate your birthday number and help you achieve the lessons you are here to learn in this lifetime. So, give yourself time to think about it.

One last note: No birthday number is superior to another. If you believe in many lifetimes then you have worked with each of these numbers in the past and may continue to do so in the future. So, a birthday 9 is not superior to a birthday 4, and a birthday 6 is not superior to a birthday 8. They just *are*!

I have pondered on these thoughts for years. With the opportunity to rewrite this second edition of *Numerology and Your Future*, I am excited to update and add to these thoughts for your consideration . . . the color of your birthday number.

BIRTHDAY NUMBER 1: RED

Red stimulates will power, strength, awareness, courage, and boldness. It is the color of energy, stirring up the blood, embodying Civil War Naval Officer David Farragut's cry: "Damn the torpedoes . . . full speed ahead." 1 is the brave pioneer setting off alone into uncharted territories. Unafraid of what lies ahead, this individual heartily welcomes the unknown. 1 is the impatient, do-it-now, let's-get-moving individual.

Red also stimulates appetites on all levels. A woman wearing a red dress or bright ruby lipstick is showing her power; she can also be seen as sexually enticing. Men often wear red power ties, the red-blooded physical prowess of the dominant male, drawing sexual attention. Red stimulates the appetite, which is why you find red the dominant color in lounges and some restaurants. Sex and food are powerful motivators.

Red is also the color of danger. Code red is a verbal directive that warns of immediate danger, a time to take action. Fire engines and danger signs are red. We wave a red flag at a bull to rile him up. We don't know if the bull sees colors but we know the red vibration instigates action. We say someone is "so angry she sees red." Why not blue or lime? Because when the red action-oriented energy is blocked, it turns to frustrated action. When we feel thwarted in our pursuits or when someone or something is blocking our progress, our auras turn red.

Then there are the "red-blooded" warriors who are true to the spirit of their country, who will fight for the right of their beliefs, even willing to spill their blood. We honor those who stand up for what they believe, who are true to the spirit of their code.

When you feel you need more energy and red-blooded spirit, wear red. At the mental level, the color red is related to individual self-awareness. Physically, it promotes excitement and energy and increases blood flow.

As a birthday number 1, you are here to stand up and stand out! Learn to be assertive, to make your own mark in the world, to stand on your own two feet, to be unafraid, and to make your own decisions. You might listen to others but basically, you are the boss of you. Action, adventure, far horizons draw you to explore. You are here to develop into a super-energy person who is always ready to take action, to explore your desires and your sexuality, to take the new road.

Even if you are surrounded by people in your life, you may still have moments when you feel you are different somehow, alone, and on your own. And granted, sometimes you do work alone. This is necessary so others don't try to influence you; that will ruffle your feathers. Knowing when to take action and be assertive and knowing when to hold that position regardless of what others say is the key to your success.

Center on yourself; that's not the same as being selfish, rather it is trusting in your ability to make your own way without outside influence. Develop your independence. Control your behavior and direct it wisely because you are here to carve new paths and leave a trail for others to follow.

If you are upset and angry and "seeing red," you could wear pink or think pink or gaze at a pink candle. You must have something pink close by that will help to calm you down. Remember color therapy—how the calming effect of "drunk tank pink" can reduce anger in as little as fifteen minutes.

You are here to be the warrior, the individual who stands out, and the person to whom others look to for adventure and new horizons, the person whose competitive spirit is to be the best and get there first whether that is physically or mentally.

BIRTHDAY NUMBER 2: ORANGE

The color orange stimulates circulation in the body and helps expand the lungs; it works hand-in-hand with meditation. Orange also promotes happiness; perhaps you should wear orange while you're meditating to enhance the positive benefits of the practice.

Meditation is important for you so that you can probe the inner workings of your mind. Trust your instincts because your subconscious will alert you to the hidden meanings in any situation. Learn to trust your flashes of insight and perhaps telepathic experiences because they will help you solve difficult problems. There is a hidden brilliance here that works well with your inventive mind.

Orange is the color of magic; magic is the act of understanding processes that have yet to be discovered. Witness someone pressing a button to open a door twenty feet away. In early Salem, that person would have been burned as a witch because those early superstitious people saw that act as magic, and that was interpreted as the work of the devil. Their reaction was the result of not understanding the natural laws of nature. 2 is the number of connecting the seen and unseen worlds.

Buddhist monks wear orange- or saffron-colored robes. The holiest colors of Hinduism are the three predominant colors of sunset—red, orange/saffron, and yellow; these are also the first three colors of the rainbow. Situated between the red and yellow colors of the rainbow, orange is the meditative stage, the time to take the seed of action (1, red) and prepare it (2, orange) for creative expression (3, yellow).

Orange (and black) is the color of Halloween. Originally a pagan holiday, October 31 marked the end of summer in the ancient Celtic tradition, a time to honor the dead and placate the mysterious forces that controlled nature. It was on this day that the veil between this world and the next was thinnest, allowing communication between the two worlds. "Hallowe'en" means "hallowed evening" or "holy evening."

As a birthday number 2, you are learning about the subconscious link between two worlds, some of you perhaps as a medium, psychic, empath, or intuitive. In any case, you are sensitive and need quiet time away from the intrusions of the outside world to renew your soul. It is during these secluded times that you contact and educate your inner being.

You may use your learned sensitivities as a mediator, parsing through surface dialogue to discover the real meaning of the conversations between two parties. You know how to unruffle feathers, to calm contentious discussions, to pour oil on troubled waters. You settle disputes with pacifying words.

You are the Magic-Maker. You may prefer to remain in the background as the peacemaker who can settle disputes and bring about peaceful settlements. You intuitively understand the balance point between two forces and learn how to join opposing points of view; you resonate to the needs of others and are able to see both sides. Because of these qualities, relationships are extremely important to you.

You are here to understand the true meaning behind verbal communication, to learn to interpret language at a deeper level than the superficial context, and to meditate upon the meaning of how language connects all people in meaningful ways. You should use that ability to bring separate bodies together in harmony.

In color therapy, orange encourages communication between people. Be like the yam, that sweet orange vegetable that grows underground. Become aware of the roots of life; use your ability rooted in a deeper understanding of the essential meaning of the words exchanged between parties, and your efforts will produce sweet harmony. This is the signature of the peacemaker.

In regards to the yam, add a taste of butter and honey . . . they're delicious!

When I read this number to my grandson who is a birthday number 2, he replied: "I yam that I am." He is so clever!

BIRTHDAY NUMBER 3:
YELLOW

Yellow vitalizes our bodies and minds and stimulates activity. It is the color of the Sun, the life force that shines for everyone, that brings a smile on a gloomy day. Yellow is stimulating and cleansing and is known as an antidepressant. This color stimulates confidence and optimism and awakens an enthusiasm for life.

Notice that when the days are cloudy for long periods of time our energy lags. When the sun reappears, we feel reenergized and renewed; without apparent reason, we just feel happy. In the palette of colors, yellow is the most obvious; it's the one color we notice first.

Psychologically, as one holistic site mentioning color therapy put it, yellow is the color of perception rather than reasoning. Perception is defined as the ability to become aware of something through the senses, to see what is not evident. In this sense, yellow is the color of faith. You have the perception to see beyond those who say, "How can you believe in that? What proof do you have?"

Well, you can believe and you don't need proof; you see beyond those tangibles. You know that faith can move mountains. And the reason you know is because 3 is the number behind the manifestation of life and form; it is the most creative of all the numbers.

Metaphysically, the ancients saw yellow as happiness and merriment, and more importantly, they saw yellow as the animating color of life. Note our common expression . . . things happen in 3s. 3 is the underlying foundation of life and is embodied in the shape of the triangle. It takes 3 parts to energize and give life to the whole as shown in just the following few examples: It takes the trinity of mother-father-child to create the family; it takes past-present-future to create time; it takes breadth-width-depth to create the three dimensional world we live in; it takes rhythm-harmony-tone to create music; it takes red-blue-yellow to create the primary colors.

As a 3 birthday number you are the energizing force in life. You should don your party hat, pick up your palette to paint, write that script for the puppet show, invite your friends for high tea, plan an around-the-world cruise with 100 of your closest friends—just join the party wherever it is happening. This is your life. You are here to use that creativity through expressing optimism, joy, enthusiasm, and faith in life. You need the space and freedom to grow and experience life. 3 stimulates artistic expression and brings the little child inside you out to play.

Learn to be confident socially, reaching out to others through groups, organizations, parties, and various other venues where your happy smile draws others to you and encourages them through your uplifting spirit. Amusement and fun enhance your spirit. Your enduring optimism and good humor gives hope to other people. To paraphrase the original Annie, whose faith in life was unsurpassed, you sing a slightly different tune: "The sun is out today!"

Your number represents birth and fertility through creations from your body, your children, and/or through creations from your mind using any variety of artistic pursuits. You may work with children because they embody the power of believing that all things are possible, reminding you of the same message. You can express your creativity through any medium: from writing, painting, and music to dance and acting; from jewelry making to interior design; from planning social events to cooking those deliciously delicate hors d'oeuvres. Please . . . invite me over!

Don't scatter your energies or waste them through extravagance and overindulgence. Find a purpose where you can shine in your own right, and then inspire others with your faith in life. Remember, things do happen in 3s.

Wear that smile every day; it is the universal expression of happiness and joy. Psychologically, yellow is the happiest color in the rainbow's palette of colors.

Green is the color of nature, and is related to the earth and earthly things. It's easy on the eyes and promotes a feeling of rest, health, safety, and balance. Green relieves stress and thereby promotes healing. This "feel good" color soothes the nervous system as anyone knows who spends a day away from the stresses of their everyday world out in nature. Before appearing on a television program, guests wait in the "green room" because green has a calming effect.

Connecting with nature is important for number 4 birthdays. Walking down a wooded path where the birds tweet and the squirrels scamper, where you converse with wood spirits and little people who

BIRTHDAY NUMBER 4:
GREEN

hide under the mushrooms, or sitting in the vast silent desert before the ruins of the Anasazi cliff dwellings of the Southwest, or by the eternal ocean listening to the waves splashing over the sand: these experiences renew your spirit, sooth your nerves, and create a feeling of peace and balance.

You are here to be a steward of the earth, to build strong foundations, to take care of your body, to experience physical and sensual relationships, and to enjoy your senses through touch, taste, and smell.

You lay the foundations upon which society is built. Material possessions are important to you because they give you a sense of ownership of part of life's bounty. If you work well and wisely, you will be rewarded. When someone is "green with envy," they are envious of the material successes such as money, goods, and positions of others in this material world.

Many environmental groups use the color green in their logos and advertising. You may put your time, effort, and money into groups that work to heal the planet like Greenpeace and the Sierra Club and the Nature Conservancy. Perhaps you feel the need to get involved.

Or you might decide you want to manage the financial resources that keep the Earth running in professions like accounting, banking, and money management. Or you could decide you want to be a farmer, close to the land, growing healthy crops to feed the people of this planet; or maybe you plant a small garden where you put your hands into the warm earth to plant, weed, and harvest the food to feed your family, the "green thumb" activities. Or perhaps you are in the trades, working with your hands; you may like to tinker and fix things.

Work, order, security, money (or cows and pigs if that is your medium of exchange), gardens, and pantries filled with food, a warm cozy abode inhabited with a warm cozy companion, and a healthy connection with the earth are essentials for a birthday number 4 like yourself.

Green is healing. For many years, surgeons wore white scrubs until an early twentieth-century influential doctor switched from white to green scrubs because he thought it was easier on his eyes. According to an article by Susannah F. Locke (September 1, 2008, "Ever Wondered?") ". . . looking at green can refresh a doctor's vision of red things, including the body innards of a patient during surgery . . . staring at red during an operation causes the red signal in the brain to fade, which makes it harder to see the nuances of the human body." Green, the harmonizing color of red in the color palette, balanced the doctor's vision. I'm sure we all appreciate a surgeon with "refreshed" vision. That original doctor's instincts were correct!

Today, scrubs worn in surgery are almost always light green, light blue, or a green-blue. Non-surgical scrubs can be any variety of colors.

If your color is green, you are a healer of some kind. You should use your green thumb in whatever life path you have chosen. Green means solid comfort in the things of the earth.

In color therapy, blue is said to control the throat, which allows freedom of expression so that you can communicate more easily with others. It improves verbal skills so that you can intelligently interact with people in social settings. It also enhances your ability to listen, not only to others but to your own thoughts and feelings as well. Blue inspires integrity and honesty.

When we speak of people who are true to their beliefs, we say they are "true blue." This color evokes feelings of loyalty and faithfulness, perhaps alluding to the color of the sky, reliably above us every day. Some companies require their salesmen to wear blue shirts—perhaps they know this color inspires trust in their customers.

This color also relates to the fastness of a blue dye that will not run. Blue dye is not soluble in water; it stays true to its color, thus "true blue."

Another idiom relating to blue is when a person is down or depressed. We say this person is "feeling blue" or having "the blues." They are having a "cloudy day." This means, of course, that mentally they have lost touch with the outside world in some aspect; they feel cut off from verbal interactions with others. Or they are having some kind of internal dialogue that they can't resolve at that time in their life.

As a birthday number 5, you are here to gather information and learn how to communicate on many levels. Education is essential for you: You may be a teacher or a lifelong student, reading books, and continually asking questions; or you could be involved in social media dialoguing, or you may enjoy buying and selling; or you might express your restless nature through the outdoor classrooms of life's experiences. Curiosity compels you.

Words are your life line. As a result, you can speak many languages in the sense that you pick up on conversations and always have something to offer. Perhaps some of you do have a talent for learning foreign languages because your mind is so agile. At any rate, you seem to know what to say and how to say it. You sense that others need to speak what's on their minds so you become a good listener as well, as long as the topic interests you. Often, you are able to help others because of that vast mental library of yours.

BIRTHDAY NUMBER 5:
LIGHT BLUE

You are the communicator. Information, curiosity, and verbal exchange are essential for you this lifetime. Whether you are a librarian, receptionist, salesperson, writer, teacher, or a social individual, entertaining others with your wit and cleverness, you are expressing your need to learn these skills. You may have a library of books, or are constantly searching or communicating on the Internet, or traveling the byways and highways of life, always seeking out new contacts and ideas and experiences.

You may have been a member of the Blue Stocking Society, founded in the early 1750s as a women's literary discussion group—a revolutionary thought back then when women's activities were expected to be needlework and knitting (although they are honorable creative enterprises). It was considered "unbecoming" for women to learn Greek or Latin or to be an author. As a truly feminine enterprise, the Blue Stocking Society was open to women and men.

Education, however it is obtained, is the key for you.

One of the most popular and prolific western novelists in the world, Louis L'Amour, left school at age 15 to go to work. He traveled through the American West, eventually writing more than 100 books. Awarded the Medal of Freedom by President Reagan in 1984, he died in 1988. His autobiography, *Education of a Wandering Man,* is the perfect verbal definition of the individual whose intelligence is fed by life's experiences rather than by formal education.

Yes, you are the celestial postman, collecting and disseminating information. You need to make verbal and intellectual contact with the world . . . the sky's the limit . . . especially if it's light blue.

BIRTHDAY NUMBER 6:
INDIGO

Indigo (dark blue mixed with dark purple) is used in meditation to achieve deep levels of consciousness; it is related to the "third eye," the chakra (a center of spiritual power in the body) that is located at the exact center of the forehead. Indigo stimulates the third eye and awakens integrity, responsibility, loyalty, duty, devotion, and deep intuition.

The words "responsibility" and "duty" evoke thoughts of organizations like the police who keep the peace and protect their citizens from criminal activity, and the firefighters who charge into burning buildings without thought of their own lives to save trapped people and pets. These principles also involve social groups who band together to help the underprivileged and those in great need.

Dark blue promotes peace, reliability, and a sense of security. Notice that the uniforms of the police are often dark blue. We call the police, "the boys in blue." The current popular televisions series, *Blue Bloods* is about a New York City family of police officers. Note the "gut feeling," the intuition that comes from a deep level within, that some crime fighting professionals learn to trust.

Law and order, responsibility and dedication to home, family, community, and country, are key words involved in maintaining balance in this world. You are here to learn to honor your responsibility for others. Peace and security are the necessary key elements in your life. You may find yourself involved in the courts where judges and prosecutors and lawyers work to maintain justice.

The military is also found under this number's influence. These are often the people who have a cause to which they will sacrifice themselves because of their dedication and belief in liberty and freedom, sometimes even unto death.

You may find you are concerned with the domestic scene where you focus on home and family, taking care of loved ones by providing a comfortable home and nourishing meals. Cooking might be one of your creative talents. You would teach your children love and respect so they would grow to be good world citizens. "The hand that rocks the cradle is the hand that rules the world."[7]

You may find that people come to you with their problems because they know you will offer a shoulder to cry on. This could extend beyond your family and neighborhood into the public in general as a career as a counselor or therapist because of your compassion and understanding and your ability to make things right and to cure their blues.

Domestic occupations appeal to a 6 birthday number: building and the trades, occupations that require a certain artistic labor. Think of the skilled laborers who worked on ancient temples and churches with stone chisels creating awe-inspiring art. 6 professions seek to beautify through such occupations as interior decorating, beauty makeovers, art, landscaping, and master gardening that provide a sense of well being in the lives of others.

One of my clients, working with a charity, gave free beauty makeovers to women in third world countries. These women got to be queen for the day. As a result of the change in their self esteem, these makeovers showed them what their futures could be because of the change in their attitudes about themselves. My client created small miracles in terms of numbers but huge impacts in terms of consciousness.

You should find an artistic expression through any profession that creates beautiful spaces where love and beauty and harmony can fill the senses so that your corner of the world brings the Yin and Yang into full glorious bloom.

It's the daily effort that you put into caring for others that are the miracles in life.

In fact, during your life, you may often hear someone say: "It's a miracle how you changed my life."

BIRTHDAY NUMBER 7:
VIOLET

In numerology, the number 7 indicates a period of rest, a retreat from the business of the outside world to a quiet place where your energy is focused on your thought process. It's a period of time to activate the mind, a time to think. The 7 period fits in beautifully with the color violet.

As opposed to infrared, ultraviolet is the other end of the color spectrum. Violet influences the central nervous system, thus the need for periodic rest periods. It also stimulates the blood in the upper brain and the pineal gland, which *"encourages the flow of imagination and the integration of ideas."* (My italics.)

This key phrase—"the flow of imagination and the integration of ideas"—is a perfect description of the 7th step process where you fit together the pieces of the pattern, where you weave the individual colored threads from the first six steps, where you integrate your ideas. If you're not sure what this means, please read the earlier section on The Rainbow, page 49.

Violet stimulates inspiration and dream activity so you would be wise to keep a book by your bedside to record your dreams every morning. We do dream every night, even though we may not remember them; however, you can train yourself to recall and record them. One method is to tell yourself when you fall asleep: "I will remember one dream." If you do this each night, it will happen. Then write it down immediately before you get out of bed; they are slippery devils. Many great ideas and inventions have come to those who listened to their dreams.

Born under a 7, your strength is your mind. Had you been born in another time, you would have been placed in the temple to train to become a priestess, because those in that field would have recognized the mystical powers of your mind. Introspection and perfection are key words.

Today, in our busy society, you need time by yourself in which to think, meditate, and ponder upon the ideas that flow freely through your mind. Periods of isolation are necessary for you so that you can strengthen your mind. These quiet, more isolated spaces allow you the time to explore disciplines such as philosophy, science, technology, religion, or metaphysics. In this way, your fine mental capabilities can be developed more fully.

If you are often tired or you hear others questioning why you seem tired all the time, that's an indication that you aren't being true to your 7 birthday number. Examine what you have been doing. Have you spent too much time running around in circles when what you really need to do is get a running start toward that hideaway, whether it be the ocean, the mountains, or your woman cave? You need time to think!

You also need those retreat periods to strengthen your body. Healing periods are necessary. Spend time away from the disruptive noises of society and the constant stimulation of the air waves that bombard your mind every day through the television, business meetings, traffic jams, cell phones, "Twitters" and "Tweets."

Rather, you need to detach yourself from the wires of society and listen to the tweets of nature through the voices of those little feathered creatures that bring us such joyous melodies, along with the voices of the moose, the whales, the prairie dogs, "the lions and tigers and bears! Oh, my!" Nature's spaces allow your imagination the freedom to roam, unfettered by interruptions.

We find the number 7 birthday in the lives of philosophers, writers, poets, teachers, inventors, scientists, spiritual leaders, environmentalists, and creative thinkers (and we're all creative in some way), and those individuals who seek the truth in their perspective fields.

You may be busy in your respective profession however you still need that independent space where your can pursue your quest for knowledge. You are the mental explorer who never stops seeking; this is the food that nourishes you. Post a sign on the door to your life that reads: Out to lunch!

BIRTHDAY NUMBER 8:
RAINBOW

Your color is the rainbow, the mantle that has been woven with the threads of the past seven vibrant colors. You wear that coat of many colors for the entire world to see. In the best sense, you are the social conscience of how to use power in this material world. You are the promise that there is reward for hard honest work from your past efforts.

Your rainbow body, this coat of many colors, is the aura that surrounds you. Those sensitive people who see auras recognize you immediately as a power person. Those who do not see auras still sense and recognize your power; it emanates off you in waves. You presence brings with it the power to achieve.

Years ago, I stood next to a candidate for political office. When he started to speak, I could literally feel a wave of power emanating from his body. It was neither good nor bad; it was just there. He had free will to use it the way his conscience dictated.

There are those who use power for their own ends and, in the process, trample over those who are powerless. The knowledge that "absolute power corrupts absolutely" is the theme with this birthday number. The figure 8 is drawn with two equal circles; balance is the key. What you send out comes back to you in equal measure. It's called karma.

You are here to attune to the physical world, to experience life directly. Yours is a number of strength and responsibility, which you must wield with awareness because your use of these qualities affects not only your life but the lives of those over whom you have power.

You can be recognized for your deeds. As a power person, you are a leader in whatever profession you choose in the "real" world: in politics, in business and finance; as an executive in charge of a corporation; an environmental or social leader; a builder or military leader; a community organizer, a mother on the march, on whatever path you walk in this life. You not only hold the architectural plans of life, you are here to become the master builder in this material world.

Money is certainly a part of your cycle because, at least in our society, money moves mountains and bestows power. In another society, you could be a powerful figure depending upon the number of cows and pigs you owned. Money is the means of exchange that represents how people value your services, your talents, and what they are willing to pay for those talents. Once your abilities reach their peak, others will seek you out and pay their tributes.

Power is an aphrodisiac that draws others to you because your position can bestow favors and a high lifestyle that others may desire, even if they can only rub shoulders with your rainbow body. Relationships can be formed with other power sources. Again, the number 8 is drawn as two equal but connected circles; the power must be evenly shared. Difficulties arise when relationships, personal or business, are out of balance.

It takes knowledge to know how the world works, and how you should work within those parameters. You need to be aware that what you give out will come back to you in equal measure. If you operate your business or home or relationships with a caring commonsense approach, treating others with the respect they deserve, they will love you for it and work twice as hard for you. You can leave a lasting legacy in whatever profession you choose.

While some people in this life may be behind the 8 ball, you hold the cue stick!

POT OF GOLD

Your color is the promise of the pot of gold at the end of the rainbow.

As a birthday number 9, you are in possession of the metaphorical gold and jewels in the pot at the end of the rainbow. Your lesson this lifetime is to share the precious metals in that pot with others regardless of their beliefs or attitudes. You must sow the seeds of wisdom; some will fall on fallow ground while others will take root and blossom. Yours is not to select the terrain but to speak what you know whenever and wherever the opportunity arises and to do so with compassion and understanding.

You should be an example for others. You must be the humanitarian in the sense that you don't discriminate against others because of race, religion, sexual orientation, philosophy, or background. The knowledge you have gathered, perhaps even from past lifetimes, is now translated into wisdom and is meant to be given out. Know that you know! You have the gift of wisdom to guide you in this life, a gift that must be shared.

One thing you are here to learn is that you must teach others through whatever role in life you choose. You are the guiding light, like the Tarot's Hermit on the mountaintop shining the Light of Wisdom for others to follow. You will also find that not only will you find a way to speak truths in your every day living, but you must also live by those truths. You are not one who can preach one way of living, while you do just the opposite behind the scenes, for surely, that curtain will be swept aside and you will be exposed. You must live your life by what you teach.

Sharing your wisdom requires that you recognize that not everyone is on the same path as you. Every person has their own valid road to walk. There is a belief that there are three paths in life: the path of work, the path of faith, and the path of knowledge. Don't be discouraged when you encounter those who don't want to hear what you have to say. A little of your message will be embedded in their minds for future examination along their path.

Be charitable; be kind; be compassionate. You may work as a teller at a bank with a friendly smile that uplifts customers; or a parent who raises her children to love and accept others, thereby sending good citizens into the world; or a politician who truly cares about the people she represents; or a tradesman, a teacher, a writer, or philosopher. All professions have people who are wise in their own ways, and who make impacts on a daily basis, impacts they may not ever realize are happening.

You may find that people gravitate to you because they find you easy to talk with, and they value your insights. They see in you a universal acceptance of life in all its colors and flavors so they realize that you don't judge them; therefore, they can be more open with you.

9 is the cycle of endings, of completions, the culmination of the knowledge gained from the past 8 cycles. 9 has a curious mathematical quality in that any number multiplied by 9 returns to 9; any number added to 9 returns to itself. It's circular in that sense. It's the universal number that keeps returning or, you might say, keeps the wheels turning. 9 keeps "the wheel of life" rolling on.

Be that shining light on the top of the hill that keeps life rolling on, a beacon in the darkness, a hand held out to those who falter. Lead the way into the future with wisdom, humility, and compassion.

**

If you're interested in the traditionally basic tones:

- Black is associated with power, authority, and intelligence, magic, and mystery. Think of power figures like ministers, nuns and priests, along with witches and wizards, those figures who are in touch with the mystical world. Too much black can be overwhelming. However, it also has a slimming effect when used in clothing and in marketing products.

- Grey can be neutral and indifferent, or refined and timeless. It can also suggest old age and perhaps feelings of emptiness. A gray area is when the discussion is stuck between two differing points of view and it's either hard to clarify the points or it can mean one can choose to go one way or the other.

- White is associated with purification, cleanliness, and innocence . . . white as the driven snow. It also symbolizes completion. We start over when we want "a clean slate." In ancient Egypt and in China, white is associated with death and mourning, experiences that suggest a clean slate and a new beginning. White is the color of perfection, the Light of Spirit.

This section is offered to you as something to think about.

The concept of a birthday gift came to my attention many years ago when I gave a lecture at an all-day seminar at a church. The minister, a dear man named Reverend Paul Higgins, asked if I could tie my numerology lecture in with the theme of the day that was "Gifts of the Spirit," from I Corinthians 12: v. 7–11.

To my surprise, but perhaps not really, I discovered there are nine gifts of the spirit, but none of these are meaningful without the greatest gift of all . . . Love. Nine gifts of the spirit, I reasoned, had to be tied in with the nine numbers, and the greatest gift of them all, Love, had to be the 0, the symbol of all that is, was, and ever shall be. The mystical symbol for the Cosmic Egg of the Goddess and for God is a circle.

The 9 gifts reflect the underlying pattern of the universal steps 1 through 9 and are the fundamental laws of nature. As mentioned earlier, groups of 7 and 9 in metaphysical literature often relate to celestial and terrestrial measurements that we weave into our philosophies because we know these truths at deeper levels.

Following are the verses from I Corinthians that the minister asked me to weave into my lecture. The verses below are from the Lamsa Bible, translated by George Lamsa, a man who spoke the original Aramaic language of Jesus. His is the most accurate translation, unlike other versions, which where translated by those who had to learn the language first thereby losing the nuances of the original.

A case in point is the mistranslated verse in Matthew 19:24, which in the King James Version was translated as: "And Again I say unto you It is easier for a camel to go through the eye of a needle than for a rich man to enter the kingdom of God."

The word for "camel" is a mistranslation of the word for "rope."

Lamsa corrected this passage to read: "Again I say to you it is easier for a rope to go through the eye of a needle than for a rich man to enter into the kingdom of God."[8]

Here is the Lamsa translation of the gifts of the Spirit:

I CORINTHIANS, CHAPTER 12, V. 7–11

Verse 7. But the manifestation of the Spirit is given to every man as help to him.

Verse 8. For to one is given by the Spirit the word of wisdom; to another the word of knowledge by the same Spirit.

Verse 9. To another faith by the same Spirit; to another gifts of healing by the same Spirit.

Verse 10. To another the working of miracles; to another prophecy;

to another the means to distinguish the true Spirit; to another different languages; to another interpretation of languages.

Verse 11. But all of these gifts are wrought by that one and the same Spirit, dividing to every one severally as he will.

If this is a gift, we have not "earned it" in the traditional sense. Therefore, might we be here to learn to use this gift along with learning the lessons of our Birthday Number? Think of the Gift of the Spirit as a birthday gift that might have been presented to you at the moment of your birth.

As you know, each of us is born under one of the 9 numbers. We know that every number beyond 9 can be reduced to a single number. The goal of the 9 numbers eventually is the perfection found in the 0. 0 is the symbol for the circle. As Voltaire wrote, "God is a circle whose center is everywhere and circumference is nowhere." Also, the circle is the symbol for the love of the Creator.

So, you might think on the following associations which I present to you for your consideration. See if they work for you.

Birthday Gift Number 1: to distinguish the true Spirit

Birthday Gift Number 2: the interpretation of languages

Birthday Gift Number 3: faith

Birthday Gift Number 4: healing

Birthday Gift Number 5: different languages

Birthday Gift Number 6: the working of miracles

Birthday Gift Number 7: prophecy

Birthday Gift Number 8: knowledge

Birthday Gift Number 9: wisdom

The Goal-0-Love

Because the root connection between your "birthday color" and your "birthday gift of the spirit" is your birthday number, you will find that the following discussions about the gift of the spirit necessarily repeat some of the previously described qualities of the number itself.

1 represents individuality, and also unity. 1 is a centered number, ego-centered in the lower sense; ego-centered in the highest sense. Red is the fiery energy behind the number 1.

An ego-centered individual is not divided by outside interests but is rather totally centered on self, aware only of self, much like a child who, in innocence, demands her personal needs above all else. A child is closer to her original source than an adult, therefore, she often speaks or lives out the true essence or spirit of life, totally immersed in enjoying each moment to the exclusion of all else. "Out of the mouths of babes" come words of wisdom. A child lives the oneness in life, and becomes one with it. The child can distinguish the true spirit of life because of her centeredness.

1 also represents unity. We stand together as one when supporting a cause, a policy, a nation. There is strength in unity. You can easily break one strand of uncooked spaghetti but try breaking the entire box. (It's early; food's on my mind as I wait for my hubby to bring my traditional breakfast of toast with peanut butter and honey.)

As Abraham Lincoln said in his 1858 acceptance speech upon receiving his party's nomination for president: "a house divided against itself cannot stand." His law partner, though supporting the idea, said it was "politically incorrect" to be using the words of Jesus from the gospels.

If you are living a true birthday number 1, you should be expressing your total individuality with all your being, even if it is politically incorrect. You should be number 1 in the sense that you can, by example, show how best to enjoy every moment of living your life with a single mind . . . "if thine eye be single, thy whole body is full of light." You can show how to experience the world with an eye full of wonder, and a zest and enthusiasm and total absorption in your pursuits.

There's a quote that I believe came from Thomas Edison: "Give me an uneducated man who doesn't know it can't be done and he'll go ahead and do it. Give me an educated man and he'll give me a thousand reasons why it can't be done." You're the uneducated "man" in the sense that you are not influenced by what others say is, or is not, possible. Your true spirit guides you.

You don't look for leadership but others will follow you in worthwhile causes because they sense your singular spirit and will look to you for direction. You message is direct and clear; there is no ambiguity. You are able to find the true spirit of life and carry it with you through whatever journey you undertake.

BIRTHDAY GIFT NUMBER 1:

THE MEANS TO DISTINGUISH THE TRUE SPIRIT

BIRTHDAY GIFT NUMBER 2:

THE INTERPRETATION OF LANGUAGES

As we know from the meaning of the numbers, 2 is the peacemaker and mediator, the companion who settles disputes because she must have harmony. Orange is the color of the magical 2.

The interpretation of languages involves a sort of translation. When we translate, we reword an idea so that others may understand what was formerly unintelligible. Often the understanding comes in a flash, like lightning, a bolt out of the blue. What was once totally confusing suddenly becomes clear as a bell.

And is it not the misinterpretation of another's words that can cause division. Have you ever taken what someone has said in an entirely different context from the way it was intended? Case in point: A family member was negotiating a business deal when she remarked that the price was too high. The man on the other end of the deal hesitated, then reluctantly agreed to the price with the comment, "Well, if you won't spread it around . . ." She took his comment to mean that she was too tight with her money. It turned out he merely meant that he would agree to her terms if she would not spread around the fact that he had made an adjustment in his fee.

Language is often a poor means of communication. Words are loaded with different meanings; a word can be a trigger mechanism that sends people off on tangents, depending on their past association with the word you happen to be using. These word associations are deeply embedded in our subconscious as a result of our past experiences. We find the connection to this truth in Key 2, the High Priestess in the Tarot. She rules the hidden workings of the subconscious mind.

If your birthday is a 2, you are here to become the translator, the mediator, who is the connector between opposing ideas, opposing factions, and opposing parties. You are the calming influence who often works behind the scenes, the figure behind the veil who does not want or accept public accolades for your work. Your gift is one of the most important of all, the peacemaker and the interpreter of languages.

You understand the nuances in conversations; you can see through the words to the intent behind them. You know when someone is telling the truth, or speaking half truths, or even just confused. Because of this, you cannot be easily fooled by smooth talk. You take it all in, interpret the meaning and then, deftly, handle the individuals involved to bring about peaceful solutions.

3 is the number behind the manifestation of the physical world of 4. Nature unfolds in 3s; things happen in 3s. 3 is the life behind the form, the moving force we cannot see but we know is there and is real. 3 is the trinity of life. Yellow is the sunshine of faith.

Faith is believing that something will manifest even though you cannot see it at the moment; faith is believing without visible proof. You don't have to adhere to a specific religious belief. You just believe in life.

A scene from a 1950s television series had a reporter speaking with a priest in the basement of an old European cathedral. The reporter was tormented because he had lost his faith. The priest put a comforting hand on the man's shoulder and said, "Only the truly faithful dare to question their faith."

This is a profound statement! What the priest was saying is that if you have a deep inner core of faith, then you have the courage to question the outer trappings of any religion or philosophy created by man because that inner core cannot be shaken.

This is you. You have that inner core of faith.

As a birthday number 3, you don't have to adhere to a religious belief; you can express your birthday gift in many ways. Nurseryman John Chapman, dubbed Johnny Appleseed, introduced apple trees to the eastern United States at the turn of the nineteenth century by traveling the countryside spreading apple seeds along the way. You can become a modern day Johnny Appleseed spreading your seeds of faith throughout the land.

You can spread joy and goodness as you walk through life, touching others with your good feelings and optimism and hope for the future. You might be a motivational speaker or write books that inspire others to more self-awareness, which helps them attain their goals; or the kind neighbor with a ready smile and a helping hand whenever needed; or a teacher who buys supplies for her class of happy eager faces; or a fireman rescuing a beloved cat from forty feet up a tree; or a person who wears a welcoming smile in her everyday encounters.

Your faith in life can move mountains. You are a beacon of light for those who have lost their way. Your example inspires others to see and feel the joy in life . . . a butterfly gently kissing daylilies or a brisk fall breeze that stirs the colorful palette of the autumn leaves. You see the life behind the form and have faith that butterflies and fall leaves will return.

BIRTHDAY GIFT NUMBER 3:

FAITH

BIRTHDAY GIFT NUMBER 4:

HEALING

4 is the square with four sides. It represents the world, the Earth, which we can see and touch and smell. Nature unfolds in patterns of 3s; the physical world unfolds in 4s. The color is green.

It is the world of form that suffers the illusion of division, of separateness, of disease or dis-ease (out of ease). It is through the faith of number 3 that the healing can begin. It is through the physical efforts of the birthday number 4 that healing takes place.

The gift of the number 4 birthday is that of healing hands. It may be that your touch can soothe a troubled friend or a sick child. You may find your gift valuable in working with animals; certainly they can heal you as well. Animals are natural healers who bring joy and healing to those they touch.

Your gift requires that your healing efforts produce tangible results. You may choose to be a mother, a holistic healer, or a surgeon, or an environmentalist, an accountant or a closet organizer, a mason or a cook. Your ability to restore order, to create comfortable and organized spaces, to be steady and dependable, tends to settle internal anxieties and spreads a calming influence over those benefitting from the results of your efforts. These qualities create external order as well as an internal healing.

My daughter, Sarah, runs a home cleaning business. She arrived at work one morning to be met by the homeowner who was almost in tears. The woman was stressed because she had family coming for the holiday weekend and her home was in total disarray. Stressed by her work situation and a personal relationship, the woman needed to present a clean home to family, some whom were coming from a distance. Sarah put her arms around the woman to comfort her. The woman was so grateful that her home would be cleaned and put in order; it boosted her self-esteem. This is the number 4 gift of the spirit, the gift of healing.

You are the healer who provides comfort and security in this world whether you build with your hands or you heal with your hands. You provide the safe continuity of day-to-day living that diminishes the fear of chaos. With you at the helm, others don't feel at dis-ease with the world; they can relax knowing that you are at hand.

This gift is connected to light blue, the color of the sky. The gift of different languages, or the ability to speak anyone's language, seems a natural for the number 5, the easy communicator: speaker, salesperson, public relations expert, teacher, newscaster, reporter, office manager, writer, and so on. This number aptly applies to Mercury, the messenger of the gods, the character who carries messages from one place to another, the celestial postman.

5 is the midpoint between the numbers 1 through 9. As such, it has the ability to look at the past and learn from those experiences. This number, therefore, allows more choice and flexibility than that of the other eight numbers. 5 can adapt easily to any given situation.

Those of you with the birthday number 5 have the gift of languages, the ability to influence countless other people, not only because of your ability to sense and communicate what others feel, but also because of your curiosity. As a result of this curiosity, you are either on the go, mingling with others from all walks of life in order to gather information, or you're buried in a great library where you can peruse the wisdom of the ages and then dispense it, the master librarian.

The gift of different languages refers not only to languages spoken in various countries, but also to the different manners of speaking. You've heard the expression, "You speak my language." That means you understand me and I understand you; we can communicate. You can become the polished conversationalist able to converse on a myriad of topics from sports to metaphysics, and thus you can engage others.

This gift allows you to understand what others are trying to say, and to be able to respond on the same level. Indeed, the right word can change history; even punctuation can cause havoc. Take the case of the comatose comma:

> A misplaced comma cost Canadian Radio-Television and Telecommunications Commission $2.13 million dollars. Because their hired lawyers put a comma in the wrong place, the meaning of the paragraph changed, and the Canadian firm had to pay the party on the other end, Aliant, Inc., $2.13 million dollars. (Toronto's *Globe and Mail*, August 6, 2006)

And take the example of comma placement from the delightful little book, *Eats, Shoots and Leaves*, by Lynne Truss:

> "A woman, without her man, is nothing.
>
> A woman: without her, man is nothing."

Ah, yes. The gift of language. So, my friends, do watch those dangling participles and comatose commas.

BIRTHDAY GIFT NUMBER 6:

THE WORKING OF MIRACLES

According to *The Random House Dictionary*, the word "miracle" means "an effect or extraordinary event in the physical world which surpasses all known human or natural powers and is ascribed to a supernatural cause." Indigo, the color associated with 6, stimulates duty, devotion, and deep love.

In numerology, love of family and community is ascribed to the number 6. The power of love is an extraordinary power that rises to the level of a supernatural cause in the physical world. Love can and has been known to work miracles as its effect can surpass all known human powers. The working of miracles can only be connected to the number 6.

As a 6, you could be the homemaker, the judge, the lawyer, the politician, the artist, the writer, the psychologist, the landscaper, amongst other professions; those who seek justice, balance, and beauty in their environment. These are the types of people who work miracles by enforcing the rule of law or by inspiring awe through their abilities with paint or words or by performing transformations in the minds of the troubled or who use the Earth as their landscape.

Miracles do happen. Case in point: A mysterious voice led rescuers to a child who survived 14 hours hanging upside down in a car seat just above frigid river waters. Just before finding her, police and firefighters claimed they heard an adult yell "help me" from inside the car. But the young mother had died hours before from the impact. No one could explain the voice or how the little girl survived 14 hours in freezing temperatures without the proper clothing.[9]

Miracles happen every day: the woman and man who create a child, the miracle of life; the father who kneels to fix a child's broken toy and the toy works once again; a mother who kisses a cut and it doesn't hurt any more; a teenager who makes a good decision against peer pressure; a tiny seed that drops into the soil re-emerging from the ground as a growing plant; a thought that materializes into *Swan Lake* or the *Mona Lisa* or *The Brothers Karamzov*; a pair of gnarled hands that sculpts the Pieta; the human heart that pumps unceasingly for ninety years.

Miracles are not always showy. They happen every moment of the day, and you who were born under the number 6 know the miracle of life and stand as an example for us all through your practice of creating beauty and being fair, your love of family and community, and your love of art in all its forms.

Your actions in this life are to create miracles that add to the Earth's palette of beautiful color.

BIRTHDAY GIFT NUMBER 7: PROPHECY

In some ancient cultures, a child born under the number 7 was placed in the temple to become a priestess because 7 was believed to bestow heightened mental capabilities. Violet is the color associated with 7. As mentioned earlier, this color stimulates the blood in the upper brain and the pineal gland, which encourages the flow of imagination and the integration of ideas.

7 rules retreat, contemplation, and isolation where the individual has time to meditate upon the meaning of life and to investigate the higher thought processes, all of which requires quiet time to allow the mind to daydream. Scientists, philosophers, mystics, metaphysicians, and all deep thinkers, those who use their imaginations, come under this number.

As a birthday number 7, your mind is your strength, emphasizing the gift of prophecy. The Mother, the Goddess Isis, the Oracle at Delphi, and Gibran's Prophet are all manifestations of the number 7, the holders of truth, the oracles to whom the masses look for answers and guidance. They are symbols of the gift of prophecy.

Your birthday number 7 gives you the gift of prophecy, the potential to weave that information from your past into predictable patterns for the future; you have the ability to foresee trends. You are here to learn to use your mind to assemble and analyze present-day facts, and then use your intuition to create new paradigms of thought that appear to be prophetic. This process requires blocks of time away from the intrusions of the busy world.

You could be a market analyst, an advertising agent, a small business entrepreneur who taps into the public consciousness with a new product, a Tarot card reader or a psychic, an inventor with a vision of the future, a philosopher or writer whose works endure through the changes of time, or even a numerologist or an astrologer. If you're a mother, you certainly have eyes in the back of your head! You have the ability to put together disparate parts to make a whole.

The Greek figure, Cassandra, was given the gift of prophecy. One story relates that, because she refused the romantic advances of Apollo, she was cursed so that nobody would believe her prophecies. The story I like better is that, when she fell asleep in a temple, little snakes licked her ears enabling her to hear the future. Metaphysically, snakes represent knowledge.

There will always be those who won't listen to you—those with ears to hear but who don't listen—even though what you say has proven true in the past.

The number 7's gift to the world is prophecy. People should listen to what you have to say because there will come a point when you can stand back, like Cassandra, and smile. You won't have to say, "I told you so."

BIRTHDAY GIFT NUMBER 8:
KNOWLEDGE

You have power in this physical world! The 8 is a solidified square, which is the cube, a symbol of power in the physical world. 8 is karma, cause and effect; the energies you put out into the world will come back to you in equal measure. The rainbow body, the coat of many colors, is associated with this gift.

Notice that 8 is the only digit that you can draw over and over without lifting pen from paper. You might say, "what goes around, comes around"—another way of saying karma. The number 8 turned on its side is the cosmic lemniscate, the symbol of infinity. You might also visualize it as a pair of eyeglasses. The world is seeing you.

8 is the cosmic teacher, the one who shows us where we have to concentrate right now, right here, in this moment. There is no talk of the next lifetime or waiting to get your rewards in "heaven." 8 says, take care of this, right here and right now. Your rewards will come in this lifetime.

The 8 emphasizes the visible practical world of daily living. You may find your power in the world of finances and business dealings where large sums of money are involved. You could run a big corporation or be boss of your own business. You could exercise your physical strength on the field of sports. You spend years learning how to throw a fast ball, a curve ball, and a sinker, and you make it to the big leagues. You spend years going to law school before you become a noted and recognized big-time lawyer. You have the strength to achieve because you have gained the knowledge necessary to achieve.

Your knowledge doesn't necessarily come from books as much as from direct experience. You profit from the knowledge that repeating a certain act will bring an expected result: cause and effect. You learn and profit from those experiences, using your knowledge to guide you into the future.

You also know that it takes partnerships in this world to be successful. No one builds their future without help from another, at some age, at some juncture as they walk through life. Therefore, you need deep personal relationships that must be expressed on the physical level as well as on the spiritual level. Remember the 8: two equal but connecting circles.

The 8 rules things that are established and permanent: land, stone, the teeth and bones, the passage of time. Your gift, birthday number 8, is the knowledge you will gain and then express in this physical world. You will wear the coat of many colors.

BIRTHDAY GIFT NUMBER 9:

WISDOM

One definition of wisdom is "the quality or state of being wise, knowledge of what is true or right coupled with just judgment as to action, sagacity, discernment, or insight."

Here I have to quote one of my favorite authors, W. D. Buffa (also writing as Lawrence Alexander), whose character in one of his novels said: "(she) makes the mistake of believing that the aim of intelligence is the expansion of knowledge rather than the depth of understanding." Wow! That one sentence from his entire novel blew my socks off. This is the gift of number 9. Your pot of gold number is the connection to this gift.

As opposed to the number 8, which is knowledge gained through learning from cause and effect, wisdom is the state of being wise. The knowledge has already been acquired, there is no action involved; it is there, it exists, it is in a state of being. If your birthday number is 9, you have the gift of wisdom on your side.

As a birthday number 9, you don't have to shout from the mountain top rather, like The Hermit in the Tarot deck, you stand quietly and hold up the lantern of light, the lantern of truth, for those who want to find their way to a higher consciousness.

The Hermit is not shouting or waving the lantern with theatrical shows of "look at me; I know what is right." The Hermit stands quietly, does not speak, but waits patiently for those who are willing to see the truth. You are that person, the one who can work quietly, and by example, show more than those who take the stage and pontificate. The way you live your life becomes an example for others.

With wisdom comes justice, forgiveness, and love. You can express these qualities in many occupations: a parent, a teacher, a community leader, a motivational speaker or writer, the receptionist at the doctor's office, the clerk at the check-out counter . . . because you have the compassion to empathize with the suffering of others. Your quiet presence can light their days.

One thing I have found out about those with a birthday number 9 is that they can speak their truths and inspire others only if they live those truths themselves.

With the gift of wisdom, you are an example for others in whatever lifestyle you have chosen or which might seem to have been chosen for you. Others will hear your words and recognize that you live by them as well. You will truly be a beacon of wisdom in whatever capacity you choose to live your life. Then you will live in that "state of being wise" and will be the light for those with eyes to see.

THE COMBINATION OF YOUR BIRTHDAY NUMBER, COLOR, AND GIFT OF THE SPIRIT

Try on your color, explore your gift, and see how they fit. They can add another dimension to your birthday number.

For those of you who are interested in the subtle differences between the Lamsa Bible translation by a man who spoke the original language of Jesus and that of two other editions of the bible translated by non-Aramaic speakers, please turn to the Addendum to read The Lamsa Bible interpretation.

Now we're on to find out "What the heck is going on in my life?"

NUMBER	COLOR	GIFT
Birthday Number 1	Red	The gift to distinguish the true Spirit
Birthday Number 2	Orange	The gift of the interpretation of languages
Birthday Number 3	Yellow	The gift of faith
Birthday Number 4	Green	The gift of healing
Birthday Number 5	Light blue	The gift of different languages
Birthday Number 6	Indigo	The gift of the working of miracles
Birthday Number 7	Violet	The gift of prophecy
Birthday Number 8	The rainbow body, coat of many colors	The gift of knowledge
Birthday Number 9	The pot of gold at the end of the rainbow	The gift of wisdom

PART II ·
YOUR TIME MACHINE

"OUR BIGGEST FAILURE IS OUR FAILURE TO SEE PATTERNS."

—MARILYN FERGUSON,
American author, editor, public speaker

CHAPTER 4

WHAT THE HECK IS GOING ON IN MY LIFE?

IT'S ALL ABOUT CYCLES. YOU BEGIN THE GREATEST journey of your life at the moment of your birth. You embark upon your journey with a detailed map that depicts the major highways, detours, and rest stops along the way. Yet, because you don't realize you have a map tucked into the pocket of your car door (does anybody use those today?) or a GPS affixed to your dashboard, you might take off without any sense of destination. You drive straight on, unmindful of the directory signs along the way, until you hit a pothole or face a dead end and suddenly find yourself lost or your vehicle badly in need of repair.

One of these detailed maps is your numerological chart, which is determined at your moment of birth by your birthday and the particular name you were given at that time. Your journey this lifetime is then set in motion, and the wheels continue to turn throughout your life.

By examining your personal life cycles and what they mean for you, you can jump into the driver's seat and take control. You can learn to work and flow with your cycles rather than having them blindside you. When you are aware of your personal cycles, your seasons, you are prepared to make intelligent choices on your journey through life. You cannot change the cycles once you're born, just as you cannot change the seasons of the year, but you can learn to recognize your cycles and then use them as a guide. You'll know when to plant, when it's time to nurture the seeds, and when your efforts are ready for the harvest.

On every birthday you begin a new personal year cycle. Along with celebrating your birthday in your own fashion, you might take some time to examine the events that have taken place over the past twelve months to see what you have learned. Each yearly cycle adds to your life's experiences, which in turn expands your consciousness. In this way, you grow through becoming aware of how to live in a more productive manner.

You have nine basic personal year cycles, which follow the universal pattern of nature: the numbers 1 through 9. These nine cycles repeat over and over throughout your life.

The benefit of these nine-year cycles is that you learn through repetition. Just as you learned your multiplication tables in grade school by repeating them over and over . . . at least I did, but that was eons ago . . . so you learn your lessons in life by repeating the basic nine cycles over and over. History does repeat itself. Or at least it rhymes, as Mark Twain noted.

YOUR PERSONAL YEAR CYCLES

Your personal cycles begin on the day you were born. As stated, each succeeding birthday advances your cycle by one number and these cycles repeat every nine years.

In any given year, your personal year cycle begins on the month and day you were born and continues until the month and day of your birth in the next year.

To find your current personal cycle:

> Add your month of birth + your day of birth + the year of your last birthday

Let's use the following example of Jodi Ann Lee who was born July 6, 1968.

If we want to know what her personal year cycle is in May 2020, we go back to her last birthday which was in July 2019.

> Add her month and day of birth to the year 2019.
> Reduce the year 2019 first: (Refer to reasons for this on page 26)
>
> 2 + 0 + 1 + 9 = 12

Then add her month and day of birth to the reduced year 12.

TO CALCULATE YOUR CURRENT PERSONAL YEAR CYCLES

July + 6 + 12

7 + 6 + 12 = 25

Jodi is in a personal year cycle 25/7 from
July 6, 2019 until July 6, 2020.

Analyze the meaning of Jodi's personal year cycle base number first which is a 7. Then build upon that interpretation by blending the definitions of the 2 and 5 to tell a story.

**

Why not find your personal year cycle now. Remember to take the full year of your last birthday. Then turn to page 238 for a description of your personal year cycle single number. If you have a double number, blend the meaning of each number into the base number to tell your story for that year.

The colors and gifts you read about in the last chapter might also help you with your personal year cycles. Try them on for size!

Do remember that whenever you are in a cycle that corresponds with one of your five personal numbers, then the effects of that cycle are emphasized through that particular number in your birth pattern. That cycle gains more importance for that period of time.

To repeat: your personal year cycle runs from the month and day of your birth in one year to the month and day of your birth in the next year. It has nothing to do with the calendar year.

There is another school of thought that says you should start your personal year cycle with the calendar year, January 1, regardless of your birthday. With this reasoning, if you were born December 31, just before midnight, your first personal year cycle is only minutes long. That isn't enough time to imprint your life's purpose; you need a full year to do that.

The proof is in the pudding, as they say. I encourage you to try this method and then select the one you feel works best for you.

Calculate the personal year cycles of your family and friends and wow them with your knowledge. These cycles work with "anything" that has a birthday.

Understanding what family members are experiencing because of their personal year cycle will help you understand their actions thereby keeping peace in the family.

For example, you're in a 5 cycle and have been excited all week about attending the latest sci-fi film with your sister. Then, that morning, she decides she's too tired, and all she wants to do after work is stretch out on the couch and watch the Discovery Channel. Knowing that she's in a 7 cycle and really is tired, you can understand and not get your panties in a twist. Not that you would ever get upset because you're just like me, always handling situations calmly.

(Voice: stage right) You don't always keep your cool, Mom.

Dear reader, please ignore that . . .

. . . .

Got all that information you just read? Good. If not, please go back and read it again. We learn through repetition.

YOUR BIRTHDAY NUMBER IS ALSO YOUR FIRST PERSONAL YEAR CYCLE

Let's say your birthday adds to a 7. Your birthday number indicates the type of lessons you are here to learn throughout your life.

Your birthday number is also your first personal year cycle.

For instance, if you want to know what your personal cycle was when you were six months old, go back to your last birthday before the age of one, which was—you got it!—the day you were born.

Therefore, the first twelve months of your life (from 0 to 12 months) is also your first personal year cycle.

In other words, you spend the first twelve months of life learning the message of your birthday number!

That is why the first twelve months of your life are so important. Those first twelve months imprint the meaning of your birthday number, those lessons you are here to learn, into your consciousness.

Using this example of a birthday number 7, the cycles start:

Age 0 to age 1 is a personal year 7; this is also the birthday number 7.

On the next birthday, at age 1, is a personal year cycle 8;

On the next birthday, at age 2, is a personal year cycle 9;

On the next birthday, at age 3, the cycle starts over with cycle 1,

On the next birthday, at age 4, is a personal year cycle 2, and so on throughout this person's life.

Whenever you reach personal year cycle 9, the next personal year cycle will be 1.

Since there are 9 cycles, this means that every nine years, at ages 9-18-27-36 and so on, you repeat your birthday number. These ages are extremely important therefore you should examine the events that occur when your age is a multiple of 9 or your age can be divided by 9. Those events bring you in contact with your birthday number which was imprinted upon you in the first twelve months of your life—the lessons you are here to learn. Your birthday color and birthday gift can add additional information and support.

If your birthday number is 9, the first twelve months of your life from birth to age 1 will imprint the meaning of your birthday number 9 in your subconscious. At age 1, you start your personal year cycle 1.

Since 9 means endings and transitions, so with a birthday number 9, an event between your birth and age 2 will occur that brings changes into your life.

YOUR PERSONAL YEAR CYCLE LIFETIME CHART

You can easily set up a chart that will cover your personal year cycles for a lifetime.

All you need to know is your birthday number, which you calculated in chapter 2. Remember, your birthday number is the total of your full date of birth.

For a fun experience and to prove the cyclical nature of your life in living color, you could purchase a piece of poster board or create a chart online to work with.

Let's assume you're using a poster; you might find this more convenient.

Print the numbers 1 through 9 down the left side of the poster from top to bottom spaced evenly. Then draw horizontal lines between the numbers separating them evenly. Now, make at least 11 additional columns as wide as possible across the poster.

The sample chart shown below covers ages up to 74 in order to fit on this page. If you're working on a poster or online, you may have room to add additional columns to take you past age 100!

The first column on the left shows all the birthday numbers 1 through 9.

Use your birthday number.

In the second column, beside your birthday number, write in "age 0." That's how many years old you were when you were born. It's not the year that matters in this chart; it's your age that is the key.

In this example we are using the birthday number 7. You will see "age 0" written in the block next to number 7.

Each of these blocks moving down the column represents twelve months of your life starting with your birthday each year. Again, this chart uses your age and has nothing to do with the calendar year.

In this example, move down the chart to age 1, and then age 2, and then begin at the top of the next column at age 3, and continue down the column. Repeat this process up to the age you desire.

1		Age 3	Age 12	Age 21	Age 30	Age 39	Age 48	Age 57	Age 66
2		Age 4	Age 13	Age 22	Age 31	Age 40	Age 49	Age 58	Age 67
3		Age 5	Age 14	Age 23	Age 32	Age 41	Age 50	Age 59	Age 68
4		Age 6	Age 15	Age 24	Age 33	Age 42	Age 51	Age 60	Age 69
5		Age 7	Age 16	Age 25	Age 34	Age 43	Age 52	Age 61	Age 70
6		Age 8	Age 17	Age 26	Age 35	Age 44	Age 53	Age 62	Age 71
7	Age 0	Age 9	Age 18	Age 27	Age 36	Age 45	Age 54	Age 63	Age 72
8	Age 1	Age 10	Age 19	Age 28	Age 37	Age 46	Age 55	Age 64	Age 73
9	Age 2	Age 11	Age 20	Age 29	Age 38	Age 47	Age 56	Age 65	Age 74

Now that you have created your personal year cycle poster for your lifetime, you can begin to write in the important events in your life.

Be sure to write these events in the block that shows your age at the time of the event, not the year of the event.

I tacked my poster to the back of my bedroom door. That way no one sees it but me, and maybe my hubby, but he's on a beeline for the coffee pot in the morning and sees nothing on his way.

This position behind the bedroom door is convenient. If I wake from a dream with a memory of an event, I grab a pen from my night stand and write the event in the age block at which it happened. Also, during the day at home when I'm not near my computer, it's just a few steps to the bedroom door to make an entry. During the day when I'm away from home, I can jot notes on a slip of paper and stick them in my pocket until I get home.

Start filling in the blocks with notes about major events from your past. Place them in the block that relates to your age when that event happened.

Go back over your life: How old were you when you had your first date . . . at what age did you get married . . . at what age did you take that life changing trip to Europe . . . when did you get that degree . . . how old were you when your first child was born . . . at what age did you get that promotion . . . and so on.

When you have accumulated a number of events and your poster starts to fill up, you can look, first to your birthday number, to see what events have occurred that are in keeping with that number. Those events are important because they are helping you learn your lesson this lifetime.

Then, you can look at the rest of the numbers and read horizontally across the poster. Notice how the events on each horizontal line are similar and in harmony with the meaning of the single number in the far left column.

This is an amazing experiment because you will begin to see that the same types of experiences occurred in the past when you were in the same personal year cycle number. Now, these are not the same exact experiences, of course, but they will have the same underlying lesson that relates to the personal year cycle number to which they are connected.

For instance, in your personal year 6 experiences, you may have moved, a baby could have been born, you may have remodeled, someone might have moved out, you could have been involved in a major community project, etc. All these experiences relate to the number 6 of changes in the home and duty to the community.

The poster is a good idea because it's handy, and when you think of an important event a week from now, or two months from now, you can go back to the poster and make a note about it. You can also ask other family members and friends about major events, and you can go through diaries, journals, and scrapbooks. A passage in a book or a news item on television or the Internet may trigger a memory that you can add to your record. So, make those spaces between the birthday numbers as deep as possible.

It's amazing when you notice how your life repeats itself. We say that history repeats itself; we know the planets, including our blessed

Earth, repeat their cycles around the Sun; we know the Moon repeats its cycle from new to full then back to new; we know the seasons repeat; however, we never stop to think that our lives are cyclical as well. This chart can show you the truth of your involvement in the rhythmic cycles of nature.

Turn to page 238 to discover the meaning of your single number cycles and then blend your double numbers into the base number for a more specific interpretation.

PEAK POINTS AND ACTION POINTS IN YOUR PERSONAL YEAR CYCLE

In the original printing of this book, I introduced techniques that, at that time, I had not seen or read about in numerology. I called these techniques the Peak Points and Action Points in your cycles. Once you determine your peak and action points in any cycle, they remain the same, so you only have to figure them once.

In any cycle, there is a beginning, a growing period, a culminating, a waning period, and an ending, which becomes the transition point into the next cycle. This is a vital sequence that deserves our attention in regards to numerology because it can point out particular dates when certain types of events can occur.

This process is similar to the phases of the Moon, a perfect model of the workings of the universal waxing and waning processes present in all life cycles.

Each New Moon offers a beginning, the seeds of potential. Those seeds take root and begin to grow. At the Full Moon, the seeds burst into full blossom. After the Full Moon, called the waning cycle of the Moon, the results that you experienced during its fullness send messages deep into your subconscious mind where those experiences nourish and add to your body of knowledge at that point. Your life will be richer and fuller because of what you have learned from that particular cycle. Every cycle will fulfill this universal pattern of waxing, culminating, and waning.

Every calendar year has a peak and an action point which are the spring equinox, the summer solstice, the autumnal equinox, and the winter solstice. These points represent moments in the solar year that predict changes.

As part of nature, we too experience peak and action points in our personal yearly cycles.

In this segment, we will apply this process to your personal year cycle. As we move along in this book, you will find you can apply this pattern to any cycle you are experiencing from a month to a day to an hour.

PEAK POINTS IN YOUR PERSONAL YEAR CYCLE

The peak point in your personal year cycle is 6 months from your birthday, or halfway through your personal year. This point equates to the Full Moon in a monthly cycle when that cycle's energies come to fruition. Notice how many major events that happen in people's lives cluster around their birthdays or about 6 months later around the Peak Point.

As with the Full Moon, I allow a five-day spread around the peak point—two days before, the day of, and two days after.

If your birthday is February 13, the peak point in your personal year will always be six months later around August 13. If your birthday is September 9, your peak point will always be six months later around March 9.

In our example of Jodi Ann Lee, her birthday is July 6. Her peak point will always be January 6. See the illustration below.

PEAK POINT

JULY 6TH   JANUARY 6TH   JULY 6TH

I have talked with people who, at first, could not remember anything happening in a given year on a given date but then, after a few minutes, they suddenly recall a promotion or a residential move that changed their life.

You may not at first remember an event during a particular year. And, of course, not every year brings such dramatic events. Some events or experiences are more subtle but if you allow yourself time to think, you will discover that these peak points are uncannily accurate.

For instance, you might be in a personal year cycle 8 where your energies are focused on your work and money situations, a time during which you feel more pressure and have more responsibility. These energies began when your 8 year cycle began, on your birthday; they will peak 6 months later.

At that peak point, if you have worked well, you may receive a raise or promotion. Or perhaps you received the promotion at the beginning of your personal year. At your peak point, you may receive more accolades or lose your job, depending upon how well you have performed.

If the peak point brings a job loss, this despair can be used as a point of growth if you examine what you have learned. And it might point you in a new direction that fulfills you even more than your previous job did. It's true we learn from our mistakes; we also learn from our successes.

Obviously not every year in your life has "major" events, but still, the essence of all your personal year numbers will manifest at the peak point in some way.

An introspective cycle like the 7 cycle may not have as obvious external results but rather have more to do with a profound philosophical insight that changes your perception of the circumstances in your life, a deep realization that affects you but is not recognized by those around you.

The following examples come from my files (the names are fictitious).

. . . .

CASE 1: BORN NOVEMBER 5

Samantha always had difficulty relating to her mother; she could never understand the tension between them. When she was 34 years old, she discovered quite by accident that as a 14-month-old infant she had been abandoned by her mother. Found on a doorstep, she was taken to a local welfare agency where she remained for many months.

Born under a birthday number 9, she was in a personal year cycle 1 when this event occurred. 1 represents a new beginning, a time of isolation when she felt alone even though there were many people around her. It was a time for her to learn to stand alone. Also, it was time for making decisions and, although a 14-month-old child cannot consciously make decisions, this process was ingrained as she subconsciously made certain assessments about whom to trust.

Miraculously, on May 4, the peak point in Samantha's personal year cycle 1, a family member recognized her photograph from a newspaper story. The family claimed the child and, some weeks later, Samantha was returned to her family. However, she learned a lesson in independence at the tender age of 1.

. . . .

CASE 2: BORN JULY 20

Roger had a serious cigarette habit. He had tried everything to rid himself of the problem, all to no avail. In his personal year cycle 7, in desperation, he finally took a friend's advice and enrolled in a well known course on the power of the mind, even though he had no faith that it would work. After completing the intense course, he spent that fall and early winter practicing what he had learned.

Two days before the peak point, January 18, while in his personal cycle 7, he threw a full "just-in-case" pack of cigarettes into the trash.

They had been lying on top of his refrigerator since the day he finished the course.

As mentioned above, the 7 cycle is a time of withdrawal, a time to go within to think and analyze, a time to perfect skills, a time of mind over matter. Roger won that battle. Today, he is still free from this habit.

ACTION POINTS IN YOUR PERSONAL YEAR CYCLE

In keeping with the analogy of the Moon and the seasons on their cyclical journeys, your personal year cycle has two strong points when you are called to action. To find these points, divide the personal year into quarters, beginning with your month and day of birth. These dynamic points, which I call action points, urge you to do something to relieve the pressure caused by the friction of events that occur at those times, all in keeping with your personal year cycle number. These are points that challenge you to act and assess your current situation.

The first action point is three months into your personal year cycle. It reveals any kinks in your process. This point propels you to correct any unproductive actions so that you can use the energy of that cycle to build more dynamically.

The drive then continues to build to the peak point, half way through your personal year cycle, where your actions bring about visible results.

As you pass the peak point and approach the second action point, nine months into your personal year cycle, you start to wind down. At this point, you recognize that it's time to take actions that will finish and polish this cycle. You begin to incorporate what you have learned into your subconscious library where the experiences of that personal year cycle become part of your life's book of knowledge.

With a birthday of July 6, Jodi Ann Lee's action points are October 6 and April 6. See the illustration below.

ACTION POINT		PEAK POINT		ACTION POINT
JULY 6TH	OCTOBER 6TH	JANUARY 6TH	APRIL 6TH	JULY 6TH

Upon the first action point on October 6, she can expect the energy of her personal year cycle to become strongly activated; it's a time when she feels she has to take action regarding any kinks in the issues her current personal year cycle has raised.

The energy she expends will bring visible results during her peak point date of January 6.

By her second action point date on April 6, she is once again motivated to take action to begin to close out and incorporate her personal year cycle experiences.

Once you determine your action and peak point dates, they will remain the same every year of your life.

Thomas Jefferson was actually born on April 2, 1743, under the old Julian calendar. The Gregorian calendar, adopted after his birth, added 11 days to the calendar in 1752. One of his action points was July 2.

Two of the most important events in his life occurred on July 4, in different years: The Declaration of Independence and the day of his death at age 83. See Thomas Jefferson's time line below.

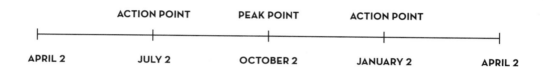

Another example:

On a personal level, one of my action points is August 5th.

Boxes of my first book, *Numerology and the Divine Triangle* (coauthored with Faith Javane), arrived at the publisher on August 3. That year, August 5 fell on a Sunday. Because there were no deliveries on the weekends, the closest dates to my action point of August 5 that the books could have been delivered were Friday, August 3 or Monday, August 6. And they were delivered on the 3rd!

August 3 was the day I was able to hold in my hands a copy of my very first book! It was a magical moment. A life long dream had been fulfilled; I had written a book. It was like the birth of a child.

On that same day, our publisher offered us a contract for the computer rights to the book. This was agreed upon and signed a few days later on Monday, August 6!

This series of events points out how the action points in your personal year cycles can work.

1979 was my personal year cycle 41/5. This meant that during that year I had important decisions to make (1) in order to achieve something tangible (4) that had to do with communication, writing, teaching (5). 5 was the base number, the purpose of the blending of the 4 and the 1.

....

A RECENT ACTION POINT:

I received the acceptance contract for the book covers and blurbs on my book, *The Beginner's Guide to Astrology: Class is in Session*, on August 5, another action point in my year. This book was published in 2017.

....

ANOTHER RECENT ACTION POINT:

After being asked in spring 2019 to update *Numerology and Your Future*, I received the contracts from Schiffer Publishing on May 7, within two days of my action point!

The proof is in the pudding, so they say. It always comes back to food, doesn't it? Certainly my pleasure point: a good book and dark chocolate at hand. Anyway . . .

....

CASE 1:

Jonathan was in a personal year cycle 6. This was also his birthday number, so it was obvious that this particular cycle was an important one in his life. He had never married because he hadn't found anyone to whom he could relate. His birthday is August 15; his action and peak points are shown in the illustration below.

At the end of this particular August, when he had turned 29 years old, he began dating a young woman. By the middle of November, his action point, she had won his heart and he asked her to marry him. They were married in a small family ceremony in the middle of February, the peak point of his personal year cycle; in May, his second action point, he left his job of some years to start a small business the two of them had bought.

Of course, not every year in a person's life is filled with such major events; however, the lessons of each of your personal years is important to your growth. Being aware of the action and peak points of each individual personal year in your life can open your eyes to events that might not seem important in their own right but, when coupled with the full year's scale, can lend great insight into your personal growth for that year.

No rule is iron clad; however, these points in the personal year cycle happen so often that they lend truth to the practice. Four distinct seasons bring life to our beautiful planet Earth; perhaps within our own yearly cycles, we also have four seasons that revitalize our earthly bodies and our minds.

FORMULA: THE PERSONAL YEAR CYCLE + THE MONTH = THE PERSONAL MONTH CYCLE

YOUR PERSONAL MONTH CYCLE

Your cycles of experience can be distilled even more with the introduction of the personal month cycle. Your personal month begins on the "day" of your birth and continues to that same numbered day in the next month.

For example: Jodie's birthday is July 6. Her personal months run from July 6 to August 6, from August 6 to September 6, from September 6 to October 6, and so on.

To determine your personal month, add the number of the calendar month you are investigating (February is 2, May is 5, etc.) to your current personal year cycle.

Using our example: Jodi Ann Lee, born 7-6-1968

To find her personal year cycle for 2015, we add her month and day of birth to the year 2015.

Add the year through once:

2 + 0 + 1 + 5 = 8
Add the reduced year to her month and day of birth
7 + 6 + 8 = 21/3

Jodi's personal year cycle for July 2015 to July 2016 is a 21/3.

Her personal month always begins on the 6th day of each month,
the day of her birth.

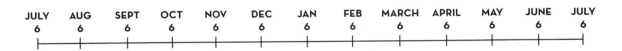

| JULY | AUG | SEPT | OCT | NOV | DEC | JAN | FEB | MARCH | APRIL | MAY | JUNE | JULY |
| 6 | 6 | 6 | 6 | 6 | 6 | 6 | 6 | 6 | 6 | 6 | 6 | 6 |

Now we add the calendar months to her personal year cycle 21/3.

Calendar Month Number + Personal Year Cycle =
Personal Month Number

Starting with her birthday July 6:

7 + 21/3 = 28/10/1:
her personal month from July 6 to August 6

8 + 21/3 = 29/11/2:
her personal month from August 6 to September 6

9 + 21/3 = 30/3:
her personal month from September 6 to October 6

10 + 21/3 = 31/4:
her personal month from October 6 to November 6

11 + 21/3 = 32/5:
her personal month from November 6 to December 6

12 + 21/3 = 33/6:
her personal month from December 6 to January 6

With the calendar change, the number sequence changes because
January is the 1st month, February the 2nd month, and so on.

$$1 + 21/3 = 22/4:$$

her personal month from January 6 to February 6

$$2 + 21/3 = 23/5:$$

her personal month from February 6 to March 6

$$3 + 21/3 = 24/6:$$

her personal month from March 6 to April 6

$$4 + 21/3 = 25/7:$$

her personal month from April 6 to May 6

$$5 + 21/3 = 26/8:$$

her personal month from May 6 to June 6

$$6 + 21/3 = 27/9:$$

her personal month from June 6 to July 6

These are her personal month numbers for her personal year cycle 3 from July 6, 2015, to July 6, 2016.

On her birthday July 6, 2016, you begin this process again because her personal year cycle changes from 21/3 to a 22/4.

Through understanding what the personal month number represents, you can narrow down the specific energies or events that will occur within your personal year cycle. The value of this technique is obvious by examining just the base number.

For instance, if you started a new relationship in your personal year 6 of love, family, community, beauty, and the arts, and you want to know how it will proceed, you might look to a 3 month when activities are growing and fun-filled. A 6 month intensifies the love and devotion aspect. During a 7 month, you might need some quiet time alone or you might want to attend an art show or the theater with that someone special. Or you might want to take some time apart to think. Each month works towards the goal of your personal year cycle 6.

The personal months are a minor vibration and may not bring major events into your life by themselves; however, when combined within a larger cycle they can reinforce the events of that cycle.

Remember that your personal month starts on your day of your birth at the beginning of your personal year cycle, and continues to your day of birth in the following month, and so on through the calendar to the end of that particular personal year cycle.

To repeat: If you were born May 9, your personal months run from the 9th of each month to the 9th of the next month; if you were born September 22nd, your personal months run from the 22nd of each month to the 22nd of the following month, and so on.

PEAK POINTS IN YOUR PERSONAL MONTH CYCLE

Now, if you are inclined to get down to the nitty-gritty, you can dissect the personal months even further by determining the peak point and action points in each month. Again, once you work out the dates of your peak and action points in your personal month cycle, they will remain the same every month as a permanent record so you only have to figure them once.

Your personal month has a peak point that occurs about two weeks after the "day" you were born. On that date, the events designated by the number of the personal month will culminate. This is similar to the phases of the moon as mentioned earlier: the beginning "day" of your personal month is the new moon: the half way point through your personal month, about two weeks later, is the full moon.

Because the number of the days varies with each month, you can estimate the date, or you could work it out precisely if you wish.

Jodi's personal month begins July 6. From July 6 to August 6, there are 31 days. 31 divided by 2 equals 15½ days. Add 15½ days to July 6, and her peak point for the month of July is July 21–22. See the illustration below.

PEAK POINT

JULY 6   JULY 21-22   AUGUST 6

Because each month except February contains 30 or 31 days, you can add 15 to 15½ days to the beginning date of each of your personal month cycles. This will give you a one-two day-period as a peak point in that personal month.

When you are working with the month of February, which has 28 days, except for leap year when it has 29, add 14 days (14½ on Leap Year) to the beginning date of your personal month to find the peak point.

You can also determine the action points in your personal month cycle by dividing the month into quarters of about 7–8 days each month.

For the first action point, Jodi, with her birth "day" of July 6, would add approximately 7–8 days to her personal month starting day of the 6th.

For the second action point, she would add 21–22 days from her personal month starting date. See the illustration below.

	ACTION POINT	PEAK POINT	ACTION POINT	
JULY 6	JULY 13-14	JULY 21-22	JULY 27-28	AUGUST 6

These dates for the peak point and action point in your personal months cycles remain the same every year as a permanent record. I know. I've said that a *"gazillion"* times, but we learn through repetition.

FORMULA: THE PERSONAL YEAR CYCLE + THE MONTH + THE DAY = THE PERSONAL DAY CYCLE

If you have an important appointment on a particular day, it may be vital that you know how you are going to feel on that day. Knowing what your mood will be on any given day can enable you to plan your calendar more in keeping with your personal ups and downs.

Your personal day cycle can help you understand why one day you feel tired and need to be alone, and on the next day you are ready to tackle the world. You will know what day is best for love relationships, that special party, the more aggressive activities such as sports, and why you spend more money on one day than on another.

To find your personal day cycle:
Add the month and day in question to your personal year cycle number.

Jodi's birthday is July 6.
First: to find her personal year cycle as of November 2015, add the month and day to the reduced year 2015 (2 + 0 + 1 + 5 = 8).

$$7 + 6 + 8 = 21/3$$
This is her current personal year cycle.

To find her personal day cycle for October 24,
add her personal year cycle 21/3 to October 24.

year cycle		month		day		
21/3	**+**	10	**+**	24	**=**	55/10/1

Her personal day number on October 24, 2015, is 55/10/1

This number indicates a day when she needs to take charge, make the decisions, be more assertive, perhaps be the person in charge. With a double 55, this certainly involves doubling her usually activity in all forms of communication: engaging in conversations, buying stacks of books, attending lectures, discussions over dinner, setting up appointments. This month keeps the revolving door spinning.

Phew! Wipe the sweat from your brow.

Got all that? Good!

The exercises covered in this chapter explained the different cycles of your life that are determined by your birthday.

If you're confused, go back over the previous material until the rules involved with each process become more familiar. You might write the rules on a 4" x 6" card to make it easier for a while. You could add this card to the other two you have created.

Practice these rules with different birthdays until it becomes second nature to you. Rome wasn't built in a day . . . but, unlike Rome, the numbers will last forever as cosmic messengers.

Oh . . . one last thing before we close this chapter. "Oh, no!" you may be saying while clutching your head in dismay. But, calm down; this one is easy.

I got to thinking one day . . . if the years and the months have peak and action points, perhaps the days do also. So, give this a try with your birth "day."

If you know the exact time of day you were born, start with that time and divide the twenty-four-hour day into quarters of six hours each.

In my case, I start with 10:38 p.m., my birth time. Six hours later is 4:38 a.m., the action point; six hours after that is 10:38 a.m., the peak point; and six hours after that is 4:38 p.m., the second action point. See the illustration below.

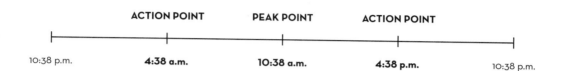

	ACTION POINT	PEAK POINT	ACTION POINT	
10:38 p.m.	4:38 a.m.	10:38 a.m.	4:38 p.m.	10:38 p.m.

This works beautifully for me.

My action point, the waxing moon phase, is 4:38 a.m.

I am up early every morning, anywhere between 3:30 and 5:00, to start the day. First I greet my cats, Sashi and Elvis, as they tumble over my feet, glad to have someone finally up so the action can start. I check their water and food, clean the litter box, and watch them scramble across the room as I toss a few of their toys about for a few minutes of playtime.

Then it's to my desk with a glass of water, Sashi at my elbow, to send birthday notes to my clients and check my e-mail. Finally, I begin writing on whatever project is at hand. The writing absorbs a few hours.

My peak point, the full moon phase, is 10:38 a.m.

If at all possible, I schedule client sessions at 10:00 a.m. I have done this for years before I even thought about action and peak points for the day. This is the time when my energy seems to peak. I have more energy to give to the clients during their sessions.

My 2nd action point, the waning moon phase, is 4:38 p.m.

After lunch, I do the daily chores, then read and relax, and, by late afternoon, I check my desk once more, filing away papers, double checking any writing that I have done during morning and perhaps adding a bit more of that which has come to me during the day. Then I save my work on my Word program and on a thumb drive, and I print it out on paper. I don't want my hard work to disappear in that computer heaven never to be seen again. I've heard too many horror stories about material that was lost because it was not saved.

By 9:00 p.m., I am in bed with a book, a glass of water on the night stand, to read for as long as my eyes stay open.

The peak and action points in your day's cycle will remain the same every day.

If your peak point or one of your action points is in the middle of the night, I don't even want to know what you're doing . . . even if it's in your dreams.

Now you know what the heck is going on in your life—and what the numbers have to say about your future activities and events.

One last note about life cycles:

UNIVERSAL YEAR CYCLES

The world experiences what is called the Universal Year Cycle, which also repeats every nine years. This cycle depends upon the calendar in use. Most of the world uses what is called the Gregorian calendar, and the entire world does use this calendar when it comes to global communication. This is the calendar we are most familiar with.

To find the Universal Year Cycle, simply add the year through once.

For example: the year 2020
2020 = 2 + 0 + 2 + 0 = 4.

The year 2020 is a universal year cycle 4.
Time to get our ducks in a row!

This means that the entire world is experiencing a period of organization when it's time to pay the piper and get down to business and create stability. The basics of life need attention—food, water, health, and finances. This period requires that we work to build a strong solid foundation for the future.

There is much more information about how the numbers affect events here on earth in the chapter in this book entitled "Numerology's Influence on the Decades" . . . particularly the sections discussing the 2000 millennium and its decades of 2000, 2010, and 2020.

. . . .

Are you ready for some more? Okay then . . . onward and upward!

CHAPTER 5
ADDITIONAL TECHNIQUES

NUMEROLOGY IS BY NO MEANS A CLOSED FIELD. As in any endeavor, there is always room for questioning, searching, and discovery. Some of the techniques offered in this book are not ironclad rules. They have worked well in the past, but that does not mean they cannot be improved upon in the future.

We are on the doorstep of the Aquarian Age, said to last about 2,100 years, when there is a demand for more intellectual freedom with the promise of discoveries that will result in new and innovative ways of thinking and communicating, ways that will change the consciousness of the world. It has already started with the birth of the Internet.

So, as you work with these additional techniques, you may come up with innovative methods, ideas, and techniques of your own, techniques that can be used to discover more about yourself through applying the methods not only to your personal birth pattern but also to the changing cycles in your life.

Play with the numbers and see what happens. The future is not written in stone but it is written in the cycles.

This chapter also includes a few of my "wonderings." I am constantly thinking of different ways to work with the numbers. Perhaps there will be enough information in this chapter to trigger in your mind a thought that will lead you toward a new discovery.

So . . . abracadabra! Let's see what magic we can pull out of the numbers hat.

ABRACADABRA: MESSAGES FROM MOM

In today's world, we associate the word abracadabra with a magician pulling a rabbit out of a hat. Hundreds of years ago, people believed this word was a magical spell. The word was written in a triangular shape and worn around the neck to ward of negative forces.

This word does have magical powers rooted in a mystical history.

One of the oldest records of the word "abracadabra" being used is from a Roman sage named Serenus Sammonicus, second century AD, from his *Liber Medicinalis*. To ward off a deadly sickness, he wrote, "On a piece of parchment, write the so-called 'abracadabra' several times, repeating it on the line below; but take off the end, so that gradually individual letters, which you will take away each time, are missing from the word. Continue until the (last) letter makes the apex of a cone. Remember to wind this with linen and hang it around the neck." This was his idea of how to combat the deadly disease of his time for which there was no name.

One of the theories of the origin of "abracadabra" comes from the equally magical Greek word "abraxas" whose letters add up to 365—the number of days in the solar year. From the Theosophical Glossary: Abraxas is a "Mystical term used by the Gnostics to indicate the supreme entity of our cosmic hierarchy or its manifestation in the human being, which they called Christos."[10]

Alternatively, the word might have come from the Hebrew words for "father, son, and holy spirit": *ab*, *ben*, and *ruach hakodesh* respectively. This is the male trinity in Christianity.

What this boils down to is that "abracadabra" is related to a solar cycle, a year, one spin of the Earth around the Sun (365 days), and also the trinity, the three-sided triangle, a mystical symbol that is behind creation.

As written earlier: Things happen in threes—beginning, middle, and end complete a cycle; maiden, mother, and crone are the three stages of life; width, depth, and height form the physical world; rhythm, tone, and harmony make music; red, yellow, and blue create color; and so on.

"Abracadabra" derives from the Gnostic name for the Supreme Being, making it a word of power. The Supreme Being created the world and its cycles: the yearly cycle of the Earth around the Sun (365 days) and the triangle, the symbol behind the physical world.

Patriarchal history has awarded this Supreme Being status to the male.

However . . . before patriarchy, the world worshipped the Great Mother who created the world from her Cosmic Egg. Tiny female statues of women with extended bellies and large breasts have been found all over the world suggesting the Great Mother ready to give birth and prepared to nurture her children from her full breasts.

The beginning of chapter 3 in my book, *Astrology's Hidden Aspects: Quintiles and Sesquiquintiles,* reads: "Three is Time . . . Three is symbolized by the triangle, which has long been a religious symbol of the trinity. The Tantric Yoni Yantra, or downward pointing triangle, is the symbol of the Primordial Mother, the source of all life. This triangle, a revered and adored symbol, represented the Mother's genital area from which all life emerged."[11]

Therefore, the downward pointing triangle was a symbol of the Primordial Mother's genital area through which she created the world. This is the power symbol, the symbol of three.

The powerful name "Abracadabra" placed on the inverted triangle, the Primordial Mother's symbol, and reduced numerically reveals a hidden message.

To find that message, place the single numerical value below each letter. Then, add the first two adjacent numbers and total them below those same two numbers. Continue across the line and repeat until you reach the base of the inverted triangle. Reduce the double numbers to their single number as you go through this process. Keep the double number at the bottom of the inverted pyramid.

What is the Cosmic Mother's message?

To begin:

Add the numerical value of the first two letters in the name
abracadabra:
1 (A) + 2 (B) = 3.
Center the 3 under the 1 and 2.

Then add the number value of the B to the number value of the next letter in the name, R.

2 (B) + 9 (R) = 11
Reduce double numbers to the single number.
11 = 1 + 1 = 2
Center the 2 under the B and R.

Continue in this manner.

A	B	R	A	C	A	D	A	B	R	A
1	2	9	1	3	1	4	1	2	9	1

3 2 1 4 4 5 5 3 2 1

5 3 5 8 9 1 8 5 3

8 8 4 8 1 9 4 8

7 3 3 9 1 4 3

1 6 3 1 5 7

7 9 4 6 3

7 4 1 9

2 5 1

7 6

13/4!

We find the mystical number 13 at the base of this triangle. The number 13 represents the birth, death, and transformation of all earthly things, the 4; this is the cycle of life. 13 is the mystical number used in witches covens and lunar calendars. It is the number of power and magic and a link to the Source of Creation. The Cosmic Mother's message is the promise of transformation and rebirth.

The full word, "Abracadabra," adds to the mystical number 7.

You can place your full name at birth on the inverted triangle to discover your Abracadabra number, your mystical message from your Mom, Creator of the Universe.

Let's use the example of Jodi Ann Lee that we have used throughout this book.

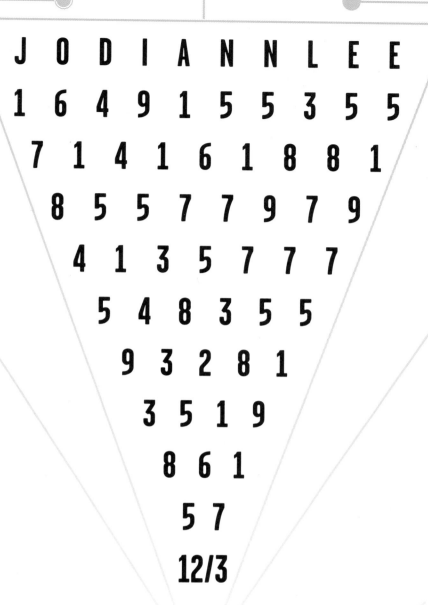

```
J  O  D  I  A  N  N  L  E  E
1  6  4  9  1  5  5  3  5  5
 7  1  4  1  6  1  8  8  1
  8  5  5  7  7  9  7  9
   4  1  3  5  7  7  7
    5  4  8  3  5  5
     9  3  2  8  1
      3  5  1  9
       8  6  1
        5  7
       12/3
```

Jodi's Cosmic Mother's message comes through the 3 family.

We know Jodi's birthday number is 37/10/1, the lessons she is here to learn are to stand on her own two feet and forge ahead. The Cosmic Mother's message to Jody comes through as a 3, which means Jodi has the most creative of all the numbers behind her. Things happen in 3s. If she listens, the positive growth-oriented energy of the 3 will sustain her through life regardless of the ups and downs. Her belief in herself and her positive attitude can bring her the success she desires.

PERIOD NUMBER CYCLES

The period number cycles allow you to look into the future of any year you want to investigate. To set this up, you will use your personal year cycle, your age, your birthday number, and your vowel number.

First, create an illustration with four blocks. Then divide your personal year cycle of twelve months into blocks of four months starting with your birthday month.

Once again, we'll use the example of Jodi Ann Lee, born July 6, 1968.

To find her personal year cycle in 2015, add her month and day to the year 2015:

Reduce the year first:
2015 = 2 + 0 + 1 + 5 = 8
Add her birthday to the reduced year:
7 + 6 + 8 = 21 or 21/3

Insert her personal year cycle 21/3 into the first block on the left.

Personal year cycle July 6, 2015-July 6, 2016 7 + 6 + 2015 (2015 = 2 + 0 + 1 +5 = 8) 7 + 6 + 8 = 21 21 = 2 + 1 = 3 or 21/3			

The divisions of her personal year into four-month periods are called the period numbers. They start with the day of her birth. Insert those dates into the three blocks to the right of the personal year cycle.

In those three blocks, also write the year that is being examined: in this case, 2015.

See the illustration below.

Personal year cycle July 6, 2015-July 6, 2016 7 + 6 + 2015 (2 + 0 + 1 + 5 = 8) 7 + 6 + 8 = 21/3 21 = 2 + 1 = 3 or 21/3	**Period Number** July 6-November 6 2015	**Period Number** November 6-March 6 2015	**Period Number** March 6-July 6 2015

In the second block to the right of the personal year cycle: Add Jodi's age at the time of her personal year cycle 21/3. Jodi was 47.

In the 3rd block, add Jodi's birthday number 37.

In the 4th block, add Jodi's vowel number 26.

See the illustration below.

Personal year cycle July 6, 2015-July 6, 2016	Period Number July 6-November 6	Period Number November 6-March 6	Period Number March 6-July 6
7 + 6 + 2015 (2 + 0 + 1 + 5 = 8) 7 + 6 + 8 = 21 21 = 2 + 1 = 3 or 21/3	2015 47 ——— 2062 2 + 0 + 6 + 2 = 10/1 Add age	2015 37 ——— 2052 2 + 0 + 5 + 2 = 9 Add birthday number	2015 26 ——— 2041 2 + 0 + 4 + 1 = 7 Add vowel number

In Jodi's personal year cycle 21/3, during the months of July 6 to November 6, she would do best to close the circle on some creative (personal year cycle 3) situation or project and make a stand on her final decision to begin again (10/1).

During the months of November 6 to March 6, she needs to share her knowledge and experience (9) from some kind of stage or platform (personal year cycle 3). The 9 requires that she shine her light of awareness to show the way for others.

And during the months of March 6 to July 6, she needs to retreat, rest her body and activate her mind (7). Maybe take a vacation to a place where she can enjoy the success of her creativity (personal year cycle 3). She needs time alone or perhaps with one or two others with the same quiet introspective mind set (7).

The theory behind the choice of the age and the birthday number and the vowel number in that order is: The first thing you recognize and are asked on your birthday is how old are you. Then the experiences of each year are incorporated into your birthday number or what you are learning. Every year you learn a bit more about why you are here. And finally, the experiences of the total year are absorbed by your vowel number, your inner being, and embedded in your Akashic Records, that great library in the sky where everything that has ever happened to you in this life and all past lifetimes is recorded.

PINNACLES AND CHALLENGES

Another numerological technique is called the pinnacles and challenges.

Your pinnacle numbers reveal the circumstances and events that occur during the ages indicated, which we will calculate shortly. These are helpful sign posts along the highway of your life, showing you what energies are available during your pinnacle periods of time. These numbers reveal what the road ahead has to offer: the smooth sailing highways, when to turn off for the scenic views, where the gas stations are, and when to focus on staying at home curled up by the fire and surrounded by little energetic creatures. Pinnacle numbers assist and encourage you in accomplishing your goals.

We all have challenges in our lives, things that we have to work on and work out. This is what brings meaning into our lives. If things went along swimmingly all the time, life would be boring. How many pina coladas can you drink while lying on a velvet sandy beach while the blue waves lazily lap the shore and tickle your toes?

Well, that could last quite a while . . . but after some time, your body calls out for movement in order to experience a sense of accomplishment and to develop your spiritual muscles. The challenges answer your call, alerting you to the timing of their visit.

To find the ages at which your pinnacle and challenge numbers will operate, you first have to subtract your birthday number from the number 36.

"Why 36?" you ask. I'm sure I heard you ask that . . .

Metaphysically, the life current, the Creative Force in the universe, is represented by the number 36. For example, 9 is one complete cycle, and 4 is connected to the four seasons of the Earth, and the four elements—Fire, Earth, Air, and Water. 9 x 4 = 36. Many of the multiples of 36 are considered sacred numbers because they relate to terrestrial and celestial measurements.

In the ancient mystery schools, 36 was the number of the Sun whose serpentine movement over the equator created the four seasons ensured that life would flourish. If the Sun remained stationary in one spot on our planet, there would no life as we know it. However, because our Earth is always tipped toward the Sun at the same angle all year, from our point of view it appears that the sun moves up over the equator and then down over the equator, creating the motions of a snake or a serpent.

The serpent, the snake, and dragon and its forms have always represented the life force. In the Garden of Eden, the serpent is the life current circling the tree. Similarly, the caduceus, the medical symbol, depicts the snake as the life force circling up the staff which is symbolic of the spine.

It has been written that the Pythagoreans swore their oaths of secrecy on the number 36. The addition of the first 8 numbers—1 through 8—equals 36. The numbers 1 through 7 are the pattern behind the physical world. The 8 is the physical world; the physical world relies upon the movement of the Sun over our equator, thus the Solar Logos, the Word, the linking principle between Spirit and matter.

Every circle has 360 degrees (drop the 0 and we end up with the number 36). We circle the Sun once every year, that's 360 degrees.

There are more metaphysical explanations; however, these are some that show why the pinnacles and challenges of life start with the number 36 as the base from which to operate.

From our geocentric point of view, (with the Earth as the center), does the Sun literally circle us? I asked that question online hoping for a simple yes or no and found a video, of which I grasped about 1/50th of the information provided, in which the professor suggested an article by Luka Popov titled: "The Dynamical Description of the Geocentric Universe." I have no thoughts of tackling that but perhaps you might. If you come up with a simple answer, please let me know.

Now that you're probably glassy-eyed with all these explanations . . . I know I am . . . take a breather. If you're interested in learning more about the hidden aspects of many numbers, you might want to look at my book, *Astrology's Hidden Aspects*, the first half of which is all numbers and symbols. There is no knowledge of astrology needed in that section of my book.

CALCULATIONS FOR THE AGE GROUPS OF THE PINNACLES AND CHALLENGES

Now let's calculate the age groups of the pinnacles and challenges.

The pinnacles and challenges are divided into four age groups. To find your four age groups, start with your birthday number.

To find our friend Jodi Ann Lee's age groups,
start with her birthday:

July + 6 + 1968
7   + 6 + 24/6 = 37/10/1

Her birthday number is 1.

. . . .

REMEMBER: in this exercise we start with the number 36, as explained above.

STEP 1: Subtract Jodi's birthday number 1 from number 36 to find her first age group. Her first age group is from 0 – 35.

STEP 2: Add 9 to the 35 which equals 44. Her second age group runs from age 36 – 44.

STEP 3: Add 9 to age 44. Her third age group runs from age 45 – 53.

STEP 4: The fourth age group then runs from age 54 until the end of life.

Another example:

If your birthday number is 7, you subtract 7 from 36 which equals 29.

STEP 1: Your 1st age group runs from your birth to age 29.

STEP 2: Add 9, the 2nd age group is 30 – 38.

STEP 3: Add 9, the 3rd age group is 39 – 47.

STEP 4: Add 9, the 4th age group starts at 48 until the end of life.

In the chart on the following page, you will see that I have done the calculations for you. All you have to do is find your birthday number in the left hand column, and follow across the chart horizontally to find your age groups.

Chart for Pinnacles and Challenges

YOUR BIRTHDAY №	AGES OF 1ST PINNACLE/ CHALLENGE	AGES OF 2ND PINNACLE/ CHALLENGE	AGES OF 3RD PINNACLE/ CHALLENGE	AGES OF 4TH PINNACLE/ CHALLENGE
1	0 to 35	36 through 44	45 through 53	54 on
2	0 to 34	35 through 43	44 through 52	53 on
3	0 to 33	34 through 42	43 through 51	52 on
4	0 to 32	33 through 41	42 through 50	51 on
5	0 to 31	32 through 40	41 through 49	50 on
6	0 to 30	31 through 39	40 through 48	49 on
7	0 to 29	30 through 38	39 through 47	48 on
8	0 to 28	29 through 37	38 through 46	47 on
9	0 to 27	28 through 36	37 through 45	46 on

Now that we have determined the age groups, let's find out what the number messages are within each age group.

To find Jodi Ann Lee's pinnacle numbers, start with her birthday:

(July) 7 + 6 + 1968 (1 + 9 + 6 + 8 = 24)
Her birthday number is 1. (Left column)
To find her first pinnacle number experience:
add her month and day of birth:
7 + 6 = 13/4
Her first pinnacle number is 4:
it will be in effect from birth to age 35.

To find her 2nd pinnacle number experience:
add her day and year of birth:
6 + 24 = 30/3
Her second pinnacle number is 3:
it will be in effect from ages 36 to 44.

PINNACLE NUMBERS 1-9

To find her 3rd pinnacle number experience:
add the 1st and 2nd pinnacles numbers:
4 + 3 = 7
Her third pinnacle number is 7:
it will be in effect from ages 45 to 53.

To find her 4th pinnacle number, add her month and year of birth:
7 + 24 = 31/4
Her fourth pinnacle number is 4: it will be in effect from age 54
until the end of life.

Jodi's pinnacle numbers are 4, 3, 7, and 4.

Find the meanings of your pinnacle numbers below:

PINNACLE NUMBERS 1-9:

THE HELP YOU CAN EXPECT.

PINNACLE NUMBER 1: You have help when you stand up to make your own decisions. This behavior will carve a path for the future that satisfies your need to go, to do, and to dare. All things being equal, put yourself first and you will gain confidence in your leadership role at whatever you are doing. Be brave, courageous, and dare mighty things.

PINNACLE NUMBER 2: Cooperation and diplomacy will serve you well during this period. You don't need to be top dog, rather exercise your power from behind the throne. As Teddy Roosevelt quoted from an African proverb, "Walk softly but carry a big stick." There is hidden magical energy here; nurture those things that are stirring beneath the surface.

PINNACLE NUMBER 3: Express your creative ability through the use of your imagination. Birth new ideas. Positive thinking and an optimistic outlook on life change the world around you and bring you success. Reach out to others and expand your horizons. Travel, change your image, be more flamboyant, and find a platform from which to express yourself.

PINNACLE NUMBER 4: "Work is love made visible . . ." Organization is the key to your success now. You have help building strong foundations to support the material goals in your life. Put your plans into effect and work hard to implement them. Financial and material success can result. Keep a tidy home and work area: Organize your closets, basement, and garage. If there is order around you, your life will flow more smoothly.

PINNACLE NUMBER 5: It's time to move around, interact with others, communicate, and experience life. Your curiosity opens doors to more information that will help you make choices in your life that can get you out of a rut, and perhaps alter the direction you have been going in. Sexual encounters make life more interesting. Take courses; get out in the community and mingle.

PINNACLE NUMBER 6: Love is the answer here. Your home and family can be a source of comfort and nurture. Your sense of beauty is heightened so you can produce beautiful works of art in any projects in which you are involved. Kindness, compassion, and sensitivity to the needs of those around you bring love in return. There can be changes in your home, people moving in or out, remodeling, and residential moves that can be beneficial.

PINNACLE NUMBER 7: You need periods of quiet time to think. Even though you may have a busy schedule, you should retreat occasionally to rest your body so your mind has time to contemplate current situations. This is the "7-year itch" syndrome so, by scratching those itches, you will arrive at the answers you need. Your mind is your greatest ally now. If you don't rest, the higher forces may tap you on the shoulder to remind you where you belong.

PINNACLE NUMBER 8: You have the strength now to achieve the worldly goals you have set for yourself. 8 is the "power and the glory"; therefore, the efforts you put out now can manifest in public recognition equal to the amount of work you have put in to this point. Raises, promotions, a kitchen makeover, whatever rings your bell, can be yours. What you have put out will come back. Karma is Queen.

PINNACLE NUMBER 9: Letting go of those things that are no longer necessary in your life can be done gracefully and with ease. Now you recognize that change is a part of life so you go with the flow, comfortable in the knowledge that only the best awaits you once you walk through that door into the future. You give back so that you have room to gain in the coming cycles.

You can combine a personal year cycle within a pinnacle time span to learn more about the energies available to you within that specific year.

CHALLENGE NUMBERS 1-9

Keeping the same age groups you calculated above, use the following formulas to find your challenges.

To find Jodi Ann Lee's challenges, start with her birthday:

$$July + 6 + 1968$$
$$7 + 6 + 24/6$$
$$7 + 6 + 6$$

For the first challenge number, use the month and day of birth
Subtract the smaller number from the larger number: 7 - 6 = 1
Jodi's first challenge number is a 1, and will be in effect from birth to age 35

The second challenge number uses the day and year of birth.
Subtract the smaller number from the larger number: 6 - 6 = 0
Her second challenge number is a 0, and is in effect from ages 36 to 44

The third challenge number uses the numbers of the first and second challenges.
Subtract the smaller number from the larger number: 1 - 0 = 1
Her third challenge number is a 1, and will be in effect from ages 45 to 53

The fourth challenge numbers uses the month and year of birth.
Subtract the smaller number from the larger number: 7 - 6 = 1
Her fourth challenge number is a 1, and will be in effect from age 54 on.

Jodi's challenge numbers are 1, 0, 1, and 1.

Find your Challenge Numbers beginning on the next page:

THE CHALLENGES TO OVERCOME.

CHALLENGE NUMBER 0: There is no specific challenge with a 0. This is a period when you can concentrate more on discovering yourself without any particular agenda. Like the shape of the 0, this period is more about fully exploring who you are, going full circle, to meet all the aspects of your being. It is wise not to waste this spiritual exploration period.

CHALLENGE NUMBER 1: This is not a time to hide in the background. You need to take a position now and make yourself heard. Learn to be more assertive when the situation requires such action. Be more courageous and reach out to travel paths you wouldn't have ventured before. It's time to stand out and stand up and be noticed for who you are.

CHALLENGE NUMBER 2: Take the back seat now and then. Learn to cooperate and be more companionable. Relationships require a more sensitive touch on all levels—personal and professional. Others will react positively to you when you learn to reach down inside yourself to nurture the magical seas that reside there. Learn to be the power behind the throne.

CHALLENGE NUMBER 3: Welcome the opportunity to learn how to express yourself in any creative manner you see fit. Take acting lessons, practice in front of the mirror, do whatever it takes to get out on to the world stage. Even if you are naturally shy, find a way to shine during this period, even if you do so incrementally, one step at a time.

CHALLENGE NUMBER 4: Pay attention to organizing your life so that you have a floor plan. Avoid clutter in your environment because that constant reminder clutters your mind and affects your decisions. Don't give up because you think the work is too much. Stick at it, and you will eventually see the results in tangible forms like money and a healthier body.

CHALLENGE NUMBER 5: Avoid scattering your energies by spreading yourself too thin. Too many irons in the fire means that too many things going on at once so some are bound to fail. This can also affect your nervous system so take stock of what you want to accomplish and approach it with a calm mind. Learn to focus.

CHALLENGE NUMBER 6: Home and family responsibilities, and even community involvement, can be a challenge. Whether you've taken on more family because of elderly parents or a new relationship, or you're moving or remodeling a home, you should attend to these issues with love in your heart. Creative outlets can help.

CHALLENGE NUMBER 7: Separating yourself from others, retreating into your mind, will not answer your problems at this juncture in your life. Although getting away can be helpful, now is not the time to use it as a crutch that isolates you from life. Rather, use your mind to explore philosophies and think about solutions to current situations.

CHALLENGE NUMBER 8: Your challenge is to embrace and learn how to use power in the physical world. If you are a person who naturally takes charge, use that position carefully and wisely or it can corrupt you. If you fear authority, now is the time to find your own power through taking courses that give you the courage to be noticed for your accomplishments.

There is no Challenge Number 9 because it is the highest number. The other nine numbers are subtracted from it.

You can combine any personal year cycle number with a challenge number to learn more about the challenges that will help you grow during that particular year.

TABLE OF EVENTS

Another technique is called the "table of events," which reveals the general trends under which you will be operating for given periods of time in your life. The personal year cycles reveal what any given year will bring, but the table of events will group a number of these cycles under one number vibration that will operate during an extended time period. With the table of events, you can pick a specific age—25 or 48 or 63 for instance—to determine what number influences will be in effect.

This is a lengthy process but once it is set up, it remains a permanent record for your lifetime, so hang in there.

To set up your table of events, use your full name at birth. Place the value of the letters above your name in single numbers.

For instance: Jodi Ann Lee

1	6	4	9	1	5	5	3	5	5
J	O	D	I	A	N	N	L	E	E

The numbers above your name indicate the number vibrations that will be in effect at any given age. The numbers that you place below the letters in your name will be the ages at which those numbers above your name will be in effect. Work each name in your full name independently.

Start with your first name. In our example, we start with Jodi.

Remember, the numbers we place below Jodi's name will indicate her age for this set up. These ages are the result of addition. (See chart that follows.)

The value of the first letter of her name is 1 therefore we place a 1 under the first letter of her name, J.

The value of her second letter in her name is a 6.
Add the 6 to the 1 for a total of 7.
Place 7 under the O in her name.

The value of the third letter in her name is a 4.
Add the 4 to the total of 7 which equals 11.
Place 11 under the third letter in her name.

The value of the fourth letter in her name is a 9.
Add the 9 to the previous 11 for a total of 20.
Place 20 under the fourth letter in her name.

Jodi's first name will now look like this:

1	6	4	9
J	O	D	I
1	7	11	20

If you have a long name like former Red Sox players Garciaparra and Saltalamacchia, this may take you some time. (See table that follows.)

Now . . . take the age 20, at the end of her first name, and start again with the first letter of her first name.

To her age 20 add the value of the first letter of her name, 1, for a total of 21. Place age 21 under the letter J to start the second row.

To the age 21, add the value of the second letter, 6, for a total of 27. Place age 27 under the letter O in the second row.

To the age 27, add the value of the third letter in her name, 4, for a total of 31. Place age 31 under the letter D in the second row.

To the age 31, add the value of the fourth letter in her name, 9, for a total of 40. Place age 40 under the letter I in the second row.

Jodi's name now looks like this:

1	6	4	9
J	**O**	**D**	**I**
1	7	11	20
21	27	31	40

Then we start on the third row.

To the age of 40, which is the end of the second row, add the value of the first letter in her name, 1, for a total of 41.
Place the age 41 under the letter J in the third row. (See table that follows.)

To the age of 41, add the value of the second letter in her name, 6, for a total of 47.
Place the age 47 under the letter O in the third row.

To the age of 47, add the value of the third letter in her name, 4, for a total of 51. Place age 51 under the letter D in the third row.

To the age of 51, add the value of the fourth letter in her name, 9, for a total of 60. Place the age 60 under the letter I in the third row.

Jodi's name now looks like this:

1	6	4	9
J	**O**	**D**	**I**
1	7	11	20
21	27	31	40
41	47	51	60

Then we start with the fourth row. (See table that follows.)

To the age of 60, add the value of the first letter in her name, 1, for a total of 61. Place the age 61 under the letter J in the fourth row.

To the age of 61, add the value of the second letter in her name, 6, for a total of 67.
Place the age 67 under the letter O in the third row.

To the age of 67, add the value of the third letter in her name, 4, for a total of 71. Place the age 71 under the letter D in the third row.

To the age of 71, add the value of the fourth letter in her name, 9, for a total of 80. Place the age 80 under the letter I in the third row.

Jodi's first name now looks like this.

1	6	4	9
J	O	D	I
1	7	11	20
21	27	31	40
41	47	51	60
61	67	71	80

People are now living well past eighty so continue this process as far as you want.

We repeat this process with Jodi's middle and last names, working with each name individually. Let's work out her middle name, Ann.

Her name Ann works out as follows:

1	5	5
A	N	N
1	6	11
12	17	22
23	28	33
34	39	44
45	50	55
56	61	66
67	72	77
78	83	88

Then we work out her last name Lee.

3	5	5
L	E	E
3	8	13
16	21	26
29	34	39
42	47	52
55	60	65
68	73	78
81	86	91

Jodi has a three-part name therefore, at any given age she will be influenced by three numbers, one from each name. If you have a two-part name, at any given age you will be influenced by two numbers.

For example: if Jodi wants to know what three numbers will influence her at the age of 34, she looks for that age.

In her first name, age 34 is found between ages 31 and 40. Therefore she is under the influence of the letter D or number 4.

In her middle name, age 34 is under the letter A. Therefore, she is influenced by the letter A or number 1.

In her last name, age 34 falls under the letter E. Therefore, she is influenced by the letter E or number 5.

So, at age 34, Jodi is operating under the influence of a 4, a 1, and a 5.

You could say that at this age she needs to be organized (4) and take charge (1) of some project that allows her mobility and freedom of expression (5). This could manifest as teaching, lecturing, writing, traveling (5). This influence will last as long as she is age 34.

. . . .

Zounds and forsooth! You've done it.

The beauty of this pattern is that it is permanent. Once you've gone through the work of setting up your table of events, you don't have to do it again. It's set for your life. Thank goodness!

Now on to a few simple techniques. Honestly!

YOUR POWER NUMBER

There is a number called your power number that is said to indicate the motivating force behind your entire being in this lifetime. It is your source of energy, your battery so to speak.

This number does not come into play until your middle thirties, after you have "gained your soul." I read somewhere that Plato said you gain or recognize your soul in your late twenties. Astrologically this seems to hold true because around the age twenty-nine, the planet Saturn completes one entire transit around your horoscope, crystallizing all your character traits. It is at this time in your life, at age 29 or so, that you become a whole person with the capabilities of exercising your potential to its fullest. Major events occur around this age in everyone's life.

Therefore, your 30s are the real testing ground astrologically and numerologically when the power number begins to become more apparent in your life. Talents and abilities you never knew you had or were capable of can surface at this time in your life. Your whole being shines through.

To find your power number, add the highest value of your name number at birth to the highest value of your birthday number.

Using Jodi Ann Lee as an example:

Her name number from her full name is 44/8.
Her birthday number from her birthday is 37

44 + 37 = 81
Reduce: 8 + 1 = 9

Jodi's power number is a 9.

The effects of this number vibration will come to fruition through her thirties.

You may notice that the power number is the same as the whole number from you birth blueprint.

Example: my power number is a 3.

I was a timid child throughout school, never raising my hand to participate in class. Through my 20s, I never spoke out at public meetings.

My power number 3 came into effect in my thirties when I began to lecture and appear on radio and television discussing numerology, astrology, dreams, and other metaphysical subjects. In order to prepare for this journey, I programmed myself.

Way back before the internet and cell phones, when tape recorders were the high-tech item, I made a tape so that it was my voice and not someone else telling me who to be. The taped message went like this: "I am calm and confident. I speak before groups and organizations. People respect my opinion. I am a capable woman."

These four sentences were spoken using the present tense—not "I *will be* calm and confident." *Will be* never comes.

I repeated these four sentences over and over until the half-hour tape was filled. Over the ensuing months, I played this tape every night in preparation for my first public appearance. The process was simple because all I had to do every night when I slipped under the covers was to press the rewind button then the play button and I was off to dreamland and let my subconscious do the rest. Just two buttons to press and I changed my life.

So, my husband is now calm and confident . . . but then, he always was.

Eventually, I appeared on numerous radio and television programs and was able to speak before small and large audiences with relative calm. My career began to blossom with more conferences, lectures, and then the publication of my books.

YOUR HABIT NUMBER

A habit is something done without reasoning or thinking; it is automatic or second nature.

When circumstances arise suddenly, we often revert to a habit. When too much work piles up, even if it should be shared with others, we might dig in to take care of it all and work ourselves into exhaustion. Or, if relationships get contentious around us, even if we're not involved, we automatically step into the role of peacemaker. Knowing your habits can make for an easier life.

To arrive at your habit challenge, count the number of letters in your full name at birth, and reduce the total to a single number.

Jodi Ann Lee has 10 letters in her name.
10 = 1 + 0 = 1
Her habit challenge number is 1.

HABIT NUMBERS 1–9

HABIT NUMBER 1: You are a natural leader; just as long as you don't think "my way is the highway" with your laser vision.

HABIT NUMBER 2: You are cooperative and need to bring things into balance; just don't get tangled in the little things that are not so important.

HABIT NUMBER 3: You are extremely creative; just don't get so caught up that you take too many dreams and they remain just that: dreams.

HABIT NUMBER 4: You are organized and a good worker; just don't get so obsessive about it that you get sloppy or give up.

HABIT NUMBER 5: You are mentally curious and intellectual; just don't be so changeable that your mind bounces from one thing to another.

HABIT NUMBER 6: You are loving and artistically inclined at home and in business; just don't become so immersed in your search for love and beauty that you become overly protective and imbalanced.

HABIT NUMBER 7: You search for truths and want to perfect your skills; just be sure that your solitude doesn't keep you separated from others.

HABIT NUMBER 8: You are a power person in the material world; just be sure that you don't dominate others. The pursuit of power can corrupt you.

HABIT NUMBER 9: You are an example, the light of knowledge that shows the way; just be sure you don't get discouraged when others don't "see" it your way.

YOUR HOUSE NUMBER

Your house has a personality. The number attached to your residence influences how you live in that house, what activities happen there, the general tenor of the family dynamics, even if the number invites or rejects visitors. Your home's personality has been reinforced over the years. Unless, of course, the house is new. Even then, the new house number still applies.

To find your house number, add the numbers of your address until you arrive at a single number. If you have a single house number to begin with, then you're all set.

Examples:

236 = 2 + 3 + 6 = 11; 1 + 1 = 2. This is a house number 2.

1427 = 1 + 4 + 2 + 7 = 14; 1 + 4 = 5. This is a house number 5.

The number personality applies to apartment numbers as well. The building overall may have a number, an address, but the apartment number is the most important.

You react subconsciously to house numbers. For instance, the mood created by an address of 666 has a different flavor than the mood of a 333 residence or a 777 home. Even now, you're feeling the difference, right?

On a "dark and stormy night," how would you feel approaching the door of an unknown residence and, when reaching for the door bell, seeing the number 666 emblazoned over the button. Would you flinch, step back, or run for your life?

Sounds silly, I know, but numbers are embedded in our consciousness, and we all know the story of the 666 through books and the media, incorrect though it is. (For the true story of the 666, see chapter 7.)

You could match your vowel number to the number of the house you want to live in because that personal number is your comfort zone. But perhaps you don't want to get too comfy and cozy; then you'll just curl up in that pillowy recliner, eat bonbons, and get nothing accomplished.

If you're attached to your consonant number, then it may be all show to impress the outside world. That's okay if your agenda is to set the tone in your neighborhood while living an entirely different existence behind closed doors.

If you like the idea of your name number matching your house number, then you desire that your house is a showcase that stands for the brand that your name represents in the world: names like the Hilton Hotels, Phillips 66, Anheuser-Busch, Walmart and Sam's Club (a combination of the founder's name: Sam Walton). The family name is important to you.

Probably the best number from your birth pattern to use when looking for a meaningful house number is your birthday number because it represents what you are here to learn this lifetime. And you might as well have help from the place where you presumably spend most of your time, your home.

If you find you are living in a house with a number that does not gel with your birthday number, that does not mean you have to move. Rather, you could first make adjustments to the house so you can live in it comfortably.

Example: Say you birthday number is a 7, and you require peace and quiet and rest to fulfill your lessons, but you happen to live in a house number 4 which says get organized, work on repairs, take care of the landscape.

Your first step could be to do the 4 first: Organize the interior of the house from top to bottom, take care of any necessary repairs, and hire someone to mow the lawn and do the weeding. Then, because the 4 is taken care of, you could settle into your 7 routine.

Give this arrangement time to work. If after a reasonable amount of time, you find you're still uncomfortable in that house, then it could be time to move.

Houses do carry the energies from one family to the next.

What follows is a description of the home if the occupants of the house are in harmony with the house number.

HOUSE NUMBERS 1-9

HOUSE NUMBER 1: This is a home that supports independent types of people who are always heading out the door or doing their own thing or working independently within the house, a sort of "my space, your space" arrangement. They don't want anyone telling them what to do or how to live. They may have their own work area and their own bedroom. This promotes their need to stand on their own and not be influenced by relationships. One well known writer lives in a brownstone in Boston: he lives on the bottom floor; his wife lives on the second floor.

HOUSE NUMBER 2: This is a private home with people who desire to live away from the hustle and bustle of life, who like a quiet peaceful environment. They are tactful types who desire to live in harmony with each other. They don't want trouble so their sensitive natures keep them from allowing arguments to take over their conversations. They are also sensitive to any controversy with neighbors; they believe that "good fences make good neighbors." But then, who knows what goes on behind closed doors?

HOUSE NUMBER 3: This is a joyful house. The people who live here are fun loving and ready to party; mark the dates on your calendar. This is a place where creative talent is nurtured and positive thinking and love of games are expressed. Members of the family have the freedom to come and go with ease. Because this is a welcoming home, the occupants will greet you at the door with a big smile and a "come on in" and "don't mind the clutter; I've been so busy lately." And you will smile too.

HOUSE NUMBER 4: This is home for practical residents, the salt of the earth types who enjoy working on their home and are also willing to lend a helping hand to build, repair, or organize a project in their neighborhood. Their homes reflect a respect for time and space: hangers facing the same way in closets, spices alphabetized in the cupboards, furniture arranged optimally. They tend to be economical, believing that "a penny earned, is a penny saved" so they make good managers.

HOUSE NUMBER 5: This house has a revolving front door to accommodate the constant traffic flowing in and out. The occupants are constantly on the move, planting a peck on the cheek and grabbing a microwaved sandwich on the way out the door on their way to meet their friends or to the next community meeting, and they're already late. This house never seems to sleep: lights shine through windows late into the night. Cell phones, TVs, and gaming devices keep them in the loop.

HOUSE NUMBER 6: This house is a home. Filled with love and contentment, it draws occupants who are family oriented and who care for each other. The interior design speaks to the beauty of well-designed comfort with a love of art and music, candles and flowers. The occupants are responsible for family and will also work for the welfare of the community. They see fair play as a paramount duty to family; therefore, they respect each other; disagreements are settled fairly.

HOUSE NUMBER 7: No parties held here. But there may be a laboratory filled with foaming glass tubes buried in the bowels of this basement so the residents can search for the secrets of transmuting lead into gold. This is a place of rest, sleep, retreat, and quiet contemplation where the residents are not interrupted by the stresses of the outside world. Their minds are replenished and their souls nourished by the simplicity of their lifestyles. This setting is conducive to educational and metaphysical pursuits.

HOUSE NUMBER 8: This home is the showcase for successful business people. In fact, business could be conducted from the house in which case the residents make it a place where they can advertise their importance and accomplishments to those who enter. Pick up a business card on the way out. The friends they cultivate may also have important friends who can further their careers. The exterior of their house speaks of money and makes an impression of success and good judgment on those passing by. This house may be more an office than a home.

HOUSE NUMBER 9: These residents could place the statue of liberty on their front lawn that says "give me your huddled masses, yearning to breathe free." They want to help others and their home supports the compassion and unconditional love they express; their door is open to anyone in need. It's a home that nourishes art and music and spiritual pursuits. Their family may consists of not just their own but may also be a home for those who have been cast off by society.

Years ago, during a radio talk show, a numerologist asked one of the listeners to give him three single numbers quickly without thinking about it. The woman did so, and he proceeded to explain what thoughts were paramount in her life and on her mind at that time. He did this with several subsequent callers with great accuracy.

I thought: He could be psychic and using the numbers as a point of focus, or the numbers themselves are giving him all the information he needs, or it's a combination of both.

The numbers themselves do tell the story. As far as how much psychic ability is involved is hard to say. Everyone is psychic to a degree, so it's difficult to separate our psychic ability from any conversations we have or acts we perform.

However, with just a basic knowledge of the numbers 1 through 9, you could do the same thing as the numerologist did with the radio audience.

We all have an innate understanding of the meaning of the single numbers, even without a deep study of these numbers. We use them in our daily language: "things happen in threes" . . . "the seven-year itch" . . . "the whole nine yards" . . . and so on.

Great knowledge is stored in the subconscious mind; at times, pieces of this storehouse of information surface through our daily language without our conscious awareness so you will be amazed at how well you can do with this technique.

I thought about this "three number selection" for some time and finally realized that, even at this quick level, there is a process. This observation comes from the meaning of the first three numbers in the creation process: 1 is the seed, 2 is the work of cultivating that seed, and 3 is the resulting bloom from that seed. So I reasoned that the selection of three single numbers at random follow these logical steps.

Therefore, the first of the three numbers, the seed, is the idea that activates the process. The second of the three numbers indicates the underlying work needed to cultivate and care for the seed, and the last of the three numbers suggests the bloom, the final outcome. "Things happen in threes."

While giving a lecture at a seminar some time after this radio show, I decided to try this method. I explained to the group how it worked, then pointed to one of the participants, and said: "Give me three numbers—quickly—the first three that pop into your head."

The woman said 7–4–3.

I thought a moment and then responded: You need a vacation (7), but before you can take one, there are matters to be straightened out, perhaps financial ones (4). Once these are settled, you will have more freedom and perhaps the money to take a long trip

SELECT THREE NUMBERS! NOW! QUICK!

during which you will meet new and interesting people, and have a good time socializing (3).

She was as amazed as I was.

My reasoning: The first number is the impetus. The 7 she chose showed she needed rest and a retreat from the outside world so she was motivated to take a vacation.

The second number indicates what has to be taken care of before this can happen. She chose 4 as the second number which indicates work and organization and paying attention to finances.

And the third number is the final outcome. She chose the number 3 which is travel, expansion, and greater social contact.

By synthesizing her three selected numbers, a story was told.

As you experiment with this technique, you will become more efficient at this process and will soon realize that at a subconscious level you know what you need and that in reality you do anticipate what is about to happen in your life.

How else could the selection of three random single numbers tell so much about our innermost thoughts and needs? It's because numbers are the universal language. Pretty amazing!

My appearance on a Boston television show in 1979 with a panel to discuss the then upcoming decade of the 1980s brought this home to me. A gentleman from the telephone company was on the panel with me. He was asked why the WATS line was an 800 code number (this was the telephone service that businesses paid for so that the customers could call in free. Remember, this was a long time ago!). He was asked if there was a special reason the 8 was chosen. Why not 200 or 600? The man explained that the number was chosen arbitrarily and that any other number could just as easily have been used.

When it was my turn to speak, I explained that the number 8 rules the material world of big business. The officials had chosen this number code because it fit the enterprise they were introducing to the public.

Some might say that the chances were one in nine that the 8 would have been selected. This is true, although how many times could you pick the correct number from a series of nine. If this were the only instance of this kind of an occurrence with the numbers, I would agree with the skeptics, but the proof mounts day after day when you begin to observe the world around you.

Be alert and have fun with the numbers. You can surprise people with your ability to speak this universal language.

PART III·

WHAT'S BEHIND DOOR NUMBER . . . ?

Chapter 6

THE PATRIARCHAL GODS

"GOD" IS A PATRIARCHAL TERM USED TO REPRESENT the Source of creation. However, God was preceded by the Cosmic Mother who contains the Cosmic Egg in which all existed before creation. More about that at the end of this chapter.

Brought up in the Judeo-Christian world, I will be using the Bible here as a reference point.

Almost the entire Old Testament was written in Hebrew (with the exception of a few chapters in the prophecies of Ezra and Daniel and one verse in Jeremiah, which were written in a language called Aramaic).

On one level, the Hebrew language in the Old Testament in the Bible tells a human story for those who need and want to relate to their creator in a personal comforting manner. On another level, hidden behind the letters of the Hebrew language are numbers that tell an esoteric story.

Gematria is a method of applying number values to the letters of the Hebrew alphabet to reveal hidden information. It's important to remember that words often mask esoteric truths. In the past, truths were deliberately hidden to protect the information from those superstitious, controlling entities who sought to destroy any deviation from their limited belief systems.

In times past, the Creator has had a number of names, depending upon what function was being discussed. We will discuss two of those functions: the "creation god" and the "architect god."

God is a mathematician.

To the Pythagoreans, God was not a mathematician—mathematics was God! Galileo wrote, "Mathematics is the language in which God has written the universe."

Paul Dirac, theoretical physicist and 1933 Nobel Prize winner in physics for fundamental contributions to the development of quantum mechanics and quantum electrodynamics wrote: "If there is a God, He is a great mathematician."

Philosophers and scientists alike from the past and into the present understand this concept. Let's examine this mathematical god further.

As stated, the Old Testament of the Christian Bible was written in Hebrew. Hidden behind the letters of the Hebrew alphabet are number values.

Genesis 1:1 reads: "In the beginning God created the heavens and the earth . . ."

In the Hebrew language, the name of the god used here is ALHIM or elohim. The numerical values hidden behind this name are 31415, a mathematical value of huge significance—not only mathematically but spiritually.

Pi, Π, or 31415, is the mathematical constant that represents the relationship between the circumference of a circle and its diameter: C = circumference; D = diameter. The formula is written as C = Πd.

By the way, pi is an infinite number and never settles into a repeating pattern. One internet site asked if I wanted to see the first million digits!

"So, what's the big deal?" you might ask. Well, geometry is a language based upon numbers, and the big deal is that this name of god contains a cosmic mathematical message.

The discovery of pi is popularly attributed to the Greek mathematician and engineer Archimedes (280 BCE). Archimedes may have used pi in 280 BCE, but Moses, the said author of Genesis who was trained in Egypt by masters, also knew the value of pi. He incorporated this value into the first sentence of the Bible in the form of the name of God. Pi is also found in the measurements of the Great Pyramid in Egypt, constructed some say 6,000 years ago.

Frank C. Higgins, 33rd degree Mason and author of *Hermetic Masonry* (a book I highly recommend to number addicts) writes: "The pi proportion is something that is never absent, in one form or other, from everyone of the world's primitive religions . . ."[12]

Higgins also wrote that "Almost all the ancient names of Deity, when their letters are resolved into numbers, are found to consist of what are sometimes called 'cosmic numbers' in that they express some great planetary or terrestrial cycles."[13]

ELOHIM OR ALHIM: THE "CREATION" GOD: PI, THE LIVING LOGOS = 3.1415

As stated above, Genesis 1:1 reads: "In the beginning God created the heavens and the earth." The Hebrew word for god is ALHIM or Elohim (Elohim was originally the name for goddesses and gods, plural).

If the word ALHIM is placed is a circle and then the corresponding number values of the Hebrew word for god are placed in that same circle, look what happens! Note that the double numbers are reduced to their single number in the illustration.

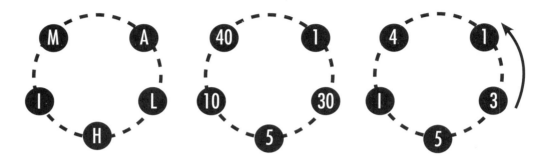

As you can see, ALHIM has a numerical value of 31415 or pi!

And pi, as mentioned above, represents the relationships between the circle and its diameter. The circle represents Spirit; the diameter or horizontal line represents matter.

Therefore, pi represents the relationship between Spirit (the circle) and Matter (the diameter), between the "creative" aspect of god and all life forms on earth, between god and humanity, or between god and you. Or, as I prefer, between Goddess and you . . . and me and everyone else on this planet.

And that's why god is a mathematician! The first aspect of god in the first sentence in the Bible is the creative god, the force that created the universe and the link between the Creator and us.

What does the term "Living Logos" mean? I'm so glad you're asking all these questions!

Logos is the Greek term translated as "word, speech, principle, or thought." In Greek philosophy, it referred to the divine reason or the mind of god. Logos suggested the idea of communication.

The creation god "thought" the world into existence and then "spoke" the world into existence through thoughts and words, the Living Logos.

Sound familiar? How many times have we heard that simple message? For every action, there is an equal and opposite reaction; as you think, so shall you be; mind creates reality; thoughts are things; thoughts create reality.

We are co-creators of this world. That's why prayer, meditation, chanting, and positive thinking do matter.

We heard from the creation god, the one who spoke and set the creative wheels in motion. Now we need a blueprint, a plan that lays out the dimensions and specifications for the building of that creation. For this step, we need an architect.

In Exodus 3:14, God said to Moses, "I AM WHO I AM." This is the architect god.

Through Gematria, the Hebrew name for the "I AM" God is Jod-Heh-Vau-Heh or Jehovah. The numbers behind Jod-Heh-Vau-Heh in the Hebrew alphabet are 10-5-6-5.

Interesting, but what does this mean?

Jod-Heh-Vau-Heh or Jehovah is the code name of the Sacred Trapezoid, a geometrical figure of specific proportions, which embodies terrestrial and celestial measurements and sets up our place in this universe.

In mathematics, a trapezoid has four lines enclosing a space of which two of the lines are parallel. (See the illustration below)

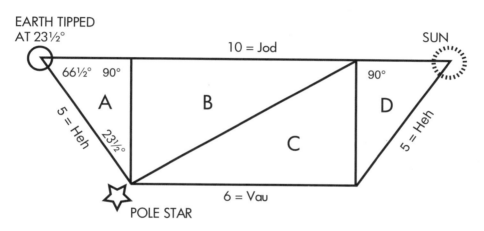

This diagram shows the Earth tipped at its constant 23½° angle to the path it travels around the Sun (the ecliptic). Since every right triangle has 180°, this creates right triangles A and D, with angles of 90°, 66½°, and 23½°. Therefore, these right triangles A and D reflect the Earth's relationships to the Sun and its polar star, the Earth's place in the solar system and in the universe.

The numerical value of the sides of this trapezoid is 10-5-6-5. As stated, through Gematria, the letter counterpart of 10-5-6-5 is J-H-V-H or Jehovah, which represents the Great Architect who constructed our Universe.

In pre-patriarchal societies, it was of course the Great Mother who was worshipped as the Creator of the Universe. As mentioned earlier, the female aspect of creation was deleted in patriarchal discussions of "god."

Jehovah as the Sacred Trapezoid shown here represents the Earth's relationship to the Sun using the tilt of the Earth's pole. If the Earth's pole was vertical to the path it travels around the Sun, then the Sun's light would always shine on the same band around the equator. Therefore, we would have no seasons.

Because of the Earth's tip, the Sun's movement undulates above and below the equator and creates the seasons we all know. This creates the life we live on our planet. Without this relationship there would be no life on this Earth as we know it.

This Sacred Trapezoid is the architect's plan that created a suitable environment on this planet in which life could thrive as it has! Jehovah is the "architect god."

When asked by Moses who he was, God's response was "I am that I am." The response was not "I am who I am," which would imply a person, but rather "I am that I am." This is a state of being.

Jehovah, Jod-Heh-Vau-Heh, 10-5-6-5, is the "I AM" god, the "architect god" behind the manifestation of the world of form. The "Jod" in Jod-Heh-Vau-Heh can also be translated as I, J, or Y, so you may see this formula as IHVH, JHVH, or YHVH.

The sacred formula 10-5-6-5 was known to the initiated in secret schools through the ancient worlds of the Middle East, South Asia, and East Asia.

In the ancient world, religion clothed science: one spoke to the emotions, to the general public who needed personal contact through familiar embodiments like human personalities; the other spoke to the mind, to the initiate who could relate to the purity of mathematics as an expression of divinity. But both messages were identical.

The exact dimensions of the sacred trapezoid can be found throughout the world in the construction of furniture, in temples and churches, on the floors and walls of buildings, and inscribed on coins and amulets. Many ancient keystones were carved in the shape of the sacred trapezoid. The Masonic apron as well as the shoulder and arms of the Egyptian sun god Ra embody these dimensions.

These dimensions are repeated in various ancient cultures and have been carried down the centuries through the arts so faithfully that we have to believe there is an innate understanding of the proportion, order, and harmony of the Universe created by the Great Architect. That's why the Masons, the Builders, and the Carpenters were sacred professions.

You might find the following chart listing the four part creation of the world informative.

The Four Elements
The Building Blocks Of Life

THEIR EXPRESSION IN THE PHYSICAL WORLD

ELEMENTS	FIRE	WATER	AIR	EARTH
Seasons	Spring	Summer	Fall	Winter
Tarot Suits	Wands	Cups	Swords	Pentacles
Playing Card Suits	Clubs	Hearts	Spades	Diamonds
Tetragammatron	Jod	Heh	Vau	Heh
Sacred Trapezoid	10	5	6	5
Serpent Signs	Leo	Scorpio	Aquarius	Taurus
Astrological Types	Ardent	Emotional	Intellectual	Practical
Apostles	Mark	John	Matthew	Luke
World Myth Figures (i.e., Sphinx)	Lion	Eagle	Woman	Bull
Nature Spirits (Paracelsus)	Salamander	Undines	Sylphs	Gnomes
Greek Philosophical Qualities	Morality	Aesthetics	Intellectuality	Physicality
Human	Spirit	Soul	Mind	Body
Human Functions (Jung)	Intuition	Feeling	Thinking	Sensation
Human Bodies	Vital/Etheric	Emotional/Astral	Mental/Casual	Physical

As promised at the beginning of this chapter, here is the text from one of my earlier books about the Goddess:

It is important to remember that the earliest known religions adored the Mother-Goddess. Followers of the Goddess can be traced back to Neolithic communities, ca. 7000 BCE, and some claim the Upper Paleolithic Mother-worshipping cultures lived as long ago as 25,000 BCE. By comparison, Abraham lived in Canaan (Palestine) somewhere between 1800 and 1550 BCE, according to most Biblical scholars.

The authors of the Judeo-Christian Bible seemed to have "purposely glossed over" the sexual identity of the female deity who was held sacred by the neighbors of the Hebrews in Canaan, Babylon, and Egypt.

The Old Testament does not even have a word for "Goddess." In the Bible the Goddess is referred to as elohim, in the masculine gender, to be translated as "god." Biblical scholars interpreted "elohim" as god even though it is a plural form meaning "goddesses and gods."

The Koran of the Mohammedans however was quite clear. It read: "Allah will not tolerate idolatry . . . the pagans pray to females." The pagans were all who would not covert to Father-God worship.[14]

CHAPTER 7

THOUGHTS FROM MY NOTEBOOK: FROM CUBES TO CRYSTALS

I KEEP A NOTEBOOK BESIDE MY BED IN WHICH, EACH night, I record ideas, thoughts, questions, experiences, and significant passages I've read during the day. In the morning, I make note of any unusual dreams. This notebook is invaluable in my work. It seems I can think better holding a pen and writing my thoughts, trying to give form to the ideas that are floating somewhere in my brain cells.

As a practice that is now a habit, this process has in the past and continues now to reveal information that, for me, is startling, exciting, meaningful, and worthwhile. My notebook is a world of free-floating concepts, from Pythagoras to the musical scale to sketches of cubes, from triangles and multi-pointed stars to various arrangements of the letters of the alphabet and their numerical values, from quotes out of fascinating books to dreams of flight and crystal chandeliers.

I sometimes wonder what and where is the hand that will unite these separate pieces into a cohesive picture. And then a moment occurs, a precious moment, which often brings tears to my eyes because it reveals a truth for me. A few pieces come together, and I begin to see and to understand the beauty and delicate intricacy of the cosmic puzzle.

Our thoughts create our reality, which in turn alters reality.

As David Spangler writes in *Revelation: The Birth of a New Age*, through experimentation in the laboratory, science has come to realize that "the observer and the observed are one," an idea long taught by mystics of all ages.

In quantum physics, the myth of the detached observer is destroyed by Heisenberg's Uncertainty Principle. Heisenberg claims that every scientist approaches experimentation with some bias, expecting certain results, and "the act of observing on a sub-nuclear level alters that which is being observed."

Physicists say that "for every action there is an equal and opposite reaction." The mystics say, "as ye think, so are ye." Or "as it is above, so it is below." We can think our thoughts into reality.

In other words, what the writers, scientists, and mystics are saying is that we control out lives through our thought forms. Mind and body (the physical body and the physical world) are inseparable.

There is unity in spite of seeming separateness and, for me, my notebook is testimony to this fact. Therefore, I would like to share some of my reality with you. Please keep an open mind and store these thoughts somewhere in the recesses of your mental notebook. You may find that some of this information will click for you now and for some of you maybe not now or ever. But there may come a moment when a few pieces might fall into place, and then you too will smile in amazement at the simplicity of it all.

THE NUMBER OF THE BEAST 666 AND THE COMPUTER

According to Revelation, the last book in the New Testament, the prophecy of the Lord through St. John, Chapter 13, speaks of the beast that shall gain sovereignty over the world for forty-two months.

Verses 16–18 reads: "and He [the beast] causes all, both small and great, rich and poor, free and bond, to receive a mark in their right hand, or in their foreheads: and that no man might buy or sell, save he that had the mark, or the name of the beast, or the number of his name. Here is wisdom. Let him that hath understanding count the number of the beast: for it is the number of man: and his number is Six hundred threescore and six [666]."

The 666 has puzzled theologians and lay person alike for centuries. That it has come down to us with an evil connotation no one doubts. Note how the 666 was placed on the head of the devil's child, Dameon, in the film *The Omen*.

Nevertheless, I had never heard a satisfactory explanation of why the number 666 was used in Revelation rather than the numbers 333 or 999. And as a numerologist, I know that numbers are not chosen arbitrarily.

Through a series of events, I found an answer that satisfied me.

At a convention, I happened to overhear a man mention the number 666. I turned and asked what he was talking about. He said he was discussing the carbon 12 atom which contains 6 electrons, 6 neutron, and 6 protons.

A flash went off in my head. Here was the 666!

He went on to say that carbon is found in all living matter. He seemed unaware of or at least did not make the connection with the passage in Revelation and the number of the beast.

I was so excited about this information that, when I arrived home, I began my research. The atomic number of carbon is 6. Carbon is a component of all living matter, and carbon 12 contains 6 electrons, 6 neutrons, and 6 protons, as the man at the convention had said.

Our bodies and the life forms on earth are products of carbon.

Carbon comes from the Latin, "carbo" which means coal. Dead plant matter decays into peat and eventually into coal. "Coal forests" were found in the former wetlands that covered most of the tropical areas of the Earth during the late Carboniferous and Permian times.

Buried deep in the earth, the heat and pressure over millions of years converts the peat into coal. When that coal is under an immense amount of pressure and heat, its atoms are squeezed and heated, and then pushed toward the earth's surface where they cool and become diamonds.

Coal, the 666, buried deep in the earth under great pressure for millions of years, turns into a diamond!

"Carbon atoms make up an immense part of our molecular structure. Without carbon, the many other elements that make up our bodies would not be able to function properly. Human beings are carbon-based 'life forms.'"[15]

There is a metaphysical message here. The unevolved human being, the lump of coal, is the beast, the 666!

When we are trapped by and act out our baser physical desires, we are stimulating the beast within us. We can enjoy the physical body and its experiences—we are meant to—but we must own them; they cannot own us to the point that we are driven to commit evil deeds in order to satiate the body's lusts and material needs. Then the temple, the human body, becomes a den of the beast, controlled by the needs of the carbon atom, the 666.

When I was a little girl, I was warned by the adults around me that if I were naughty, Santa wouldn't leave gifts in my stocking; he would leave a lump of coal. They did not know the implications of that lump of carbon.

By learning and growing through the pressure of many trials and tribulations (the pressure on the lump of coal) perhaps through many years and/or lifetimes (for millions of years), we become polished, and eventually turn into an en-light-ened human being (the diamond). Light is a symbol for knowledge.

We then become the temple not built with human hands; we become the crystal temple full of light.

Beyond the metaphysical interpretation, there is a very real beast in the world that lurks in many places under the guise of the 666. In the original version of this book in 1980, I wrote: "With the invention of the computer, it would be an easy matter to mark every person in the world with a number, and then record that number in a computer."

Back then, long before personal computers and smart phones, in the 1980 printing, I wrote what has more or less come to be: "A cashless system of exchange is seriously being considered and is actually being tested in certain areas of the world. People will go into a store and make a purchase which is transacted by running their number into a computer terminal connected to a central computer where the person's paycheck is automatically deposited each week. The computer then deducts the amount of the purchase from the customer's account. No money is exchanged." Remember, this was written in 1980!

The quote from Revelations: "no man might buy or sell save he had the mark of the beast or the number of his name."

Might the time come when, to further "protect" customers from the loss or theft of their cards, it is suggested and eventually insisted upon that each person be marked with their number on their flesh. It would be invisible, seen only under a certain light, but nevertheless the person is marked as Revelation stated.

On the surface, this might seem simpler and easier; however, the implications are horrendous. If society does away with cash as a medium of exchange, and you refuse to be branded or marked, you could not purchase the necessities of life—food, clothing, shelter, and medicine. The forces that control the computer would eventually control your actions—how you vote, how you live, what you will submit to because they have a weapon—because they can deny you the basic necessities of life.

The carbon body, the 666, is then under the control of a larger 666, the computer.

To add weight to this argument, although the pronoun used in Revelation referring to the beast is usually translated "he," the Greek passage could also be interpreted as "it." The computer is an "it."

The world ruler, the beast, could very well be a computer run by a powerful group of individuals who see to it that everyone in the world has the mark in their flesh. The people are then controlled and controllable. George Orwell's *1984* version with Big Brother may have been a warning where every citizen's move will be watched and monitored.

Today the computer through the internet, although a blessing in some ways, is disrupting people's lives on many levels.

On June 21, 2019, an article on the Bing browser titled "News about Smartphone Users Growing Horns" caught my attention. I could only think that "the devil is in the details" after our discussion of the computer, the 666, and the beast.

Does this beast live on in the form of cell phones?

The article went on to say that young people who can't seem to live without their cell phones are growing horns on their skulls from cell phone use. The forward tilt of the head shifts the weight from the spine to the back of the neck causing bone spurs. Cell phones are not only altering this obsessive behavior in terms of isolation and disruptive relationships but are also remolding skeletons with horn-like spikes at the back of the skull just above the neck.

The new tech world is a temptation.

ARE YOUNG PEOPLE GROWING HORNS?

The universal danger symbol for the presence of radiation is 666!

Every circle has 360 degrees. The radiation warning symbol contains two concentric circles, each divided into three pie-shaped segments. Each segment is 60^0. Reduce the 60 by adding: $6 + 0 = 6$.

RADIATION

60°   60°

60=6+0=6

In the radiation warning symbol we have two groups of 666! Another incarnation of the Bible's beast!

In 2019, the movie *Chernobyl* dramatized the true story of the worst nuclear disaster in history when, in 1986, the nuclear plant in Chernobyl had a meltdown and spread radiation over much of Europe. Chernobyl is one of the ten most polluted places on Earth.

In the first printing of this book in March 1980, I predicted: ". . . The 1980s might see a nuclear disaster resulting from human error at a nuclear plant . . . disasters could cause mass evacuations . . ."

THE NUMBER 26, KARMA, AND SALT

Continuing with the theory of cosmic numbers as expressed through the various names of the ancients for god, we now look at the number 26.

The English language is comprised of 26 letters in the alphabet, a language widely used and spoken in the world today, especially in global negotiations. An alphabet holds the limit of our ability to communicate through the written word.

As discussed, one Hebrew name for God is Jehovah or Jod-Heh-Vau-Heh. The value of the Hebrew letters in this name is 10-5-6-5, for a total of 26.

As mentioned, the square represents the pattern of the material world, and the shorthand for the extension of the square is the cube. Remember, the circle, triangle, and square are the patterns that create.

Extend the square into a three-dimensional form and it solidifies into the cube, into the physical world of form. The ancients used the cube as the symbol of the physical body, the stone that must be worked, shaped, and perfected. Our purpose in life is to work, shape, and perfect our lives as human beings.

There are religious/philosophical connections to building. Note that Jesus was a carpenter; the Masons work to build the temple; and we have organizations like Builders of the Adytum (BOTA), a modern mystery school. Adytum is the Greek word for Inner Shrine, the temple, the body.

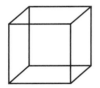

The number of the cube is 26: 8 points, 12 lines, and 6 planes = 26.

The ancients used the cube as the symbol of the physical body, the stone that must be worked, shaped, and perfected. Our bodies are made of carbon; the numerical value of the word "carbon" adds to 26.

To repeat: the number of the cube is 26: 8 points, 12 lines, and 6 planes = 26.

The name of the architect god: Jod-Heh-Vau-Heh or 10-5-6-5 = 26. And this is where karma comes in.

The definition of karma is: the sum of one's actions in this and previous existences, which will determine the fate in future existences. So, our actions while in the physical body, the cube, determine our fate through karma.

The Bible says: "Ye are the salt of the earth." Salt crystallizes in cubes—the symbol of the human body, the Earth, the number 26. Solid deposits of salt exist all over the Earth, some many thousands of feet thick. The oceans, which cover a major portion of the Earth's surface, contain salt.

Salt is an essential part of the human diet. When we perspire excessively, we lose much of the salt content in our bodies, therefore, we may need to take salt tablets to replenish the salt our bodies lose. This is especially true in hot climates. The Roman army needed salt for its soldiers and their horses and livestock. Therefore, at times they were paid in salt. The world "salary" comes from the Latin word "salarium," or the money that was paid to the soldiers for the purchase of salt, which was necessary for their survival in the hot climates in which they lived and often fought. When we use the phrase that "she is worth her salt," we are referring to this ancient practice when soldiers were paid for their work, for what they were worth.

Wherever salt is scarce, its value is very high. Some salt is impure in that it contains insoluble earthy materials. We are the salt of the Earth. Salt crystallizes in cubes; the cube is symbolic of the human body. Some of that salt contains impure insoluble earthy material, fit only "to be trod underfoot," according to Matthew 5:13 in the Bible.

The metaphysical implication here is that the human being who cannot purify herself of negative Earthly desires is trapped in a useless existence. This is karma. Remember when Lot's wife turned back to look upon Sodom, the city of sin, she was turned to a pillar of salt (Genesis 19:26). The implication is that she hesitated to leave behind her old ways; she was trapped in her old desire (karma), and, therefore, she turned into a pillar of salt, frozen in time.

On the other hand, "Salt can be grown by very slow cooling into large and perfectly transparent cubes. . . " The human being can grow, by a very slow process of hard work and understanding, into a greater purified being. A transparent cube is the body purified or the body full of light!

The number 26 represents the fullest expression on any level in the physical world.

The Great Pyramid in Egypt is believed by many to be a mathematical measurement in stone of time and space. Many also believe it was used as an initiation temple for the highly evolved souls in history. The Ascending Passage, called the Hall of Truth, has a slope of 26°, 18 minutes, and 9.7 seconds.

This upward slope, according to Peter Lemesurier in *The Great Pyramid Decoded*, represents "evolutionary progress" and the 26°-angle of ascent indicates "human evolution." Again, the pyramid is expressing the number that indicates our ability to fully attain our potential through ascending the Hall of Truth.

Angles represent points of information, such as in a graph about population growth or a company's assets for the quarter. These are points of consciousness at which certain truths can be understood. In sacred geometry, an angle represents a point of awareness. Therefore, the 26°-angle in the Great Pyramid is stating that the number 26 is a point at which we are consciously able to understand and reach our fullest expression.

Note that the full precession of the equinoxes, or the Great Year, rounded off is 26,000 years. The Great Year, metaphysically, represents one full spiritual cycle of the human race.

When people speak of the Marathon, they often mean the Boston Marathon of 26.2 miles, a distance that pushes the runners to the limit. Although there are other marathons of different distances, the Boston Marathon is still considered the ultimate achievement. Every runner knows there is a "wall" at the 18–20-mile point, beyond which physical endurance no long matters. These last miles are run on sheer determination. The 26-mile marathon is a test of the will, the total expression of the manifestation of the human will.

26, the number of karma, is also incorporated into the common deck of playing cards. 26 red cards and 26 black cards suggest the Yin and the Yang, the positive outgoing and receptive incoming cycles of life, and perhaps indicating the choices between right and wrong once we are in the physical body. 26 + 26 = 52, the number of cards in the deck, also the number of weeks in one year, one complete cycle. When you add the numbers on the cards, counting the Ace as 1 and the court cards as 11, 12, and 13, they add to 365, the number of days in one year.

There are 13 cards in each suit representing the 13 weeks in each season. 13 is death and rebirth indicating the death of one season and the rebirth of the next season. For more card symbols, see *Nuggets from King Solomon's Mine* by John Barnes Schmalz.

In numerology, the number of karma is 26 (which reduces to an 8). Karma is "the result of doing," referring to cause and effect. A certain action causes an equal and inevitable reaction. We build good karma through positive actions and bad karma through negative actions. Some believe we carry this karma from one life to the next.

Wherever you find the 26 operating, you will find karma, and the full expression of which the human race is capable.

I view "good luck" as good karma that comes back to us; it's just that we don't recognize the connection between a good deed performed perhaps weeks, months, or even years ago as the source of that good luck.

Have you ever thought how amazing it is to have the ability to read and write? How it has changed lives?

In the film, *The Black Robe*, a seventeenth-century Jesuit priest and his companion are escorted through the wilds of Quebec in the dead of winter by Algonquin Indians to find a mission settlement. At one point on their journey, an exchange takes place. (I don't recall exactly who gave the message and what was written, but the essence of that exchange in this example is correct.) It may have been the priest who told the Indian leader that he could make marks on a piece of paper, send it to his companion across the clearing, and that his companion would do what was written on the paper. The Indian leader told the priest to make the white man dance in a circle. So the message was written and delivered, and to the Indians amazement, the white man danced in a circle . . . all because of the marks on a piece of paper. This is the power of the word—which we take for granted today.

The strokes of a pen on a piece of paper or the typesetting in this book or the letters on your computer or cell phone convey a message that you understand because you were taught at an early age how to read. You first learned the letters of the alphabet. These single letters conveyed no message. You then put these letters into groups forming words, which singly had a meaning. Then those words were grouped together, and suddenly a sentence was born!

I remember the thrill I experienced when, in the first grade, I read my first sentence: See Spot run! A wave of power washed down over me when I realized I had hold of something very powerful, something that could change my life. I still recall the colored picture above the large lettering, a picture of Dick and Jane running together, followed by their faithful dog, Spot.

I was born in the age of radio. There was no television, no *Sesame Street* to teach me the letters and words in colorful, fun fashion. That sentence was a miracle in my five-year-old mind, a miracle that strokes of black ink on a page told a story.

A NEW LOOK AT LANGUAGE

THE LANGUAGE OF LINES AND GEOMETRIC FORMS

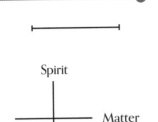

Spirit

Matter

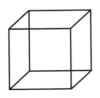

So it is with geometric shapes. This language is composed of different combinations of lines, which create a language and convey a message to those who have learned the meaning of the geometrical symbols.

Let's explore this concept of numbers/geometry as a language.

A straight horizontal line might appear to have no meaning; it has nothing to say. But in sacred geometry that horizontal line is the shorthand symbol for the world of form, the physical body, and the material world. Because that line has a beginning, a middle, and an end, it represents time.

A vertical line is Spirit, the energy from above. Where the two lines cross is where spirit creates matter, a symbol of fertility.

Barbara G. Walker, in *The Woman's Encyclopedia of Myths and Secrets*, writes: "From very ancient times, an effigy of a man hanging on a cross was set up in fields to protect crops." (By the way, I highly recommend this book! It may be out of print but worth the effort to find. Keep it handy; it's full of revelations.)

The first shape that can be constructed with straight lines is the triangle, called the first perfect form. It contains three angles, or three points of consciousness, and represents the trinity of mind, soul, and spirit. It symbolizes the energy behind the world of manifestation.

Note the trinity in religious and spiritual teachings: the mother-father-child concept. We say: Things happen in threes. This is recognition of the energy that is produced by the triangle, the energy that will eventually produce form.

The second perfect form created with straight lines is the square. The square adds the fourth line to the triangle (creating the pattern for the body and the world of form). The energy of the triangle, the energy of things happening in threes, finally manifests in form, in the square, and produces the pattern for the world as we know it.

A square can also be represented by just two sides. You find this shape in a carpenter's square.

Where the square is the pattern of the physical world, the cube is the square solidified, a symbol of the square pattern manifesting in the physical world. The cube's geometric message is the human body, the temple not built with hands. The cube is the fullest expression in the three-dimensional world.

Let's talk about the circle. The circle is symbolic of the All, the Alpha and Omega; it has no beginning and no end but is infinite; everything is contained within it. As Voltaire wrote: "God is a circle whose center is everywhere and circumference is nowhere." Or, as I like to say, the circle is the Mother's Cosmic Egg from which all life emerged.

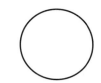

The circle, the triangle, and the square are the basic forms that comprise the language of geometry.

The circle (the 0, the Mother/Cosmic Egg/Source) contains the triangle (the 3, the Mother-Father-Child, the "three-in-one") which gives birth to square (the world of form).

In this sense, we begin to understand what is meant by the Mason's statement "God Geometrizes."

WATCH YOUR LANGUAGE: S/HE, THE WO/MAN

Be assured that the use of the male pronoun, "he" and "man," was never meant to include women. It meant "he" and "man." Let's examine these words.

A numerologist knows that each word has its own particular vibration that sets it apart from every other word. This awareness causes one to be extremely careful in the use of words: the way one writes and speaks. Words are truly energies, energies that impress themselves upon every cell of the body through repetition. This brings me to the feminist movement that has arisen in the last 100 years and continues into this new millennium, the Age of Aquarius.

Since it is not obvious from my name, Dusty, I tell you now that I am a woman. I am not a "feminist" or a "masculinist," but I am an "equalist." As an equalist, I object to God being referred to as "he" and the Christian Trinity excluding the female principle. Most trinities (the number 3, the triangle, the creative energy) contain Mother-Father-Child but, as is well known from even a cursory look at history, the early Hebrews and the early Christian sects that became dominant were extremely patriarchal or male-centered. Women were chattel, possessions, and considered inferior.

100 years ago, in the United States, the "land of the free," the vote was denied to the mentally disabled, criminals, and women. When the Declaration of Independence stated that "all men are created equal," that's exactly what it meant . . . all men! In this country in 1950, a man's home was his castle and he could beat his wife with impunity!

So, when we continually use "he" and "mankind" and "brother-hood" to supposedly include women, it does not. The vibration of these words is different. The longer we continue to use these male terms, the longer we will all be in bondage to an outdated and archaic system of thought.

Our language reflects our consciousness. Wilfred Funk, of *Funk and Wagnalls Encyclopedia*, wrote that the English language was deliberately designed to degrade women.

Let's examine the value of the word "he" and the word "she" using the single numbers.

The word: HE

H   E

8 + 5 = 13: the Death card in the Tarot

13 = The Death Card: the number of initiation, the leaving of the body, and the rebirth of life. This is exemplified in the fertilizing fluid, the male semen, leaving the body of the male to be reborn in the body of the female. The orgasm is called a "little death."

The word: SHE

S   H   E

1 + 8 + 5= 14: the Temperance card in the Tarot

14 = The Temperance Card: 14 is the number related to pi in many philosophies. Pi, or 3.1415 adds to 14. Pi expresses the relationship between the circle and its diameter. Pi, or 14, is the number that connects the horizontal line (symbol of the Earth, time, and space) to the circumference of the circle (symbol of all that is, was, or ever will be, the Creator). 14, Pi, is the creative connector.

The female principle is the creative formative aspect that receives the male semen through its death process as it leaves the male source to be received into the female body for the process of transformation and creation. The female is the transforming power after the death process. The Temperance card depicts the process of tempering or blending opposite forces.

The word "man" adds to 10, which is the Wheel of Fortune card in the Tarot. The word "woman" adds to 21, which is the World card in the Tarot. It's an interesting exercise to meditate upon the meaning of these numbers and their Tarot card equivalents.

When we continually speak of all people as "he," we emphasize the male, assertive, dominating forceful side of human consciousness while denying the female, receptive, nurturing, and compassionate side of that same consciousness. We as human beings contain both male and female expressions; however, in most cases, one side far outweighs the other, and an imbalance results. This imbalance has propelled the human race into war, death, and destruction, while ignoring the "she" side of humanity . . . the caring, gentle, protective, and nurturing aspects.

We need to use the positive aspect of both parts of ourselves . . . the Yin and the Yang, the female and the male, the receptive and assertive . . . and bring them into balance in our lives. A dominance of either side spells pain, turmoil, and disaster, not only within the human psyche but also throughout the world as we all try to live in peace and harmony.

Perhaps we should use wo/man and s/he to indicate both sexes of the human race. These terms are truly inclusive, even in the spelling.

I mentioned the number-letter code in the first chapter and suggested you make note of it on a 3" x 5" card for reference.

THE FOX

NUMBER LETTER CODE

1	A J S
2	B K T
3	C L U
4	D M V
5	E N W
6	F O X
7	G P Y
8	H Q Z
9	I R

Notice that the letters F and O and X are the 6th, 15th, and 24th letters in the alphabet. So it was natural to use fox as a memory peg for the number 6.

6 6 6
F O X

There is no other word I can think of that can be formed out of the letters f-o-x. Fox represents the 666.

The dictionary definitions of the word fox are:

. . . a carnivorous mammal of the dog family with a pointed muzzle and bushy tail, proverbial for its cunning

. . . a cunning or sly person. "a wily old fox"

. . . a sexually attractive woman

Note how we use the word fox and its qualities in our language and culture.

Remember the story of "The Little Gingerbread Man" who tried to cross the river without getting wet? It was the fox that offered its services in the form of a ride on its tail across the river. The Gingerbread Man was deceived and ended up in the fox's mouth as dinner.

Our everyday language expresses the quality we assign to this furry little creature. We might call someone "sly as a fox" or "clever as a fox" or simply "foxy." In caricatures and cartoons, we see sly, crafty people with the features of a fox—narrow eyes, long pointed nose, and wide pencil-line grin.

Our consciousness views the fox (unknowingly through the 666) as a deceiver, one who fools others into believing the actions performed are kind when, in reality, the actions can be devious.

But remember, every number is an energy; numbers are neutral.

Let's give this little creature some good press.

The fox, a small light creature, is a close relative of both the wolf and the dog, and they display the same canine quality of loyalty. Thought to be shy, they rely on their intelligence to survive. Loyalty and intelligence are admirable qualities.

ABBREVIATED GEOMETRIC SYMBOLS

THE CIRCLE:
Spirit, love, eternity, wholeness, oneness, cycles, the three in one

THE POINT:
The seed, the point of awareness

THE LINE:
Duality, Yin and Yang, female and male, a
shorthand symbol for the material world

 THE TRIANGLE:
The number 3, the trinity, past-present-future, the
creative pattern behind form, things happen in
threes

 THE SQUARE:
The pattern for the world of form

 THE STAR:
The five senses, humanity, the human with arms
outstretched, feet planted apart

 THE INTERLACED TRIANGLES:
The Great Yantra, the Philosopher's Stone, Star of
David, love on the physical plane reflecting love on
the spiritual plane

 THE CUBE:
The number 8, form solidified into matter, karma;
as above/so below, sow/reap, cause/effect, action/
reaction; the cosmic lemniscate, the only number
that can be drawn over and over without lifting
pen from paper.

The 7 and 9 seem to defy geometrical definition except in figures
that are difficult to construct. They both represent metaphysical
cycles of great import. 7 is the completion of the physical pattern
before formation in the material world. 9 is the material world that is
preparing for recycling.

CHAPTER 8

WHY DO WE SAY . . .?

I USED TO WONDER WHY WE USE A CERTAIN NUMBER in a common expression rather than another number. I mean, it would sound odd to say that a person is "behind the 5 ball," rather than that person is "behind the 8 ball." And why do we want the "whole 9 yards" rather than the "whole 4 yards."

When I began to study numerology, I found the answer. We use specific numbers in specific common expressions because the true meanings of the numbers are deeply embedded in our consciousness. We use them in our common expressions without realizing why because numbers are the universal language.

DOING THINGS BY THE NUMBERS

To arrive at a desired outcome, we have to do things in a logical sequence. The numbers 1 through 7 represent the steps that must be taken to create the pattern that will accomplish any "thing" in this material world. When we say we have to "do it by the numbers," it means there is a specific order of steps that must be taken sequentially to complete the job. The "thing" manifests under the number 8 and is eventually recycled under the 9.

See the follwoing universal pattern:

1 is the initial seed, the spark that moves out.

2 is the joining of that spark with its opposite force.

3 is the energy behind manifestation.

4 is the material pattern, the idea of how it will form.

5 is the quickening, the mental activity applied to the process.

6 is the creative balance, the artistry of fitting the pieces together.

7 is the quiet contemplative stage where the first 6 steps are connected, the pattern is sown.

8 is the number of the physical world. Only in the 8th step does the "thing" materialize.

9 In the 9th step, the things of the material world begin to give back and to dissolve for recycling.

Because we subconsciously understand the meanings of the numbers, we use them in our common expressns. You'll find a few in this chapter.

Why do we say, "YOU'RE NUMBER ONE"?

YOU'RE NUMBER ONE

We don't say "you're number 4" or "you're number 7." As mentioned above, when we say "you're number 1," we are referring to a quality. Number 1 has unique characteristics that make it stand out from the crowd. It is the beginning, the first, and the best. So, when someone says, "You're number 1 in my book," they are expressing admiration for who you are or something you have accomplished that is unusual or outstanding.

THE TERRIBLE TWOS:
IT TAKES TWO TO TANGO

Why do we say: "THE TERRIBLE TWOS" OR "IT TAKES TWO TO TANGO"?

Every parent knows **the terrible twos**, the age at which their child goes through a defiant or mischievous stage seeming to test every rule, and they get into everything and every place they shouldn't. This is the time to child-proof the house until they understand there are rules, and they must learn to cooperate. This is the time to teach them right and wrong; the Yin and Yang must balance.

It takes two to tango. Obviously it takes two people to dance the tango. To perform the dance well, each partner needs to be in perfect synchronization with the other. When this phrase is used as a compliment, it implies that the successful completion of a process was the result of both parties putting in the same amount of effort. 2 is the Yin and Yang in equal balance.

On the negative side, it takes two to tango suggests that both people are responsible for a given difficult situation so don't try to put the blame on just one party.

Why did we choose the tango specifically? Perhaps because of the alliteration; the 2 t's make it easy to say. This dance of sensuality, the tango originated along the border between Uruguay and Argentina, and soon spread to the rest of the world.

THINGS HAPPEN IN THREES:
THIRD TIME'S THE CHARM

Why do we say: "THINGS HAPPEN IN THREES"?

We say it takes two to tango, and it does, but **it takes threes to make things happen**. In 2, opposites come together, female and male. The result of that mating produces a third, an offspring. This is the triangle.

This same process happens on all levels in nature. (You'll find more about this in chapter 7: Thoughts From My Notebook.)

Think of how it takes three elements to produce a thing: past-present-future result in time; mother-father-child produce a family; height-width-depth molds the three-dimensional world; red-yellow-blue are the primary colors; rhythm-tone-harmony are the three components of music; and so on.

3rd time's the charm. When someone has failed twice, they may be encourage by the phrase "Third time's the charm" to try again. The idea of threes as good luck is ancient, most likely because three has been associated with religious trinities. Also, there is a subconscious awareness that threes in nature produce results.

The triangle, the 3, has long been a philosophical symbol of the trinity because 3 is the universal creative energy.

THE FOUR CORNERS OF THE EARTH: A FOUR-SQUARE MEAL

Why do we say: "THE FOUR CORNERS OF THE EARTH" OR "A FOUR-SQUARE MEAL"?

Although the Earth is commonly described as round, it is actually an oblate spheroid, a sphere with a bulge around the equator. The Earth bulges at its equator because of its rapid rotation on its axis.

So, why do we say the **four corners of the Earth**? We do so because the number four relates to the physical world, the pattern of the world of form and substance, including our physical bodies.

A **four-square meal** refers to having a large substantial meal, which is filling and tasty and satisfying. It nourishes the physical body.

4 is the number of the Earth and all things physical.

THE FIFTH COLUMN: THE FIFTH ESTATE

Why do we say: "THE FIFTH COLUMN" OR "THE FIFTH ESTATE"?

5 is the center of the numbers 1–9 pattern. It allows an evaluation of the past four cycles through gathering information, which can stimulate ideas about a course direction for the future four cycles. 5 is restless because it entertains many ideas that ultimately threaten those processes rooted in the past that have settled into a pattern. This free-flowing information can alter future outcomes.

The **"fifth column"** is a group of people whose different ideas undermine a larger group from within. Their activities are often clandestine and can involve disinformation, espionage, and sabotage.

The **"fifth estate"** is defined as a class or group in society other than the nobility, the clergy, the middle class, and the press. It relates to a group that differs from other members of the group. This stance sets it apart from the main system; therefore, it has a different set of rules.

Today, the fifth estate is a sociocultural reference to groups with viewpoints outside mainstream society, such as bloggers, journalists, and non-mainstream-media outlets.

I'M AT SIXES AND SEVENS

Why do we say: "I'M AT SIXES AND SEVENS"?

This expression means confusion about how to handle a situation.

And there is some confusion about where this expression came from. However, numerologists know that numbers have meanings. 6 is the number of responsibility to home and community, loyalty to loved ones. 7 represents retreat to a place of solitude where one can think.

When you're at sixes and sevens, you don't know whether you should step in, take responsibility, and try to resolve the situation (the duty of the 6), or retreat from the outside world (the duty of the 7) and leave it to others to take care of the problem.

THE SEVEN-YEAR ITCH OR I'M IN SEVENTH HEAVEN

Why do we say: "THE SEVEN-YEAR ITCH" OR "I'M IN SEVENTH HEAVEN"?

When researching the history of the **seven-year itch**, I found one source that talks about "army itch" or "camp itch," a bacterial condition referring to soldiers who caught skin diseases around the beginning of the twentieth century.

However, in today's vernacular, the seven-year itch often refers to the attitude of a person bored or dissatisfied with their current situation and who is looking for something outside the relationship; often this refers to a marriage.

Again, numerologists know that the meaning of seven is a period of retreat and quiet contemplation when one thinks about their past, the present, and what they want for the future. This can often cause one to decide to make changes in current relationships and job situations and in other areas of their life.

Seventh heaven can describe an enlightened state of consciousness such as that arrived at after contemplation and meditation. People in this state realize that mind controls matter—that what they think they are and that attitude is the key to happiness. This realization brings them a peace beyond explanation.

You may find yourself in seventh heaven when you meet the love of your life, or you experience the birth of your first child, or you get the plum job assignment at work or you win the lottery.

Astrologers know that the unpredictable and restless planet Uranus takes seven years to transit one sign. Freedom-seeking Uranus is known to upset the apple cart. As it enters a new department of your life every seven years, its job is to shake up your current status there so you can see where you need to make changes, thus the seven-year itch.

7 is one of the two "mystical" numbers; the other number is 9. Whenever we find these numbers in metaphysical or religious literature, they refer to the construction of the physical body, predominant cycles, and celestial and terrestrial measurements.

Why do we say: "I FEEL LIKE I'M BEHIND THE EIGHT BALL"?

BEHIND THE EIGHT BALL

This expression means the person is in a difficult position and doesn't know how to escape.

One reason given for the meaning of this expression is that it comes from the game of pool called Eight Ball. A player's turn is forfeited if he hits the black eight ball first or if he hits the eight ball into the pocket. The question is: Why the eight ball rather than one of the other numbered balls?

If you read chapter 7, you would know that 8 is karma. When you finish your first seven personal year cycles, you enter your personal year cycle 8. This is when the results from the efforts of your past seven cycles come home to roost, in the public, very visible to all.

For some who have not handled their cycles well or with lack of awareness, they can be in a very difficult position and don't know how to escape. They are behind the eight ball; they are facing the results of their action; they are facing karma.

THE WHOLE NINE YARDS: DRESSED TO THE NINES: I'M ON CLOUD NINE

These phrases mean "you have it all."

The general populace is not sure of the origin of these phrases . . . but those who did know were the numerologists and metaphysicians from ancient times who taught these principles down through the ages.

9 is the final digit in the series 1 through 9.
9 contains all the energies from the past eight numbers.
9 has it all.

Key 9 in the Tarot is The Hermit standing on the mountain top (an elevated level of consciousness) representing the shining light of wisdom. He has it all.

I want the whole nine yards. When you want the whole nine yards, you want it all. This usually refers to the material world of positions and possessions.

She's dressed to the nines: When you're dressed to the nines, you couldn't look any better. You are wearing the very best clothes and shoes and jewelry you own. And your makeup is impeccable.

I'm on cloud nine: When you're on cloud nine, you are in an emotional state of total happiness. You feel euphoric because something has fulfilled your inner being.

9 has curious qualities:
When 9 is added to a number, it returns to the number.
$9 + 5 = 14$ or $1 + 4 = 5$
$9 + 21 = 30: 21 = 2 + 1 = 3; 30 = 3 + 0 = 3$

When 9 is multiplied by a number, it returns to itself.
$9 \times 4 = 36; 3 + 6 = 9$
$9 \times 5 = 45; 4 + 5 = 9$
$9 \times 15 = 135; 1 + 3 + 5 = 9$

When your bank statement doesn't balance, and you're off a sum of 9, it's usually a transposition of numbers somewhere in your calculations.

As mentioned above, 9 is one of the two "mystical" numbers; the other number is 7. Whenever we find these numbers in metaphysical or religious literature, they refer to the construction of the physical body, predominant cycles, and celestial and terrestrial measurements.

Just as an interesting aside . . . Why do we say: "A baker's dozen"?

THE BAKER'S DOZEN

A baker's dozen is thirteen items rather than the normal twelve.

King Henry III of England (1207–1272) revived an ancient law that regulated the price of bread by a trade group called The Worshipful Company of Bakers. Bakers who sold breads that were underweight could be fined or flogged. Therefore, in order to be safe from such public punishment, bakers began adding an additional loaf. This practice came to be called a baker's dozen.

HOW CALENDAR CHANGES HAVE CHANGED HISTORY

THE CALENDAR HAS A LONG AND COMPLICATED HISTORY. In the beginning, certain natural phenomena gave rise to the division of time. Early people knew there would be periods of dark and periods of light, and these happened at predictable intervals they could depend upon. From the point of view on Earth, this rhythm became the 24 hour day. They also began to notice that the largest light at night disappeared, then reappeared growing to fullness, then slowly fading away to darkness once again, thus the lunar cycles. Eventually, the longer cycle of the Sun through the seasons became the year.

In order to keep track of time, the calendar was born and was made of numbers, making it easier to keep track of the passage of time, and to keep appointments whether they were for hunting parties or planting along the Nile River or peace accords in Europe.

In this section we will examine the genesis of the Gregorian calendar, the one used by the western world, and the one used internationally when it comes to commerce and communication.

In 4236 BCE, a civil (lunar) calendar was introduced in Egypt. Around 2773 BCE, this lunar calendar was superseded by a solar calendar of three seasons with 4 months each. The twelve thirty-day months were followed by five days, making the 365-day year. The Egyptians used this calendar for 3,000 years.

160

No other group adopted the Egyptian calendar until Julius Caesar's reign. By then, the Roman calendar had accumulated an eighty-day error when Sisogenes, an Alexandrian astronomer, explained the merits of the Egyptian solar calendar to Caesar. Caesar officially adopted it in 46 BCE with one modification. The new Julian calendar would alter the permanent Egyptian 365-day year to recognize the 0.25 fractional yearly error by adding one additional day every fourth year.

Even the fraction of a day was an error, however. It should have been 0.2422. This seemingly minute difference amounted to ten days by the sixteenth century. So in 1582, Pope Gregory XIII declared the Gregorian reform, omitting 10 days from the year. October 4 was followed by October 15. This brought the calendar and the Sun into sync again.

The Gregorian calendar further prescribed that only those centuries divisible by 400 would celebrate leap year, e.g., 1600, 2000, and so forth. This new calendar also designated January 1 as the beginning of the legal year rather than the former March 25. The error in the Gregorian calendar will amount to one day in 3,300 years.

Catholic countries adopted this calendar readily, but Protestant countries clung to the old calendar for a few hundred years more. England finally accepted the Gregorian calendar in 1752, and the USSR followed in 1918.

Much of the world now uses the Gregorian calendar. The notable exceptions are the Muslims and Jews, although for international trade and communications they too use the Gregorian calendar.

I believe that calendar changes represent profound shifts in the consciousness of the people affected by that change. Reviewing the history of our present Gregorian calendar, we find the following significant dates: 46 BCE, when the Julian calendar was introduced into Rome; 1582, when Pope Gregory declared the Gregorian reform in Europe; 1752, when England and her colonies finally accepted the change to the Gregorian calendar; 1873, when Japan adopted the change, 1912, when China adopted the change, and lastly, 1918 when Russia changed to the present-day Gregorian calendar.

Let's examine what happened to each of those countries following their acceptance of an updated calendar.

- **46 BCE:** One of the most far-reaching events in history occurred 46 years after Julius Caesar adopted the Julian calendar—the birth of Jesus, an event that shook the foundation of the Roman Empire and eventually caused a shift of power from the Caesars to the popes. The head of the Catholic Church now resides in Rome.

- **1582 CE:** Pope Gregory announced a new calendar in Europe and surrounding countries. This date falls in the midst of the Protestant Reformation, which officially began in 1517, when Martin Luther posted his 95 theses on the door of the Wittenberg Palace Church in rebellion against the indulgences of the Catholic Church. Historians date the reformation from 1517 to the 1555 Peace of Augsburg, which allowed Catholicism and Lutheranism to coexist in Germany, then to the Treaty of Westphalia in 1648, which had pitted Catholics against Protestants during a 30-year war. All over Europe, a profound consciousness change was taking place as people poured over the newly translated and mass-printed Guttenberg Bible. A new branch of religion was born, separate from the Catholic Church.

- **1752 CE:** In the year 1752, England and her colonies adopted the Gregorian calendar. This act foreshadowed a string of events that changed the power structure of the world. In 1775, the American Revolution began with the battles of Lexington and Concord. In 1776, the Declaration of Independence was drawn up and signed, signaling the birth of a new nation. In 1783, the British surrendered at Yorktown, Virginia; in 1788, the United States Constitution was ratified; and in 1789, George Washington became the first president of a nation that would become the major power in the world.

- **1873 CE:** Japan accepted the Gregorian calendar in 1873. Today, the old Chinese calendar is virtually ignored. The beginning of modern constitutional government began when, in 1868, a group of young samurai replaced the shogunate (hereditary commander-in-chief in feudal Japan) with a government based in part on Western political ideas. The samurai crowned the 15-year-old emperor, Meiji, as the head of the new government, using the imperial line to legitimize the new government.

- **1915 CE:** China adopted the Gregorian calendar in 1912. In 1915, General Yuan Shikai attempted (in 1915/1916) to reinstate the monarchy in China with himself as emperor. He failed; his attempt set back the Chinese republican cause for many years, fracturing China and setting off conflicts between warlords.

- **1918 CE:** Russia adopted the Gregorian calendar in 1918 upon the conclusion of a terrible and unprecedented upheaval in her history. Because of her involvement in World War I, Russia collapsed in early 1917. As H. G. Wells said in *The Outline of History,* ". . . Russia suffered first and most from this universal pulling up of civilization from its roots." Finally, in the March Revolution of 1917, a devastating war and governmental mishandling of the war effort caused the fall of the Romanov dynasty. The royal family was assassinated, bringing the Russian monarchy to an end. Much haggling ensued until the Bolsheviks under Lenin remained the sole power. The Bolsheviks were then renamed the Russian Communist Party.

- **1981 CE:** The USSR repealed daylight savings time (DST) in 1917 after only a few months. DST was reintroduced in 1981, changing time in their calendar.

- In the early morning hours of **April 26, 1986**, the Chernobyl nuclear power plant in the Soviet Union had a melt down. *Live-Science* described this event as the worst nuclear disaster in history, and Chernobyl as one of the ten most polluted places on Earth. It signaled the coming end of the USSR as a nation.

- **1991 CE:** After a coup, on December 25, 1991, Mikhail Gorbachev resigned as president of the Soviet Union. The next day, the Soviet Union dissolved. Gorbachev brought about the end of the Soviet Union and the Cold War. He was "the only leader to leave the office with his dignity in tact . . . unable to change the living standards of the people, but he changed the people" (Nytimes.org/ Archives 1991).

The Union of Soviet Socialist Republics had 15 republics; Russia was one of them.

The downfall was the result of a weak economy, political instability, Gorbachev's reforms, and the rise of nationalism. The wealthier republics didn't want to support the backward Central

Asian republics. With the fall of the USSR, the republics emerged as sovereign states. The fall of the Soviet Union created 15 new states; it changed the geography of the world map.

***

It would seem that the calendar changes not only brought nations into accurate synchronization with time, but these changes also signaled the need to start over again, to begin anew, and to change the old vibrations. Throughout history, changes in the calendar affected vast groups of people, just as the numbers on the calendar affect each individual born on a specific day.

It just goes to prove you can't fool with the numbers! Change the numbers and you change the consciousness of those adopting those changes.

CHAPTER 10

HOW NUMBERS AFFECT THE CALENDAR MONTHS

THIS IS A MORE WHIMSICAL LOOK AT THE NUMBERS. You know by now that when numbers are attached to something, they take on some of the qualities of that number. Given that premise, let's look at calendar months to see if they take on the flavor of their numerical position in the numbers from 1 to 12.

When defining the numbers of the calendar month, I realize the seasons are reversed south of the equator. When it is January in the northern hemisphere, it is July in the southern hemisphere. This problem also arises in the astrological world; when it is January, the sign of Capricorn, winter north of the equator, it is July, the sign of Cancer, the summer months south of the equator. It is said opposites attract so there is some correlation in these connections.

Years ago, I purchased a copy of *Crockett's Victory Garden* and read it diligently as my husband and I prepared our vegetable garden for the year . . . planting lettuce and peas and melons and squash. I suddenly realized that James Crockett's monthly division of gardening activities were a sound parallel to my own investigations of the meaning of the calendar months in relation to their number sequence in the calendar.

Nature follows the natural sequence of things, the rhythms of life, just as we do—although we aren't always aware of our roles in the cycles around us. We watch nature with her seasons and changes and feel somehow immune or separate from it all, without considering that we are part of this cosmic sequence. And yet, we feel energetic in the spring, lazier in the summer, more energetic once more in the fall, and

A WHIMSICAL LOOK AT THE LIFE OF THE GARDENER

withdrawn and hunkered down through the winter. We respond to the seasons and the weather as well as to all other phenomena that affect this planet. Nature is a teacher that we often overlook.

We'll also look at the origin of the months' names.

In the following chapter, I quote from *Crockett's Victory Garden*[16] because I find that Mr. Crockett's descriptions of the gardening activities for each month describe the meaning of the month's numbers and the effect this has on the consciousness of the world. Amazing!

When reading about each of the months, keep in mind the definition of the number attached to it.

1: JANUARY IS THE 1ST MONTH.

In Roman mythology, Janus was the god of doors, archways, gates, and all beginnings. His symbol was the key that locked and unlocked and opened and closed all doors. Daybreak came under his domain, and the Romans prayed to him each morning before honoring any other god. He was especially honored on the first day of every month. The greatest of all his celebrations occurred on the first day of the new year. It was at this time he was asked to bless the year ahead. He is said to have helped with the creation of the world. As a result, all initiatives and new enterprises were ascribed to him.

He is pictured as having two faces, each one looking in an opposite direction: one observing the interior and the other the exterior of homes and public buildings.

As always, mythology tells truths through hidden symbols if one looks beneath the surface. The doorway represents the spot where you step from the past into the future, a change. Every day, when we walk through a doorway, we are leaving one place and entering a new space, which is set up differently from the space we just left, even if it is in your home. Janus's two faces gazing in opposite directions indicate a time of the year when we reflect upon the past and look forward to the future.

Crockett says that January is "a good month to undertake indoor construction projects that are too time-consuming for the busier garden months." Those indoor construction projects could very well be in the New Year's resolutions we make when we set about the construct of our new self. In January, we must make time for these resolutions before we become too busy later in the year to spend time on number one: ourselves, and our needs. We must be in good shape mentally and physically before we can be of any use to others.

January, the beginning of the calendar year, the start of a new large cycle in our life, is a time for resolutions. We are imbued with a new energy, zest, and determination to make this new year better than the past ones. No matter how difficult the past years have been, we are inspired with the hope and promise of new life, knowing that we must take the initiative and make our plans. Experiences from the past years are now history, part of that store of wisdom from which we can draw the necessary experience to handle future decisions.

Conscious decisions are made as we sit alone, making mental notes or working with pen and paper. We take stock of ourselves in those solitary moments as we look in two different directions—the past and the future. Perhaps we, like the Romans, should examine the beginning of every month and every day of the month (by praying to the god Janus) and ask how well we did yesterday and how we can do better today. We could make each day and each month a new beginning by making New Day's resolutions and New Month's resolutions.

The first of anything is overseen by the god Janus who watches and observes, ready to supply us with the energy and initiative to make the necessary affirmations and enforce them.

2: FEBRUARY IS THE 2ND MONTH.

The word February seems to come from the Etruscan god Februus, who was connected with Dis Pater, the equivalent of the Greek Pluto ("phuotos" means riches). Februus's wealth came from the unceasing number of subjects who came to him through death in the never-ending cycle of birth and death. The month of February, the month of the dead, was dedicated to Februus.

February, or "Februarius mensis," means expiatory month. *The Random House Dictionary* defines "expiatory" as "able to make atonement." Febra is the Italian word for "fever"; the purpose of a fever is to purify the body, "putting an end to" an infection.

As the second month, February implies a need for balance, in our minds and in our bodies, and setting things straight. It is time for peace and mediation. Standing in the shadows, in the wings, out of the limelight . . . a number 2 position . . . February sees hidden forces at work beneath the ground and within the barren trees.

Of all the months of the year, February is the one people seem to dislike the most, although it is the shortest—28 days (or 29 days in a leap year). It seems to be a "down" month, a depressing time for many. We are caught between the "dead of winter" and the "birth of spring." James Crockett says, "In the Victory Garden, February is the bridge month between winter and spring."

In February, it seems we have to face our failings. Some of our New Year's resolutions may have failed by now, and we are beginning to feel the guilt of unfulfilled promises. While we wander around the darken labyrinths of our minds, hidden forces are at work beneath our feet, under the ground, and within all life forms that appear to be dormant. Life is still active, although it appears otherwise.

We work within ourselves to find a balance, to seek harmony, to find that part of ourselves that seems somehow missing. Perhaps that is why we have chosen February to celebrate Valentine's Day, a day when we send a special card to a special person who fills that void within us. And the 2 implies a partnership!

3: MARCH IS THE 3RD MONTH.

The word "March" comes from the Latin *Martius mensis*, or month of Mars. Some experts feel the name is connected with the root word "mar" or "mars," which represents the generative forces. Originally an agricultural god, Mars was in ancient times the god of vegetation and fertility, but those duties were eventually transferred to other gods. At that point, Mars became primarily the god of war. The word "martial" also refers to warlike attitudes.

The word "march" also means to "walk with regular and measured tread, as soldiers." On the march means moving ahead.

Mentally, we tend to feel more aggressive in March. We know winter is over and the darkness is past. Before the month is through, the spring equinox announces the season of resurrection and rebirth. Easter falls at the end of March or early April, symbolic of life "moving ahead." Life is on the march. New shoots aggressively battle chunks of ice to poke their tiny heads up through the earth, searching for the sun. Life begins to battle its way up to the light.

Gardeners look forward to March as the first month of the year when planting begins. I can still remember the first time I planted baby marvel peas on a wet March day in soil splattered with patches of snow. As a novice, I was skeptical about their survival. Some weeks later, and I still remember the thrill, I looked out over the garden to see a faint thread line of green shoots emerging from the seemingly barren soil. No wonder March is the month of miracles. Appropriately, *Crocket's Victory Garden* begins with the month of March. He says that "it's a month of promise as well as progress," a month when he can plunge his hands into the soil for the first time since winter began.

The chapter on the history of the calendar explained that March was originally the first month of the year, so in that context you can see the number 1 working. Here in March, when things are growing, the number 3 takes over: birth, growth, and expansion. Religions speak of the "three in one."

4: APRIL IS THE 4TH MONTH.

Aprilis mensis was the second month in the Roman calendar that began in March. It most likely came from the Latin verb *aperire*, meaning "to open."

April 1, commonly known as April Fool's Day or All Fool's Day, is a day for pranks and practical jokes. It became a custom in France in the 1500s after the Gregorian calendar was adopted. Previously, April 1 had been the day to celebrate the New Year with gifts and visits. When January 1 became New Year's Day, people began making fun of those who stuck with the old calendar, sending them mock gifts, and making pretended ceremonial visits to those people who objected to the new calendar.

Some pranks backfire however. My two daughters decided to play a trick on their father on April 1. As he sat unsuspectingly at the breakfast table sipping his coffee, six-year-old April said, "Look, Daddy. There's a robin on the lawn." My husband looked through the picture window, and April laughed and said, "April Fools!"

That's when four-year-old Melanie beamed and giggled, "Daddy, look. There's a squirrel in the tree."

Playing along, my husband looked out once more whereupon Melanie clapped her hands and said, "Melanie fools."

April, as the 4th month, is a time when we feel the need to organize on all fronts. Traditionally, when spring cleaning fever hit, we would charge into those dark, forbidding places—the attic, cellar, closets, under the kitchen counters, and the garage. We'd take down curtains, take up rugs, take out furniture, scrub, wash, clean, and then put everything back again. Well, not quite everything. Some of the odds and ends landed on picnic benches and folding tables out on the lawn and in the driveways as garage sale items. Eventually, they'd end up in someone else's attic, cellar, or garage, fodder for next year's lawn sale.

James Crockett says that April is perfect planning weather, and it's almost as busy as May. So, we attack our gardens with hoe and rake and shovel, battering the earth until it unwillingly begins to yield. We then sprinkle—using the proverbial coffee can—cow manure, lime, and compost until the ground is an organic quilt. Turned over, the soil is finally ready for seeds, which we place so carefully in their tiny pockets. Hours later, a quick trip to the chiropractor tops off the expenses for the weekend's activities. 4 is work, and it rules the physical body.

Less appetizing organizational chores await us, however, on April 15 . . . the income tax deadline in the United States. Heaven help the unorganized now! 4 is a money number as well as an organizational one. 4 is a square with 4 sides. Notice where individuals who try to beat the system end up . . . in a square, boxed in, in jail!

April exemplifies the 4 as a month of work and organization, a month when we all seem to be supplied with the energy and drive to accomplish the tasks that arise.

5: MAY IS THE 5TH MONTH.

The etymology of May is somewhat uncertain although some feel it comes from the Greek goddess of spring, Maia, mother of Hermes who was the messenger gods.

May as the 5th month is a time for release, change, and communication . . . a zesty, full-of-life, busy, curious month, all attributes of the number 5. We want to be rescued from the labor of the previous month. We have had it with spring cleaning and rubbish and yard sales. Now we want get happily busy in the garden we have prepared, and to investigate Mother Nature's handiwork.

For the gardener, May is the busiest month of the year. April laid the groundwork; it was the month for soil preparation and back-breaking toil. May is planting time for most seeds. *Crockett's Victory Garden* states: "May is the bridge month between the cool spring and the hot summer, and often its early days offer a little of both." The gardener is busy in the most enjoyable way possible . . . the organization is over, and the month that all gardeners love arrives when the planting begins.

Warm weather is mostly upon us in May. Besides planting seeds in our garden, we feel like kicking up our heels, getting out the convertible, taking walks in the woods or by the seashore.

In 1889, May Day was designated by socialist party leaders at an international conference as a worldwide labor holiday. It was a time to be rescued temporarily from the 4 month of April that required so much work. Even the tern "Mayday," the international distress signal used by ships and aircraft, is a call to be rescued—a needed release.

The giving of flowers on May 1 has its roots in pagan festivals that celebrated the beginning of spring. People would gather flowers in little baskets and hang them on neighbors' doorknobs or leave them on the steps. The May pole was used during the Middle Ages as the central focus of dancing and sports, a gay festive period that celebrated the birth of the new season and the fertility of all life.

6: JUNE IS THE 6TH MONTH.

Juno, queen of the Roman gods, was married to Jupiter, king of the gods. She was the queenliest of all the goddesses, and the Roman women celebrated her each year. She had her marital difficulties, however, keeping her tabs on her philandering husband who had an eye for a pretty girl.

June is traditionally the month for weddings. Many family and social activities—weddings, graduations, recitals, school awards, community banquets—take place. The school year ends in June, and we all seem to recognize the need to honor those deserving persons and to tie up loose ends before July sets in.

James Crockett states that in June, because the sun is so hot, he plants his June seeds "deeper than the early spring crops, putting the seeds in twice as deep as I do in April and May." Our June feelings run deep, just as the June plantings. Feelings of love, pride, and family unity are never stronger or deeper than those moments when we watched our child pirouette in the *Swan Lake* recital, saw them receive a high school or college diploma, or witnessed them get married, or when a loved one was recognized for community service or the publication of a book.

Summer plants can safely be set out after May 30, Memorial Day in the US, because even the evenings in June are now fairly warm. Summer officially begins this month. We feel warmer, more loving and generous, along with the earth and all of nature. We want harmony and beauty around us.

As the month of the summer solstice, June sees the peak of the solar year. 6 is the number of love and perfect harmony. It is in this month with the start of the summer season that nature attains the very peak of perfection. We respond to the universal vibration of love and harmony in June by planning our most intimate and meaningful family and community events during the month of June.

7: JULY IS THE 7TH MONTH.

Julius Caesar, who adopted the solar or Julian calendar in 46 BCE, was honored by having his birth month, Quintilis, renamed Julius. July comes from Julius.

James Crockett says, "By the time July arrives . . . the soil has been hard at work for 4 months, and it may begin to show some signs of wear."

7 is the number of retreat, rest after work well done, a time for inner repair . . . July is the month for vacations. We have been through the good intentions of January's New Year's resolution, the mental machinations of February's psychoanalysis, the stirrings of March, the April work syndrome, the May release, and June's festivities.

Now we need a vacation. We are ready for it, and we feel we have earned it. The children are out of school, we have scheduled our two weeks in July so we pack up and go off to the seashore or the mountains for those two blessed weeks when there is nothing to think about. No phones (highly unlikely though today with cell phones), no appointments, no bills to worry about . . . yet. No pressures. Just feet up, body laid out, and hand clasped around a tall frosty drink.

The mind, however, never rests. It is now, when we have set aside the noises and distractions of the outside world that we do our best thinking and soul searching. Physical activity may slow but mental activity increases in a transference of energy. Perhaps that is why we do some of our best thinking and problem solving when we daydream and remove ourselves from a situation. July is that kind of month . . . a little lost, removed from "reality" as the material world sees it, but it's a period of extreme mental activity when our imaginations can soar.

8: AUGUST IS THE 8TH MONTH.

The month of August is named after the first emperor of Rome, Augustus Caesar, 63 BCE to 14 CE. Augustus means "noble or venerated." Augustus Caesar brought much culture to Rome. He built libraries and schools, patronized the arts, and enacted just laws. His period is called the Augustan Age of Literature.

"August is the cornucopia month of the year," according to James Crockett, "a payoff month. But not a month for resting on laurels." This statement perfectly defines the number 8.

In August, under the number 8, we reap what we have sown. Our seeds have reached full maturity and we can see tangible results from our efforts. But 8 brings responsibility. We know we have more work to do. The 7th month of July gave us plenty of time to think about ourselves and our place in the sun, to rework those areas that "began to show some signs of wear."

Now, in August, it's time for action. Summer is fast ending, and boats must be put up and summer camps closed. Children are restless, not knowing what to do with themselves; even playtime can be overdone. They also sense the need for organization in this 8th month. Financial pressures arise. School clothes and supplies are purchased, colleges fees paid, and we need to take "daily trips through the garden, basket in hand," getting things done and cleaning up loose ends while we work with the results of our harvest.

Crocket says that he takes advantage of the spaces left by the harvest in August to plant cool weather crops that will produce in the fall. In this 8th month, we should look at the bare spots left as the result of our harvest, and determine how we can re-plant those spots, always remembering that we reap what we sow.

9: SEPTEMBER IS THE 9TH MONTH.

The Julian 12-month calendar fashioned on the Egyptian's solar year calendar was adopted in Rome on January 1, 45 BCE. Prior to that time, the Roman calendar began in March, making September the 7th month of that calendar. That made October the 8th month, November the 9th month, and December the 10th month of the year. The names of these months are derived from the Latin for these numbers: September came from the Latin *septem*, for seven. When the Gregorian calendar was adopted in 1582, it was decided that the names for September, October, November, and December would be kept, even though they were misnomers.

Labor Day, celebrated on the first Monday in September, is a national holiday in the United States. It originated in New York on September 5, 1882, when the Knights of Labor held a parade "to demonstrate the strength and enthusiasm of labor organizations." The idea spread and Labor Day soon became a national holiday in honor of labor.

On Labor Day, we celebrate the work we have done; we honor the effort to produce. It is curious that in the 5th month, we celebrate the release from work to have fun whereas in the 9th month, the number of harvest, Labor Day honors the work well done.

Speaking specifically of gardening, James Crockett says that: "September is a good time to record the year's successes and failures." We follow the same cycles as nature, thus September is our month to record the year's successes and failures. It is a month of endings, the transitional period. The harvest is in, vacations are over, fall is here, and winter is closing in. We try not to notice that the season is over, especially when we experience a few weeks of beautiful warm Indian summer; however, gardeners keep their ears open to the weather forecasts through September just to be sure, and to be prepared for freak frosts.

Number 9 is transitional, a letting-go period when we still try to enjoy the fruits of our past labors, knowing that their demise is imminent, knowing that we must eventually let go.

10: OCTOBER IS THE 10TH MONTH.

October is from the Latin *octo*, meaning eight. It was originally the 8th month in the old Roman calendar. It is presently the 10th month in the Gregorian calendar we use today.

In the 10th month, a full cycle has ended and we now begin the recycling process ($10 = 1 + 0 = 1$). This month represents the ending and the beginning, the unceasing cycles of life.

Hallowmas, or All Saints' Day (Halloween) has been a Catholic celebration since the 9th century, a day when all saints were honored. The trick-or-treat custom of today probably originated in Ireland in the 1600s when peasants went from door to door requesting money to buy food for the celebrations.

The *Encyclopedia Americana* attributed Halloween to the Druids in England centuries before Christ. It is said they believed that on October 31: "The lord of death gathered together all the souls who had been condemned to enter the bodies of animals. He then decided which animals the dead souls would enter the next year." This tradition reflects the truth that is so embedded in our consciousness . . . that life is unending . . . our energy goes on. Death brings only disintegration of the physical body at the same time life is transformed and reborn.

October as the 10th month, the only month of the year containing the spiritual 0 symbol, suggests completion and eternal life. As Voltaire, the French philosopher wrote: "God is a circle whose center is everywhere and circumference is nowhere."

October brings the first real frost. Wearing our heavy sweaters, we watch piles of leaves smolder in the streets, and admire the mounds of pumpkins by the side of the road; we know that summer is over and fall is solidly here.

October is a point of awareness. As James Crockett writes: "The first frost usually hits the victory garden at the end of the month, so October is the time for chilly weather preparations."

In October, a month of awareness, we take note of the transitional process. Have our efforts over the past 9 months provided positive or negative fodder for the growth of our souls? We reap what we have sown.

11: NOVEMBER IS THE 11TH MONTH.

As the 9th month in the Roman calendar, November comes from the Latin word, *novem*, meaning nine. It is the 11th month in our Gregorian calendar, the only month with a master number. (Master numbers are those numbers that repeat the same energy. $11 = 1 + 1 = 2$. As an 11, it also reflects the 2 base digit.)

"I would have to argue that November is the most important month in the gardener's calendar," James Crockett writes, "because it's the month the soil should be prepared for the next spring's plantings."

Strange that we prepare our home soil by holding presidential elections in November . . . in preparation for next year's planting when the new president is sworn into office. Our November decisions determine the quality of the following year's leadership.

As a Master number (11), November has to be a very important month in our calendar year. 11 rules sudden and sometimes upsetting decisions and conditions that bring about much-needed balance. It is an exciting period filled with surprises. Expect the unexpected is the slogan here. Presidential elections in the United States, a country with so much influence and control over the destiny of the world, qualify as a major event for the world under the 11.

Certainly, some of the election results in the United States have been sudden and upsetting in that they were unexpected. One remembers the day after the presidential election, November 3, 1948, when the front page of the *Chicago Tribune* proclaimed "Dewey Defeats Truman." When, of course, the opposite was true.

In the past, more than one presidential candidate has gone to bed on election eve thinking he would be the next president, only to awake to the reality that he had lost. A few presidents have won the electoral college but lost the popular vote. But one thing we can usually be assured of, presidential elections are exciting and surprising. And with the base number 2 (11/2), much goes on behind closed doors.

Thanksgiving, as an American national holiday, reflects the camaraderie and sharing of the number 2 base digit side of the master number 11. The need for companionship and getting together is evident by the miles people travel to share the bounty of the Thanksgiving table with their family and friends. This is the most traveled holiday every year. We celebrate Thanksgiving as an acknowledgment of our thankfulness for life's bounty. 11 as a master number brings a greater awareness, an attunement with the infinite, with the truth that lies in the cornucopia symbol . . . the ever full and unceasing bounty of life.

12: DECEMBER IS THE 12TH MONTH.

December was the 10th month in the old Roman calendar prior to the Julian calendar that was introduced by Caesar. December comes from the Latin, *decem*, meaning ten.

With the 12, we complete a mystical cycle. 12 reflects a combination of the original 7 planets with the 5 senses; the 7 holes in the head with the 5 holes in the body; the 7 white keys on the musical scale with the 5 black keys. 12 is a key number in the Christian Bible as the 12 disciples of Jesus, the 12 sons of Jacob, the 12 tribes of Israel from which the Bible says all nations sprang. And, of course, the twelve months of the year in the Gregorian calendar that are based upon the seasons of the year; 4 seasons of 3 months each equals 12.

"We leave the garden to rest for the winter and move indoors," writes James Crockett. December is that month when we leave the garden, leave the hustle and bustle of growing and producing, and move indoors, within ourselves. It is a pause in the process of living, when feelings of compassion and love arise. There is respect for the moment, a time of temporary truce, when the world feels the essence of the holy season, the reverence and awe at the process of conception, gestation, and birth of the child, the new life that resides within us all. In the Christian religion it is celebrated as the birth of the Son at Christmas; it brings renewed life with the birth of the Sun at the Winter Solstice.

7 is preparation for the physical cycle, 9 is the psychological cycle, and 12 is the spiritual cycle. 12 is a moment of suspension, a pause when the winter solstice sees the birth of the Sun as it sits still at the lowest point beneath the equator (solstice means the sun stands still) during depths of winter and then once again moves north towards spring and summer. That moment of the winter solstice is the promise of eternal life.

· ·

One last note about the calendar months: Could there be a relationship between the number of the month in which we are born and the type of internal energies that drive us? One wonders. I believe the most important ability we have is the capacity to wonder, to be curious, to ask questions, to investigate, and to explore new fields of wonder. Be curious, my friends, and never stop wondering.

Part IV·
NUMBERS RULE THE PAST, PRESENT, AND FUTURE

CHAPTER 11

NUMEROLOGY'S INFLUENCE ON THE DECADES

SECTION 1: THE NUMBERS'' INFLUENCE ON DECADES 1900 THROUGH 1970 AND PREDICTIONS FOR 1980 (PUBLISHED IN EARLY 1980)

In Section 1, you will find the numbers influence on the decades 1900 through 1970 and my predictions for the 1980 decade. This material comes from the original version of *Numerology and Your Future,* published in the spring of 1980.

. . . .

SECTION 2: WERE MY 1979 PREDICTIONS FOR THE 1980'S THUMBS-UP or THUMBS-DOWN? OR EVEN THUMBS HORIZONTAL?

In Section 2, written in 2019, you will find my analysis of the predictions I made back in 1979 for the 1980 decade. You'll find what I had right and where I missed the mark: thumbs-up or thumbs-down, or even thumbs horizontal. Please turn to page 201 for this analysis.

. . . .

SECTION 3: THE NUMBERS INFLUENCE ON THE DECADES 1900, 2000, AND 2010

In Section 3, you will find a description of how the numbers influenced the decades 1990, 2000, and 2010.

. . . .

SECTION 4: PREDICTIONS FOR THE 2020 DECADE AND A DISCOVERY THAT COULD CHANGE THE WORLD

In Section 4, do I dare? . . . You will find my predictions for the 2020 decade, which include: a cycle I discovered a few years ago while preparing for a lecture—a cycle that reveals three major events that changed history and that have repeated every 84 years since 1774. They have the potential to occur once again in the 2020 decade!

SECTION 1

THE NUMBERS' INFLUENCE ON DECADES 1900 THROUGH 1970 AND PREDICTIONS FOR THE 1980'S

· ·

THE GREAT PSYCHOLOGIST WILLIAM JAMES SAID: "Any act or thought repeated consecutively for 45 times without failure becomes a habit." A habit is something done without reasoning or thinking; it is automatic, or second nature.

I have lectured on numerology to many thousands of people over the years. The audience's response to information about their numerological cycles has been so consistent over this time frame, it has become a "habit." Audiences continue to be amazed at the accuracy of their number cycles, therefore, I know the numbers work. It has become second nature for me to think in numerological terms in relation to everything around me.

Our personal cycles are determined by our unique birth information which affects us on a personal level. The true significance of the numbers is so ingrained in our consciousness that we respond globally to the numerical significance of the calendars that we live by.

The consciousness of a people, culture, or nation is embedded in the mind of its people from the moment of birth. It is reflected in their art, language, dress, and customs through the thought processes of that people. The measurement of time, being very arbitrary, is no exception. If a people use a particular calendar, they will respond to that means of measurement. In other words, they will respond to the number vibrations they have selected for their calendar. Cultures using different systems of measuring time will react accordingly to their specific calendars.

As mentioned, the majority of the world uses the Gregorian calendar that was adopted in 1582 and is used by the western world today. This calendar is used universally when it comes to trade and communications amongst nations. Therefore, that is the system we will examine.

Each 100 years has its own particular vibrations determined by the meaning of the first two digits in the century, e.g., the 1700s, 1800s, 1900s, and the 2000s each have their overlying influence.

In any century, the first two digits of that 100-year period are repeated over and over, on documents and checks and calendars many million times more than the required 45 times as the psychologist William James said for something to become a habit.

How many times have you written, spoken, or heard the digits 19 during the years of the 20th century? The sound of your name, repeated over and over throughout your lifetime impresses a particular vibration upon the cells in your body. Imagine how strongly the vibration of the 19 in the 20th century was and is impressed upon the world body consciousness when written and spoken by millions. The same is true now in this 21st century.

The repetition of the numbers of any century, decade, or single year set up a certain frequency, a vibration, which moves around the world and influences the thinking and, therefore, the events of the entire earth. This repetition forms a habit for that time.

I have chosen the history of the United States of America rather than scattered events from around the world. I felt by focusing on one country and a larger number of major events occurring within one decade in that country, the proof would be more convincing. Ten major events in one country within one decade that describe the decade's number perfectly are more convincing than two or three events from seven or eight different countries from around the world.

The 1900 century: 1900 reduces to a 1: $1 + 9 + 0 + 0 = 10$; $10 = 1 + 0 = 1$. The 1900s as a century indicated that this century was to be a turning point, a transitional 100 years in our history, a time of birth and death, a time of testing, struggling, and cleansing through regeneration. The 1 and 9 preceding each date in the 20th century told this story: the beginning and the end. This century, of all the years of history, will stand out in terms of invention, discovery, and advancement. It is known for the beginnings (1) and the endings (9) of a way of life. The stage was set for a new millennium.

. . . .

* The quotes in this section that covers the years from 1900 through 1970 come from *This Fabulous Century* by Time-Life Books, New York.

The first decade of the 1900 century, 1900–1909, combined the 19 with the place holder, the 0. The 0 ruled the first 10 years; each year of the decade was ruled by blending the 0 with the digit that followed it. For example, in 1901, the 1 worked with the 0; in 1902, the 2 blended with the 0, and so on up until 1909.

In the 10-year period from 1900 to 1909, the 0 ruled. 0 is the cosmic egg, the creation symbol, the "I am" before creation. In the 0, the archetypes for all creation already exist. It contains all we need to create and build the world of form. The 0 decade from 1900–1909 showed us what we had to work with during the twentieth century. The circle, loving, complete, whole, and happy, bestowed a sort of "I am" pattern, a holding pattern over the first decade, as if the golden jonquils of spring had been suspended in a timeless moment, and youth and joy would last forever.

The symbol of the circle is deeply embedded in our consciousness. It has no sharp edges and implies safety and love. We carry these associations into adulthood when we arrange our chairs in a circle at a meeting because somehow we feel more comfortable that way. We sit around a campfire to enjoy the camaraderie. Many cultures had circle dances; religions contain circle imagery.

From 1900 to 1909, the encompassing symbol of the circle seemed to hold time in abeyance. We felt that God was with us, and all things were possible. "The man of the decade, President Theodore Roosevelt, was the living embodiment of the optimism and energy of this country's mood. During his 7½ years of vigorous, personal leadership, he wielded the powers of the presidency as no man had done before. Roosevelt called his crusade the Square Deal, and the people loved it. They loved him for himself, too. 'I have never known another person so vital,' wrote author and editor William Allen White, speaking for the nation, 'nor another man so dear.' Called the Cocksure Era, this was a splendid time, a wonderful country."

Most Americans felt that way in the beginning of the new century and they said so with exaggerated "references to Peace, Prosperity and Progress."

In the years 1910 to 1919, the 1 overshadowed the decade. 1 represents independence, decisiveness, aggressiveness, impulsiveness, fervor, originality, the pioneering instinct, leadership, and the need to be first and best.

Henry Ford summed up this decade best when he said he wanted: "to be known as a thinker of an original kind." These years produced much that was original. It was a decade of firsts as well as the end of innocence—a time when the 0 bubble of optimism, faith, and an almost Pollyanna attitude towards life finally burst. Historians reflecting upon this decade spoke of a period of "almost tremulous unrest," of a "reviewing of all our social conceptions," a time when "we are profoundly disenchanted." These phrases are a reflection of the number 1.

Rebellion against the past and all its traditions emerged in the new attitudes, habits, customs, dress, literary tastes, films, and dances of the decade. The new woman was born. In May 1910, the first public demonstration of women's suffrage took place. Women demanded the right to vote, which at that time was denied only to them, the mentally impaired, and criminals. The struggle ended in 1919, when women won their right to vote with the 19th Amendment to the Constitution. Ironically, the 19 of the 19th Amendment was doubly reflected in the year 1919, the beginning and the end.

Women became more aggressive and assertive. One young woman dared to smoke in public. Others invaded the male business world and raised the female working force by one million in that 10-year period. The Milwaukee women's swimming team appeared in public in a collection of men's swim suits, baring their arms and legs for the first time to the shock and dismay of clergy. One could almost hear a collective sigh of relief as tight corsets were thrown away and millions of pinched waistlines expanded. A straighter silhouette, more like the shape of the number 1, was born in style that allowed women more freedom.

The headlong and often confused rush into the future was captured by the mad movie world of Charlie Chaplin, the Keystone Kops, and the Perils of Pauline. A group of intellectuals—Anderson, Lippmann, Eastman, Dreiser, Sandburg, Lowell, and Frost—some of whom protested the lowbrow reading tastes of the public, brought on a literary revolution through a stream of purely American works and critiques.

The mass production of Henry Ford's Tin Lizzie freed millions of people from isolated farms and remote country homes. The horse and buggy gave way to instant transportation, suddenly changing the face of America. Her cheeks were now blushed with the excitement and fervor of new places to go and new sights to see. This is the adventuresome side of the number 1.

Then on April 2, 1917, war came upon the world, and America leaped to the defense of world peace. Young red-blooded American men marched off to fight, singing valiant songs of victory, and the

Martian quality of the number 1 reached its peak. Those who did not want to go to war were publicly scorned and ridiculed. The 1 proclaimed it was time to stand up and be counted.

The 1920s were under the thumb of the number 2, which represents a gestation period in which to collect, analyze, and assimilate. Secret elements, which would surface at a later time, were working beneath the surface; therefore, a quiet, nonassertive, reactive, cooperative, unsure attitude prevailed. Choices are difficult under a 2 so often decisions are deferred to a later day. Affairs fluctuate, situations change rapidly, and emotions run high, causing erratic actions at times, Poise, equilibrium, and balance are the saving factors; this is why the peacemakers and mediators are in demand. Under a 2, the seeds of creativity are planted, and artists produce deeply moving works of art.

Two principles are active: the secretive, waiting, creative energy and the suddenly explosive energy—two sides of the same coin. The number 2 is either balanced or at odds with itself. This decade had a little of both.

America was tired as she entered the 1920s. The need for peace, normalcy, and quiet was reflected in the defeat of Woodrow Wilson, who had led the country through World War I and then demanded reform at home and American leadership and responsibility worldwide, all number 1 qualities. But the time of the 1 was finished. American was disillusioned over the death and destruction of the war and its failure to bring peace and democracy to the world, so she rejected Wilson's aggressive demands and elected gentle, lovable Warren G. Harding, who proclaimed, "America's present need is not heroics but healing, not nostrums but normalcy, not revolution but restoration, not surgery but serenity." America's mood had changed from the militancy of the number 1 in the teens to the reactive mood of the number 2 in the 1920s.

The creative side of the 2 blossomed. Joe Oliver, Johnny and Baby Dodds, and Louis Armstrong of the Creole Jazz Band, some of the best musicians north of New Orleans, drove the public wild by their performances. They created "that great blue New Orleans sound." Demand for the blues increased nationwide, culminating in the most celebrated musical event of the decade, George Gershwin's premier performance of "Rhapsody in Blue" at Manhattan's Aeolian Hall in 1924. Society's elite filled the hall to hear Gershwin's "symphonic jazz."

A quote from *How to Play and Sing the Blues Like Phonograph and Stage Artists* reads: "Blues are more naturally blue when the melodic movements are treated with minor chords." It is perhaps coincidence that the number 2 relates to Key 2 of the Tarot, which is the subconscious, the roots of creativity; and the color of the subconscious is blue. The subconscious urgings could be described as minor chords, number 2, which are often drowned out by the conscious mind's major chords, the number 1, until the right moment, the right cycle, when the "outer" is stilled and the "inner" is heard.

The 20s also ushered in Prohibition, which drove the drinking public into hiding and created the underground saloon and speakeasy. 2 always lurks below the surface. Alcohol was smuggled in from ships anchored 3 miles off the coast, and moonshine was brought in from the country hills. Gentlemen carried flasks in their back pockets and ladies tucked theirs under their garters.

Al Capone, with a 700-man army at his disposal, controlled 10,000 speakeasies in Chicago and ran bootlegging operations from Canada to Florida. Out of the dark of night a secret element emerged, and racketeering was born. Emotions ran high, not only because of the furtive attempts of the public to purchase booze and avoid the law, but also because of the rackets' internal struggles to maintain supremacy over a million-dollar market (billions in today's terms).

The finale of all underground rumblings occurred in the ninth year of the decade (9, a time of endings) on Black Tuesday, October 29, 1929, when the stock market collapsed. Strangely enough, a 1921 political cartoon warned investors of shady operators angling for victims in the stock exchange. It depicted fat well-dressed male figures on top of the stock exchange building holding fishing poles, at the end of which hung those poor souls who had been caught on the financial hook. This was the supreme example of one side of the number 2 coin, the hidden energies suddenly and unexpectedly emerging to create untold chaos and loss.

1930-1939

The 1930s were under the auspices of the number 3. As with all numbers, they can be used on a lower physical plane or a higher illumined level of consciousness. The former brings disintegration, the latter transmutation. 3 is the principle of life, which activates on the physical plane. As such, its harmonious use can bestow social harmony, generosity, affability, honesty, recognition, orderly growth and expansion, and freedom from want. 3 allows planning on a grand scale, listening to dreams, and expressing talents. The inharmonious effects of the 3 wreaks destruction and chaos through exaggeration, overconfidence, wastefulness, and bankruptcy.

The first two decades raised a lean cow. The early depression years of the 1930s that followed the stock market crash caused untold hardship on many Americans who had plodded through the 1920s unaware of the loss of energy caused by insidious and hidden forces. Nature lashed the lean cow with dust storms, which buried farms and suffocated the citizens of New Mexico, Texas, Kansas, and Oklahoma. On March 4, 1933, the last bank in the country closed its doors, and financial and economic starvation loomed on the horizon. America was more frightened than she had ever been before. However, on that same day in March, Franklin D. Roosevelt (FDR) became president, moved into the Oval Office, and began issuing orders. He called special sessions of Congress, and his emergency banking bill passed through the House within thirty-eight minutes unchanged. Four days later, the banks reopened and the panic was over. People began re-depositing their money and confidence was restored. By June 16 of that year, fifteen new laws had been enacted to stabilize the economy. The New Deal, Roosevelt's alphabet soup, the National Recovery Act (NRA), the Civilian Conservation Corps (CCC), the Public Works Administration (PWA), the Works Progress Administration (WPA), and so on, nourished and slowly strengthened the weakened cow. His government programs also created jobs for unemployed artists—composer, painters, writers, and actors. One recipient was John Steinbeck who produced the major work of the decade, *The Grapes of Wrath.*

FDR radiated the confidence the country needed at that time. An associate, awed by the president, commented, "He must have been psychoanalyzed by God." Roosevelt's attitude and his social programs were exemplary of the qualities of the number 3 and its Jupiterian flavor.

In this decade, labor leader John L. Lewis held the limelight; his eloquent voice spoke for the downtrodden working class. After knowing terror, beatings, and death, labor finally secured for itself better wages, safer working conditions, and security on the job. Union membership swelled over the 7 million mark, and the once ignored and battered worker became a first-class citizen. The recognition, relaxed conditions, and affluence of the 3 began to manifest in these events.

The need for freedom became obvious in 1933 (double 3s) when Prohibition was repealed. The nation celebrated wildly. The inner need for self-expression was reflected further in the expansive events and entertainment of this decade. Music carried the tones of the Big Band sound with Benny Goodman, the Dorsey Brothers, Glen Miller, Harry James, Count Basie, Duke Ellington, Artie Shaw, and their female vocalists, Helen O'Connell, Billie Holiday, and Ella Fitzgerald.

Stage musicals flourished, and the film industry produced the greatest extravaganza of the decade, the film version of Margaret Mitchell's novel, *Gone with the Wind*. This film is still spectacular today.

Hope, faith, and optimism sprang forth in the roles played by the adorable Shirley Temple and the characters of Little Orphan Annie, Buck Rogers, and Flash Gordon, who prevailed despite obstacles. The country's exaggerated and gullible state of mind was perhaps best summed up in its reaction to Orson Welles's radio program *Invasion from Mars,* which was aired on the radio as a series of news broadcasts. Many in the listening audience actually believed the Martians had landed and were wreaking death and destruction over the countryside with their death rays.

In 1939, America put on the biggest, gaudiest, and most expensive exposition in the world. The New York World's Fair cost more than 150 million dollars (much more in today's terms), covered 1,216 acres, and boasted 10,000 trees and 1,000,000 tulips. It featured everything from transportation and Polish vodka to scientific marvels and the world of tomorrow.

The decade ended on an optimistic, rejuvenated, and well-satisfied note. Some semblance of sanity and safety had returned to the world, and life seemed more comfortable. The cow was healthy and well fed.

1940-1949

The square and its 4 sides and all that implies had precedence in the 1940s. The 4 represents solidity, security, caution, patience, thrift, industry, hard work, money, and material possessions. It upholds the traditions of the past because it is a building block, a foundation upon which law, order, and society rest. Organization is a keyword, and debts are paid on all levels. Physical relationships are emphasized. The square is a doorway to new experiences, a window through which to view the world, a boundary that defines limits and ensures safely. Notice that we say "boxed in" rather than "circled in" or "tubed in" or "triangled in." On the negative side, 4 can be limited, restrained, fearful, stubborn, and overworked, and a wall that imprisons.

Although parents usually feel their teenagers are nonconformists, bucking tradition, the 1940s produced no rebels. During this decade, teenagers "lived and dressed by rigid codes" that were quite conservative—loafers, rolled-up dungarees, and Dad's shirt for the girls; army boots, dungarees, and school jackets for the boys. Television, just introduced, came to be known as "the box." In the sense that it kept families home more often, it had a solidifying effect. Organization emerged in the clubwoman, "a ubiquitous and powerful figure on the American scene" in the 1940s. And personal relationships were explored in Dr. Alfred Kinsey's best-selling book, *Sexual Behaviour in the Human Male*, which analyzed the findings of intimate interviews with 5,300 American men.

The major event of the decade however was World War II which, paradoxically, was anticipated and prepared for—and yet caught everyone by surprise. The last issue of *Time* magazine before the surprise bombing of Pearl Harbor read: "From Rangoon to Honolulu everyman was at battle stations." The day after the attack, December 8, 1941, House Republican leader Joe Martin exclaimed, "I don't know how the hell we were caught so unprepared." Trouble had been brewing for a decade, however. The Japanese wanted dominion over the Pacific. Every graduating class at the naval academy in Japan from 1931 on was asked the following question on their final exam: "How would you carry out a surprise attack on Pearl Harbor?"

The attack on Pearl Harbor destroyed 188 planes, 8 battleships, and 3 cruisers, and left 2,400 men dead. The optimism of the 1930s ended abruptly, and America suddenly knew she must muster her forces, organize, and solidify. The 1940s had arrived.

1940 was a decade of work and production, the 4. By 1942, the amount of goods made by Americans had quadrupled and the volume of production continued until the weaponry produced defeated the enemy. Everyone worked. In the 5 months after Pearl Harbor, 750,000 women donned slacks and went to work in armament plants. The thriftiness of the 4 showed in various ways: Women collected and saved silk stockings and bacon grease, children saved empty toothpaste tubes and bought war stamps in school, men saved worn tires, old radiators, and scrap metal—all to be recycled for the war effort. Rationing was put into effect and stamps were issued for food and gas.

Victory Gardens, small squares of earth, sprang up in the most unlikely places. Anyone who had even a small square plot of earth grew a few vegetables. Although farmers were producing enough food to feed half the world, the Victory Gardens made Americans feel they were contributing. War bonds raised the necessary money to fund the war. Money is a vital issue under 4, and the economy boomed. People were working, and some were making "a killing" on the war. One bombardier home on furlough in 1944, remarked bitterly that he had heard a man on a bus say, "If this war lasts for two more years, I'll be on easy street."

In the early war years, an unfortunate public reaction caused the internment of Japanese American citizens. War hysteria influenced many West Coast residents fearful of a Japanese invasion to publicly refuse to deal with the 110,000 Japanese living in that area. Americans refused to sell them food or cash their checks, and companies cancelled their insurance. Eventually, with no charges leveled at them and with no trial, they were herded off to "camps," usually on old Indian reservations known for having the worst land and being in the most desolated locations. They were paid a pittance for their labors, yet the Japanese as a whole kept their spirit and family unity.

The square of security and protection became a prison of fear and distrust, and America succumbed to her anxiety.

On August 6 and August 9, 1945, the United States dropped atomic bombs on Hiroshima and Nagasaki, and 106,000 Japanese died. The war was over.

After the war, returning soldiers had to face another kind of reality: how to get a job and where to live, basics of the number 4. It turned out to be less of a problem than anticipated, for the public responded enthusiastically. Atlanta bought a hundred trailers to help their married GIs. In North Dakota, they converted surplus grain bins into housing units, and Benny Goodman's band played a benefit requesting rented rooms instead of money. On the work front, government aid assisted veterans in setting up their own businesses, while others went back to old jobs or to college under the generous GI Bill of Rights. The readjustment was handled well in most cases, and America finished the decade in stable condition.

The country emerged as a world leader after the war, and even though the horror of the atomic bomb lurked in the background, America felt some sense of stability and security. The war was over, and America was the only one with the A-bomb.

1950-1959

Number 5, the ruler of the 1950s, represents restlessness, freedom, change, curiosity, experience, travel, and choices. 5 is the central number in the 1 to 9 series, so it indicates a point at which one tends to look back as well as forward. Uneasiness arises. It's decision time. 5 needs information and all sorts of new experiences upon which to base decisions that arise. Therefore, all forms of communication are emphasized: socializing, travel, reading materials, culture, radio, television, and so on. It is a time of mental growth and versatility; wittiness and enthusiasm, a restless seeking and experiencing. Since the nervous system is activated under number 5, drugs and alcohol that stimulate the body should be avoided. 5 meets so many new and varied personalities in its seeking that sexuality is an issue. Because there are 4 numbers on each side of the 5, it is called "the keystone in the arch of the structure of life," and as such represents the 5 senses, which dominate our lives and demand satisfaction. 5 is the number of life, and it lives fully.

In 1951, Louis Kronenberger in his book, *Company Manners* stated: "The moving van is a symbol of more than our restlessness; it is the most conclusive possible evidence of our progress." Surely, the moving van is a symbol of restlessness, a perfect description of the number 5 and the 1950s. It was a time of movement and experience, with life as the teacher. Recreation seekers more than doubled, and the sale of camping equipment, braziers, and lawn furniture soared. Alcohol consumption in suburbia mushroomed along with the sale of aspirin: gin, from 6 million gallons in 1950 to 19 million in 1960; vodka, from 0.1 million to 9 million gallons; and aspirin, from 12 million pounds to 18 million pounds.

"Suburbia was not only a new place to live, it was a new way *to live, with more active sports, more simple fun."* I have italicized this *Time-Life Books* statement because the italicized words are keywords for the number 5. Suburbia created more than a healthy cultural environment for the children; it also created a commuting problem for the family breadwinner who was faced with unreliable train schedules and crowded highways. People were on the move . . . towards the cities to work and towards the country to escape.

The decade's curiosity and eagerness for new experience peaked in its search for cultural enrichments: encyclopedia sales rose from 72 million in 1950 to 300 million in 1960, musical instruments from 86 million to 149 million, and juvenile books from 32 million to 88 million. Six major magazines were born in the "once stable world of legitimate magazine publishing: *Flair* (short lived), *Playboy, Mad, Jet, Sports Illustrated*, and, to the surprise of many, *TV Guide.*

Elvis Presley's nervous gyrations exemplified the decade's mood in music, but TV dominated the entertainment field. It came into its own with the premier of a half-hour news show, *See It Now*, with Edward R. Murrow. Murrow took "vigorous editorial stands," which eventually prompted a simultaneous comment from the *St. Louis Dispatch* and the *New York Herald Tribune*: "Television has come of age." This program received twenty awards in 1954 alone. To fill in the empty time slots on television, live drama was introduced and won acceptance by the public . . . shows like the *Kraft Television Theatre, U.S. Steel Hour, Philco Playhouse*, and *Hallmark Hall of Fame*. The world of entertainment was in full swing.

The dark cloud on the horizon was the knowledge that Russia now also had the atomic bomb. The USSR exploded its first A-bomb in the late summer of 1949 and stunned the world. America suddenly realized that the horror of Hiroshima and Nagasaki was on her doorstep. Nobel Prize-winning chemist, Harold C. Urey, said: "There is only one thing worse than one nation having the atomic bomb . . . that's two nations having it." Part of the restlessness of the time was Russia's reneging on its wartime agreements. The Bear had devoured half of Europe and continued feeding its war machinery. By 1950, she had 3 times as many military planes as the United States, 4 times as many troops, and 30 tank divisions to our 1. And she had the atomic bomb.

It was a time of uneasiness. The film *On the Beach*, from Nevil Shute's novel depicting in horrifying detail the end of all life on Earth as a result of nuclear war, dramatized the nation's fears. James Dean's portrayal of a lost teenager in the film *Rebel without a Cause*, further reflected the quandaries of youth. For most teenagers, it was also a time of desperate innocence, as if the lightheartedness and clean fun of their Lilliputian world of beach parties, record hops, and hula hoops could erase the looming destruction of atomic war. It was moment suspended between the sanity of the past and the madness of the future.

1960-1969

The 1960s decade was perfectly summed up in 1965 in the lyrics of Bert Bacharach and Hal David's best-selling song, "What the World Needs Now Is Love Sweet Love." 6 is the number ruling the need for love, balance, harmony, and justice. In 6 there is duty, service, responsibility, and commitment towards home and community, and a need to help others by establishing human rights, equilibrium, and peace. A deep appreciate of art and music emerges because of the 6's fine sense of balance. Beauty and adornment become important. The home, marriage, and intimate personal relationships are emphasized in order to bring greater understanding of universal love through the experience of personal love. 6 is the Cosmic Mother, sex, and regeneration.

A wall poster in the Haight-Ashbury section of San Francisco in the 1960s read, "Haight is love." It was the hippie generation of love children. "And love was indeed the dominant mood—not only physical love, though currents of eroticism hung like incense in the air, but a kind of indiscriminate love, all embracing brotherliness." To a reporter's inquiry as to who he was and why he was part of the scene, a hippie responded: "God is. Love is. I am."

In the summer of 1969, on a rented 600-acre dairy farm in Woodstock, New York, 400,000 young people gathered for three days of music, talk, dance, drink, and love. "Despite traffic jams, lack of food, shelter, and sanitation, and blustering rainstorms that turned the crowded hillsides to mud, there was not a single fist fight, nor even a disparaging word. In fact, all was love."

Community families sprang up in the hippie communes and in the "retirement towns" exclusively for people over fifty. The need for love, companionship, and sharing reached both ends of the spectrum.

The Beatles beguilingly proclaimed the message of love. Their first hit, "She Loves You" swept the country and started Beatlemania. It was a time of feathers and bangles and baubles and beads. Psychedelic color splashed across faces, across the model Twiggy, and over bodies, automobiles, posters, and places of entertainment.

The drug culture emerged with Dr. Timothy Leary, a former professor at Harvard University, as its guru. LSD was said to bring a "new expression of love and freedom."

Though panned by critics, Jacqueline Susann's "raunchy sex novel," *Valley of the Dolls*, which brought the author more than one million dollars, dominated the 1960s. Her second novel, *The Love Machine*, doubled that total. Helen Gurley Brown's *Sex and the Single Girl* was an overnight best seller in twenty-eight countries and seventeen languages.

The singles subculture was born: singles bars, resorts, publications, apartment houses, tours to Europe, and cruises to the Bahamas. It began in 1962, when Grossinger's Hotel in the Catskills sponsored a singles-only weekend, the first event of its kind. Junior Officers and Professional Association (JOPA) was created by an on leave and lonely officer Mike O'Harro. 3 years later, it had 47,000 members and a million-dollar operation, which promoted singles travel and entertainment.

The decade began with a wave of idealism, a "spirit of commitment" exemplified by the Peace Corps. Young President Kennedy and his wife Jacqueline brought a "magical blend of elegance and vibrancy" to the White House. It was a glamorous time, a time of Camelot, with an appreciation of beauty and the arts. Kennedy remarked in his inaugural address, "America . . . will not be afraid of grace and beauty." On November 22, 1963, Camelot crumbled when President Kennedy was assassinated. President Johnson took over with promises of a Great Society.

A routine commitment to defend Vietnam from communist aggression escalated into the third most costly war in American history at the time. Skepticism arose during the 1960s as to the "justness" of the war, a war that showed children burned with napalm, prisoners threatened with torture, chemically defoliated landscapes, and over half of American aid siphoned off to black markets. America was used to fighting "just" wars; wars that were clear and had a cause. No one knew when the war began or why. Antiwar protests began and culminated with Major John Lindsay's campaign for reelection supporting the war protests.

Justice was demanded on another front. Blacks, historically deprived of voting privileges, subjected to segregation and menial jobs, emerged under the nonviolent leadership of Martin Luther King Jr. "We shall overcome" rang across the land. In August 1963, 200,000 people gathered in Washington, DC, to demand civil rights. Riots broke out in black communities across the nation. In Detroit, in 1967, the worst race riot of the decade exploded with 42 dead and 386 injured in nine days of fire and looting. In April 1968, Martin Luther King Jr. was assassinated. Two months later, Robert F. Kennedy was also assassinated.

On July 16, 1969, the United States space mission Apollo 11, piloted by Neil Armstrong, Edwin Aldrin Jr., and Michael Collins, landed on the Moon. It is curious that the first stop on the Moon, a symbol for lovers, would occur under the 6, a Venus and love decade. The 1960s began with a search for love, hope, and peace, and found instead hate, despair, and war. The scales had tipped and society set about to balance them once again.

1970–1979

During the 1970s, the number 7 ruled. 7 represents rest, reflection, analysis, deep thought, and an inner search for answers. It is a time to retreat from the outer world, which mysteriously will take care of itself. Under a 7, it is not a time to push external affairs because illness can result. One is then forced to take it easy, slow down, and reflect. Events climax on their own because the energy has been released. During a 7, it is time to perfect what is already in motion. Metaphysical, religious, and philosophical topics are highlighted. It is a time to avoid crowds and find the time and space to contemplate through intuition, visions, dreams, and spiritual realizations. Mental analysis awakens knowledge, and knowledge is power. 7 is the reformer presenting ideas to the world. On the negative side, 7 becomes suspicious, cynical, aloof, and a law unto itself, demanding acceptance of its ideas.

The first paragraph of an article from the January 7, 1980, issue of *Time* magazine capsulized the decade of the 1970s. The third sentence read "The American gaze turned inward." Social critic Tom Wolfe called the 1970s the "Me Decade." Waves of self-awareness disciplines—Rolfing, EST, Transactional Analysis, Silva Mind Control, Transcendental Mediation—washed over the country. Everyone's question in the 1970s was: "Who am I?" It was a decade of "dreamily obsessive self-regard," a time to "soothe troubled psyches and spirits," "to get it all together."

Organized religion experienced a revival. Spiritual study groups sprang up all over the country and born-again Christians proclaimed the gospel. Bumper stickers directed: "Honk if you love Jesus" and "May the Force be with you." Sinister religious cults kidnapped and brain-washed young followers who were often "re-kidnapped" and deprogrammed by concerned parents. This religious insidiousness culminated at Jonestown, Guyana, where more than 900 followers of Reverend Jim Jones died in a mass suicide.

The shrinking dollar caused America to pause and question its immersion in capitalism. The Arab oil boycott of 1973 and the ensuing lines at the gas pumps presented the possibility that the United States' "astonishing material indulgence" might end. In 1979, productivity actually decreased, showing the influence of the number 7's retreat and rest influence.

The number 7 brings to a head issues that have been brewing from the beginning, in this case from the 1900s into the 1970s. In the 1970s, we had the "biggest women's protest marches since the days of the suffragettes." Song like "I Am Woman" by Helen Reddy, declared the female sentiment. In March 1971, Indira Gandhi won a landslide victory in her bid for prime minister of India with two-thirds of the Parliamentary seats. In 1979, Margaret Thatcher became Britain's first woman prime minister.

The tax issue hit a peak when California voters approved Proposition 13, which cut property taxes in half. Antiwar sentiment came to a head when young students were killed at Kent State. Sixty percent of all Americans were then against the war in Vietnam . . . a pressure that helped to end US involvement in the war in 1975. President Sadat of Egypt visited Israel in an unprecedented move towards peace, breaking 29 years of hostility. Jimmy Carter, a dark horse candidate who proclaimed "a special relationship with God," became the president who would mediate in this peace settlement in the years ahead. "Blessed are the peacemakers," he said, as the Middle East Peace Treaty was signed in September 1978.

Moral issues emerged. Watergate revealed the hidden machinations of government leaders and resulted in the resignation in disgrace of an American president and prison sentences for a number of his aides. In 1974, President Nixon "found himself posturing in limbo" as he waved the victory sign as the helicopter "lifted him away to exile."

Another moral issue surfaced in the enormous unknown risks of nuclear power. The partial meltdown at Three Mile Island nuclear plant in Pennsylvania in March 1979 became a symbol of the insanity and total destruction some people felt nuclear power would wreak upon the world. Organized masses gathered at nuclear plants around the country to protest their construction. And the issue of cloning touched off controversy over its morality and the responsibility to God and country.

Eerily, the film *The China Syndrome* opened on March 16, 1979, a film in which the reporter persuades one engineer at a nuclear plant to blow the whistle on the possibility of a meltdown that could "render an area the size of Pennsylvania permanent uninhabitable." An exact quote! Twelve days later, a partial meltdown occurred at the Three Mile Island Nuclear Plant in Pennsylvania!

The racial issue culminated in the most celebrated book and subsequent television drama of the decade: *Alex Haley's Roots*, viewed by 130 million Americans. The cinema touched the pulse of the nation with *All the President's Men*, *Raid on Entebbe*, *The Deerhunter*, *Boys from Brazil*, and *The China Syndrome*.

Star Wars, the biggest success in movie history, was an exercise in the mental reaching and philosophical needs of the decade, the number 7: the forces of good versus the forces of evil. The blessing—"May the Force be with you"—spoke an eloquent plea in our inner call for divine guidance.

PREDICTIONS FOR 1980

(PUBLISHED IN EARLY 1980)

We have just begun a new decade ruled by the 8. Number 8 is karma: as ye sow, so shall ye reap; as it is above, so it is below; for every action, there is an equal and opposite reaction. In other words, we are going to get exactly what we deserve. 8 is balance, strength, discipline, fortitude, intelligence, and respect. It is practical, tough, fair, just, and careful. Under 8, we move more cautiously, implementing big ideas and plans. It is a time of work, unity, organization, and authority. The number 8 implies restriction and responsibility, a shaving down, a cutting of losses, a shedding of excess. The shape of the figure 8 implies a pinched waistline, a time to tighten our belts.

8, Scorpio, Pluto, and Saturn work together changing the "Me Decade" of the 1970s in the "We Decade" of the 1980s. 8—two circles together. The rainbow, representative of the number 8 (see page 49) may become the decade's most popular symbol, now splashed over T-shirts, posters, advertisements, jewelry, and business emblems.

Because they relate to the number 8, areas such as taxes, birth, death, underground activity, the masses, insurance, sex, justice, money, business, and finance will be key issues. The negative side brings fear, loss, and unnecessary restriction.

We are only three months into the decade (as of this writing, March, 1980) [this manuscript was turned in the end of April 1980] and I have just heard President's Carter's first major address of the year. The nouns, verbs, and adjectives in his speech can be used as keywords for the number 8. His economic message to the nation was delivered on March 14, 1980, a 35/8 day, and the issue was inflation. Because of the strain in the financial market, restraints will be imposed on the use of credit cards and on the lending policies of banks not with the Federal Reserve and on other money-lending institutions. Federal loans and guarantees will be cut by 4 billion dollars. A ten-cents-per-gallon tax will be imposed on foreign oil (for gasoline use only), and the funds will be used to reduce the national debt. A team of experts will track and investigate increases in wages and price developments that are out of line. These are just the first tough measures to fight inflation in the coming 1980s. The budget must be balanced in this decade.

President Carter went on to remark that our excessive dependence on foreign oil, the price of which was doubled in the last twelve months (March 1979 to March 1980) must end. Increased conservation and production of home oil and other sources of energy must be instituted. "America's extravagant gasoline use" must be curtailed. He spoke of "long-term structural changes" that will not be easy. The "new budget is very tight: There are some things we cannot afford." Balancing the budget is the first order of the day. Tax relief may follow to encourage the economy. He used words like pain, cost, inconvenience, discipline, and patience—all keywords for number 8. He warned that we should not look for massive changes next week, that we must "take control of the problem, which means take control of ourselves," "that we must put aside fear, face the world as it is, be honest about hard decisions, and with courage carry them out" and that we must build a strong America. His last sentence had 8 written all over it: "With the proper discipline, we will prevail in our fight against inflation."

Because we are no longer in the mood for extravagance and waste, the presidents we elect this year and in the coming two election years of this decade will be serious, strong, confident, older perhaps, and tough. We will want individuals who speak plainly and honestly, and who means business. There will be few give-away programs in this decade because we are ready for discipline. "Like a spoiled child having a tantrum, we are demanding a hard hand."

The March 24, 1980, cover of *Time* magazine read "Carter vs. Inflation . . . The president's demand: 'discipline . . . discipline . . . discipline.'" A major keyword for number 8 is discipline.

Numerous articles and news items now speak of the energy crises. The gasoline crunch will produce "fuel frugal vehicles" that will get many more miles per gallon. Companies are planning to trim down cars, reduce weight, build smaller engines with more efficient fuel management systems, and design "cleaner" bodies for lower wind resistance. Sources of fuel will change drastically in the 1980s. A southern university professor has produced, after 15 years of research, a synthetic gasoline which is a nonpollutant and which can be extracted from US coal reserves. His work was inspired by the Germans who produced gasoline from coal during World War II. The cost in now $1.25 per gallon. This could eventually be reduced to 80 cents.

Garbage may be another fuel source. I envision receptacles built into kitchen counters, one marked paper goods, the other food refuse, into which homemakers can discard "garbage" items. These feed into a system in the basement that converts the garbage into fuel to heat the home. This process would eliminate unsightly dumps and free many acres of land for other uses; it would do away with garbage collection (and strikes that leave garbage piled high on city streets), costly equipment, and maintenance; it would free a labor force for other jobs, as well as relieve our dependence on other energy sources.

The 1980s may see nuclear disaster resulting from human error at a nuclear plant. Criminal plant takeover or hijacking of nuclear wastes for extortion is possible. Disasters could cause mass evacuations. All this will turn the public away from the use of nuclear energy toward solar power as the safest, cheapest, cleanest, and most natural source of energy.

Total reliance on solar energy is feasible in the 1980s. Homes are being built right now that can store solar energy up to 3 days without the sun, and heat an entire home comfortably, efficiently, and inexpensively. The public will become aware of these methods, regardless of the efforts of vested interests to prevent it. The year 1980 is formed with four 0's: one in the 9, two in the 8, and one in the 0. The 0 is the God symbol, the Light: the Sun has always been a symbol of the God power. This is the decade of the God power, the Light, the Sun's energy. Businesses that produce and install proper solar energy systems will prosper, some becoming very wealthy.

Groups to fight taxes will continue to rise, gain power and will eventually bring about a complete overhaul of the tax structure in this country. The world of finance and our basic monetary system seems to be gasping their last breaths. By the end of the decade we may not recognize our means of exchange. Gold, historically valuable, will always be so, but it will temporarily lose its value over the next decade, perhaps two. We cannot eat it, live in it, wear it for protection, or ride on or in it. Only useful commodities will be valuable.

It is said there are built-in safeguards against another stock market crash and that banks are insured; however, underground rumblings are shaking these foundations as well.

Marriage and "old fashioned morality" is back in style. Stricter ideas regarding matrimony will prevail, providing solidity to this now shaky institution. A new respect for sex and love relationships will surface. On the negative side, disease of generative organs may appear in epidemic proportions, reflecting our misuse of the creative power and our basic resources. Changes in the law regarding prostitution may surprise many.

The legal system is ready for an overhaul. This has already begun with the publication of Woodward and Armstrong's best selling book, *The Brethren*, an expose of the Supreme Court. These judges are no longer sacred cows and will be subject to new laws that require mental health checkups as well as ethical conduct.

Organized crime, a quietly powerful entity, will have internal conflicts along with public confrontations. Having already infiltrated many areas of public life, crime will emerge in the most shocking places, and mass confrontations may cause difficulty. Power struggles of great magnitude are possible. No institution, from organized religion to the banking community, will be exempt.

Underground insects, poisonous snakes, and scorpions may emerge as the decade's heroes, providing serums for the "social diseases," sterility, arthritis, paralysis, and acne. They may provide a serum that will enable severed limbs and joints to regenerate themselves.

Archeological digs may uncover fabulous lost cities and civilizations, some unknown to us today. Many secrets of the ancient past may be revealed, perhaps through natural disasters that open or rearrange the contour of the earth.

Burial ceremonies will change drastically. Cremation may become the only plausible answer to crowded land conditions, and traditional burial procedures may be cast aside as people choose more meaningful methods. Death and birth will take on new meaning as the metaphysical aspects of both are revealed.

Work, organization, unity, and respect for authority—all number 8 attitudes—are already evident. An article by Lance Morrow in the March 10, 1980, issue of *Time* magazine eloquently states: "A complicated impulse has stirred in America's thinking about their country and its place in the world. Patriotism has reappeared. He goes on to speak about "the emergence of a new patriotic impulse in America," that "the villains have moved overseas again," and how Americans now "find they are in an unexpected kinship of common interests." He speaks of America's finest feeling of patriotism as "uniquely difficult and valuable: It is a devotion to a political and social vision, a promise and the idea of freedom—an idea not much honored elsewhere in the world or in history." This renewed patriotism should bring about a rise in the sale of American flags, military paraphernalia, and changes in hair and clothing styles that will reflect the military.

Athletics will become even more important in the 1980s as we feel the need to test our strengths. I see the martial arts as a rapidly growing area of interest as well as fencing, ballet, and all the aesthetic athletic pursuits that stress balance and beauty, where mental and physical aspects of the self must work together. The athletic system itself will be tested as athletes and their managers undergo stressful relations.

Gardening may take on a new shape. The tiny square plots of land called Victory Gardens in the 1940s exemplified the productivity of the 4 and the square with its four sides. The 4 is even drawn much like a square when it is written with top open. The number 8 is a solidified square, or double 4. Productivity is again important. Since the 8 is formed with circles, we may discover that somehow growing foods in circular arrangements becomes important. A friend just last week told me about a woman who has come up with an idea for growing potatoes in a barrel (round), which can produce enough for a family for an entire winter. This same friend of mine has a relative who is growing her vegetables in a pail. Shapes have their own peculiar energies, and since the circle is the God energy, perhaps we will find we have been growing our food within the wrong outline, and that somehow even the seed will react to the circular shape as we do. All is consciousness. Who are we to define the limits of the God consciousness, especially when we are living in the 8 for a decade?

We are only 4 months into 1980 (as of this writing) and so far the rewards from this karmic 80 decade are not encouraging. 50 American hostages are still being held by Iranian militant students at the American embassy in Iran, and the Iranians are threatening to kill the hostages if America steps out of line. The United States promises retaliation if one American is harmed. Russia has invaded Afghanistan and set up a puppet regime threatening the borders of other oil-producing nations. The world economy is in serious jeopardy; the Catholic Church is attempting to silence its intellectual priests who are openly questioning certain church tenets, and although difficult international negotiations continue, war seems more imminent each day.

We sit on a powder keg, waiting for one rash action to send the world into pandemonium. The negative thinking of the past years constantly sent out from our minds into the environment has accumulated into a heavy cloud, which now surrounds the Earth, disturbing the harmonious flow of the natural rhythm of things. We cannot expect the Earth, or the elements, to remain silent. The Earth in retaliation will speak most eloquently as she unleashes her power. Mt. St. Helens in Washington State has been rumbling and smoking for weeks as if parodying the rumbling and smoking of world leaders. Iran has suffered a number of earthquakes since the hostage situation began. We can expect more from the elements now and in the coming years. They will speak in the areas that are the most troubled.

It is apparent that we may all suffer because of the actions and ensuing results in a tiny section of the world. Events today are no longer isolated acts; they send repercussions around the world. We are all under the Universal Year Cycle 9 $(1 + 9 + 8 + 0 = 18/9)$, and we must all clean house, let go of worn out ideas, be charitable, have compassion, and be ready to change. It is time to act and we as a world know it, feel it, and must comply, or it will be forcibly enacted by Cosmic Law. We need to change—for the better. This could be our last chance before Armageddon.

In the latter part of 1982, an unusual perfect alignment of all nine planets on the same side of the Sun occurs in our solar system. In their book, *The Jupiter Effect*, John Gribbin, science editor of *Nature Magazine*, and Stephen Plagemann of NASA's Goddard Space Center in Maryland, bring out interesting points, which make one wonder if this effect is the apocalyptic prediction of Revelations. The authors point out that the planets have an effect upon each other and upon the Earth. Earthquakes are one of the effects of certain planetary conjunctions. It has been noted that conjunctions of two or more planets (Mars, Jupiter, and Saturn) cause sunspots, which in turn are directly related to war, economic crashes, and earthquakes. These three planets are in Virgo this year, and Jupiter and Saturn make a conjunction as well. Earthquakes have been hot and heavy since the fall of 1975, and certainly no one can deny the possibilities of economic depression and war (the Iranian-Afghanistan-Russian crises). The authors go on to point out many possible effects of this total planetary alignment: firestorm activity in the Sun, a change in the Earth's ionosphere, changes in wind, rain, and temperature patterns, an altering of the rotation of the Earth thus effecting the day's length and causing more earthquakes. The long predicted California quake may result from this 1982 alignment.

Pluto, the power of transformation, enters Scorpio in late 1983, retrogrades out, and returns in 1984. (Do you recall George Orwell's novel *1984*?) Pluto, the destroyer, was discovered in 1930 in the sign Cancer. A slow-moving planet, it will enter its own sign, Scorpio (the house of birth, death, and transformation) in 1983–1984 for a fourteen-year transit. A planet is always the most powerful in its own sign. This is the first time since the discovery of Pluto that it has been in Scorpio. A brief examination of the planet Pluto and the sign Scorpio reveals what the possibilities are in the coming years. Pluto and Scorpio rule such things as atomic energy, plutonium, the power struggles, and mass destruction, as well as rebirth and new life.

I am an optimist. I believe in never-ending life, in the continuance of our energy and the goodness of the Cosmic Force, God. I know that no matter what happens we will be all right, we will survive, we will learn, and we will grow and be reborn—even if this process must occur upon the ashes of atomic warfare. We have probably done this before—with the terrible crystal in Atlantis (perhaps even before that in the shrouds of history long lost to us). But now, we have the awareness, we know what the possibilities are. We can see the trends, and there are many who pray and work every day to counteract the negativity in this world.

Perhaps this time around the goodness will prevail; the positive energy will counteract and absorb the negative, teaching us that division is only an illusion. This game of life is just that—a game—and if we could see ourselves desperately struggling for power in this material world, we would laugh at the emptiness of it all. Perhaps we will learn, this time around, that life is to be lived joyously, completely, with reverence and respect for all peoples and all ideas.

. . . .

There you have the 1980s decade as written in late 1979/early 1980 in the first edition of *Numerology and Your Future*.

SECTION 2
ANALYSIS OF MY FORECASTS FOR THE 1980 DECADE

. . . .

In 1979 and the first three months of 1980, I wrote about the types of events that could occur from 1980 to 1989 because of the influence of the number 8. The manuscript was turned in to the publisher and out of my hands in March 1980.

In that first edition, I explained that 8 means discipline, strength, caution, authority, maturity, restriction, and the big word, "responsibility." I also used the words taxes, birth, death, insurance, sex, justice, money, business, and finance as key issues.

IN THIS 2ND EDITION OF NUMEROLOGY AND YOUR FUTURE, I ASK:
WERE MY 1979 PREDICTIONS FOR THE 1980s DECADE THUMBS-UP OR THUMBS-DOWN? OR EVEN THUMBS-HORIZONTAL?

The page numbers in parentheses are from the original edition of this book so you can find my predictions there if you happen to have a copy of that first printing.

***

In 1979/early 1980, I wrote: ". . . changing the 'Me Decade' of the 1970s to the 'We Decade' of the 1980s . . . 8, two circles together. The rainbow, representative of the number 8 may become the decade's most popular symbol . . ." (p. 95).

Thumbs-Up: "Rainbow Brite. If you were a young girl growing up in the 80s, then you know all about this craze. Almost every little girl had a Rainbow Brite doll and watched the cartoon that went along with it."[17]

***

In 1979/early 1980, I wrote: "8 is balance, strength, discipline . . . is practical. . . we move more cautiously, a time of work and a cutting of losses, a shedding of excess, and a pinched waistline, a time to tighten our belts (p. 95) . . . a decade that will require discipline, strength, and responsibility—certainly a much more conservative trend than the 1970s when we 'let it all hang out.'". (pp. 161–162)

Thumbs-Up: On March 14, 1980, Democratic President Jimmy Carter gave his economic message, and the issue was inflation. He spoke in terms of a "strain" on the financial market, "restraints" that must be imposed, "tough" measures to fight inflation, extravagant gasoline use must be "curtailed," the new budget is "tight," long term "structural changes" that would not be easy, but with proper "discipline," the country would prevail. These words and phrases have 8 written all over them.

The March 24, 1980, cover of *Time Magazine* read: "Carter vs. Inflation . . . The President's Demand: 'Discipline. . . Discipline. . . Discipline.'" These words were chosen by those in power at *Time Magazine*. And this magazine was on the newsstands the 3rd month into the year 1980, setting the tone for the 80s decade. 8 is discipline.

***

In 1979/early 1980, I wrote: "Because we are no longer in the mood for extravagance and waste, the president we elect this year and in the coming elections of this decade will be serious, strong, confident, older perhaps, and tough. (p. 96) . . . I wonder if in the fall we will elect a 40th president or stay with our 39th, Jimmy Carter, for another term. All indications at this moment point to a Ronald Reagan–Jimmy Carter contest in November. If I had to guess, I would say Ronald Reagan will win the presidential election . . . not because of any personal affiliation . . . but because the evidence points towards a strong, abrupt swing to the right . . . Ronald Reagan is a conservative; a tough-talking, no-nonsense man. The country's conservative trend may swing the election towards him." (pp. 160–162).

Thumbs-Up: On Tuesday, November 4, 1980, Ronald Reagan was elected the 40th president of the United States and remained in office for two terms, spanning almost the entire decade.

***

In 1979/early 1980, I wrote: "Will this end the death cycle for the presidents? We all pray that it will . . . Ronald Reagan is a conservative; a tough-talking, no-nonsense man. The country's conservative trend may swing the election towards him. He is also an Aquarian. We had four Aquarian presidents, all of whom have died in office . . . Reagan is in his late sixties. If he is elected, and the change of the Jupiter-Saturn conjunction into another element has no effect upon the death cycle, will the strain of the office be too much for him?" (p. 162)

Thumbs-Horizontal: Speaking of toughness . . . On March 30, 1981, two months into his presidency, 70-year-old President Ronald Reagan was shot by John Hinckley while leaving the Washington Hilton Hotel after giving a speech. The bullet missed his heart by one inch; his quick recovery earned him the reputation for toughness and strength.

Regarding Reagan's toughness, the number 8 proved more than correct on this event. And by changing signs, the Jupiter-Saturn conjunction brought Ronald Reagan close to death, but fortunately he survived.

The so-called "20-year presidential death cycle" refers to the Jupiter/Saturn conjunction in Earth signs that began in 1840 and repeated every 20 years through 1960. Every president elected in those years died while still in office. In 1980, when Reagan was elected, the Jupiter/Saturn conjunction shifted from Earth signs to an Air sign.

1841: William Henry Harrison died of pneumonia in 1841
1861: Abraham Lincoln was assassinated in 1865
1881: James Garfield was assassinated in 1881
1901: William McKinley was assassinated in his 2nd term in 1901
1921: Warren G. Harding died in 1923 of a suspicious heart attack
1941: Franklin D. Roosevelt died in his 4th term in 1945 of a cerebral hemorrhage
1961: John F. Kennedy was assassinated in 1963

***

In 1979/early 1980, I wrote: "Garbage may be another fuel source. I envision receptacles built into kitchen counters, one marked paper goods, the other food refuse, into which homemakers can discard 'garbage'; items. These feed into a system in the basement that converts the garbage into fuel to heat the home." (p. 97)

Thumbs-Down: Didn't happen, but what a great idea!

***

In 1979/early 1980, I wrote: ". . . the 1980s might see a nuclear disaster resulting from human error at a nuclear plant . . . disasters could cause mass evacuations . . . " (p. 97)

Thumbs-Up: In the early morning hours of April 26, 1986, the Chernobyl nuclear power plant in the Soviet Union had a meltdown caused by human error. Live-Science described this event as the worst nuclear disaster in history and Chernobyl as one of the ten most polluted places on Earth. In 2019, the film *Chernobyl* dramatized this event.

***

In 1979/early 1980, I wrote: "Total reliance on solar energy is feasible in the 1980s." (p. 97)

Thumbs-Down: Not so. I'm still living in an oil-heated home, much to my dismay. In my state, that is mostly forested, I'm surrounded by woods, and with a climate that gets hot weather perhaps 2 months of the year; solar heating has not yet happened to any extent.

***

In 1979/early 1980, I wrote: "It is said there are built-in safeguards against another stock market crash, and that banks are insured; however, underground rumblings are shaking these foundations . . ." (pp. 97–98)

Thumbs-Up: On Black Monday, October 19, 1987, the Hong Kong stock market was the first to crash, a sound which resounded around the world. The Dow Jones fell 508 points in one day, which doesn't seem like a disaster in today's term with the fluctuations over the past few years, but back then it was huge.

As noted by Economic analyst, Jesse Colombo, who wrote on August 3, 2012: "The Stock Market Crash of 1987 or 'Black Monday' was the largest one-day market crash in history. The Dow lost 22.6% of its value or $500 billion dollars on October 19, 1987."

***

In 1979/early 1980, I wrote: "Marriage and 'old fashioned morality' is back in style. Stricter ideas regarding matrimony will prevail . . . " (p. 98)

Thumbs-Up: The Moral Majority, a political organization founded by televangelist Jerry Falwell, rose up to oppose abortion, the Equal Rights Amendment (ERA), and gay rights in the 1980 decade. It helped establish the religious right in politics. It was disbanded in 1989.

***

I also wrote: "On the negative side, disease of generative organs may appear in epidemic proportions . . . " (p. 98)

Thumbs-Up: The *Time Magazine* cover for July 4, 1983, read: AIDS Hysteria.

"HIV/AIDS in the 1980s. The history of HIV/AIDS goes far back to the early 20th century when the first leap of the virus is hypothesized to have transferred to a human from primates in Africa. However, the issue of HIV/AIDS did not fully hit America until the 1980s."[18]

***

I also wrote: "Changes in the law regarding prostitution may surprise many." (p. 98)

Thumbs-Down: I found no indications of this to be true.

***

In 1979/early 1980, I wrote: "The legal system is ready for an overhaul." (p. 98)

Thumbs-Up: In 1981, President Ronald Reagan nominated Sandra Day O'Connor, the first woman to the United States Supreme Court. A male preserve for 192 years, her bestselling biography, *First, An Intimate Portrait of the First Woman Supreme Court Justice,* was a *New York Times* best seller. She shattered many glass ceilings.

The number 8 rules law and order, justice, and balance. So that nomination was a huge overhaul!

***

In 1979/early 1980, I wrote: "Organized crime, a quietly powerful entity, will have internal conflicts along with public confrontations . . . and mass confrontations may cause difficulty. Power struggles of great magnitude are possible." (p. 98)

Thumbs-Up: "A look at the 1980s mafia, when drugs, informants, and money ruled the day—and the organization's downfall was just around the corner.

"The 1980s mafia was in many ways the last gasp of an antiquated criminal empire. Though there was plenty of money to be made, the mafia faced unprecedented pressures from both outside and within, signaling that its glory days were far behind it.

"Like wise, with the high stakes of drug trafficking and the rise of a glitzier generation of gangsters, betrayal and deadly internecine fighting became the norm.

"At the same time, the Racketeer Influenced and Corrupt Organizations (RICO) Act gave law enforcement increased powers and resources to combat organized crime. This meant stiffer criminal penalties and more incentive for mafiosos to break omerta, the sacred mafia code of silence."[19]

***

In 1979/early 1980, I wrote: "Underground insects, poisonous snakes, and scorpions may emerge as the decade's heroes providing serums for social diseases, sterility, arthritis, paralysis, and acne. They may provide a serum that will enable severed limbs and joints to regenerate themselves." (p. 98)

Thumbs-Horizontal: "There is a good reason why the snake is a symbol for the medical profession in America," says Dr. Naftali Primor, who claims snakes can help relieve the pain of arthritis sufferers. (The medical symbol he speaks of is the caduceus which depicts a staff twined about with serpents and mounted atop with wings.)

Dr. Primor, head of the Shulov Institute for Sciences (SIS), has "unlocked the chemicals found in deadly viper venom to help treat arthritis." Primor has always been fascinated by snakes and started working with viper venom when his colleague, Prof. Aharon Shulov, noticed a strange practice by Russian immigrants new to Israel. They used a healing salve made out of viper venom which they spread on the skin to ease chronic pain (ISRAEL21c, March 19, 2006).

His company was founded in 1986.

The regeneration of limbs has not happened but the seeds of understanding how poisonous snakes can aid in healing had stimulated the birth of Dr. Primor's company.

***

In 1979/early 1980, I wrote: "Archeological digs may uncover fabulous lost cities and civilizations, some unknown to us today. Many secrets of the ancient past may be revealed, perhaps through natural disasters that open or rearrange the contour of the Earth." (p. 98)

Thumbs-Horizontal: The "find of the century": I couldn't find any records of fabulous lost cities and civilizations; however, the Rogozen Thracian Treasure, called "the find of the century" was unearthed in 1985 in Bulgaria. It consists of 165 receptacles, including 108 phiales, 55 jugs, and 3 goblets dating back to the 5th–4th centuries around 359–323 BCE. The objects are silver with golden gilt, a combined weight of 44 pounds.

***

In 1979/early 1980, I wrote: "Burial ceremonies will change drastically. Cremation may become the only plausible answer to crowded land conditions . . . " (p. 98)

Thumbs-Down: It didn't happen in the 1980s. "In 1980, the cremation rate around the US was just under 10%, and the percentage has been shifting toward cremation since." ("Cremation Is Now Outpacing Traditional Burial in the U.S.," an article in *Time* magazine by Josh Sanburn, August 1, 2006)[20]

***

In 1979/early 1980, I wrote: "Work, organization, unity, and respect for authority—all number 8 attitudes—are already evident." (p. 98)

Thumbs-Down? The 1980s were an era defined by conservative politics, the rise of computer technology, and the end of the Cold War. The economy was growing, a time when yuppies began to flaunt their wealth. "Greed is good," declared Gordon Gekko (played by Michael Douglas, in his award-winning performance in the film, *Wall Street*).

8 is also the number of wealth and greed. There were, of course, people working hard and following the law, but I couldn't find a clear expression of "respect for authority" as defining of this decade.

***

In 1979/early 1980, I wrote: "Athletics will become even more important in the 1980s as we feel the need to test our strengths." (p. 99) 8 is strength and endurance.

Thumbs-Horizontal: In February 1980, the American men's ice hockey team, a group of amateurs from around the country, won gold after first beating the heavily favored professional Russian team in a stunning 4–3 upset at the Winter Olympics held at Lake Placid. This event happened just before I sent my manuscript to the publisher so I was aware of it.

However, this win, called "Miracle on Ice," is still deemed one of the greatest moments in sports history. It was made into a movie in 1981. In 1999, on their 60th anniversary, *Sports Illustrated* narrowed down over 3,000 covers of their magazine, and asked readers to vote on the most iconic cover. The winner by a landslide was their March 3, 1980 cover: "Miracle on Ice" with an accompanying photo of the team celebrating.

***

In 1979/early 1980, I wrote: "Gardening may take on a new shape. The tiny square plots of land called victory gardens in the 1940s exemplified the productivity of the 4 and the square with its four sides. . . the 8 is a solidified square . . . Since the 8 is formed with circles, we may discover that somehow growing foods in circular arrangements becomes important." (p. 99)

Thumbs-Down: In 1980, the World Vegetable Center hired its first nutritionist to develop home gardens. Studies done that year showed that a 4 m x 4 m [about 13' x 13'] garden plot could produce enough vegetables to feed a family of five with the required daily does of vitamins A and C and a significant percent of protein, calcium, and iron.

***

Other events in the 1980s: the assassinations of John Lennon, Anwar Sadat, and Indira Ghandi, plus the attempt on President Ronald Reagan's life. We watched in horror as the space shuttle *Challenger* exploded, and students were massacred in Tiananmen Square. We also welcomed the introduction of personal computers by IBM. The first internet domain was registered, and in the late 1980s, the World Wide Web was invented.

An event of great import in the last two months of the 1989 was the fall of the Berlin Wall. Construction on this wall began in 1961, dividing the city into communist-ruled East Berlin and democratic West Berlin. The citizens of East Berlin suffered untold hardships and death until November 9, 1989, when the wall fell. This is the date that is celebrated as the fall of the Berlin Wall. The demolition of this wall officially began on June 13, 1990, and took a number of years.

Therefore, the fall of the Berlin Wall straddled the line between two decades: 1989–1991.

SECTION 3
THE NUMBER INFLUENCE ON THE DECADES 1900, 2000, AND 2010

· ·

Let's see how the number 9 influenced the events of the decade 1990–1999.

9 is a time of transition; it represents endings, a complete cycle, and a letting go. It's a humanitarian cycle when it is time to give back to the world some of what was gained in the past eight cycles.

The theme of this decade was major endings in order to prepare for the new millennium. Hindsight offers answers to what needs to change and what needs to be eliminated before entering the next decade, the 2000s. The 1990s involved huge transitions because, in the next decade (the 2000s), we entered not only a new century but also a new millennium dominated by the 2, the 2000s. On top of that, we were also in and are still experiencing the 2,160-year transition into the Age of Aquarius.

Therefore, the history-changing events of the 1990s were clearing the way for a triple whammy . . . the new decade, the new millennium, and the New Age.

But first, how are the 1990s viewed today?

"The 1990s is often remembered as a decade of relative peace and prosperity: The Soviet Union fell, ending the decades-long Cold War . . . ". Bill Clinton was president for most of the 1990s.

Two big events of the 1990s changed the world; one changed the world map.

In 1990, the world witnessed the end of the cold war between the USSR and the United States, two world dominant countries who had been pointing nuclear weapons at each other for some forty-five years. We had been on the brink of nuclear war. Plus, the

1990s: MAJOR TRANSITIONS

Berlin Wall, the symbol of the Cold War, had just fallen in 1989. This dismantling reunited Germany after 45 long years of cruel separations.

In 1990, the world watched in amazement as the Soviet Union dissolved into fifteen separate countries. Some hailed this as a victory of capitalism over socialism. World maps were redrawn. The end of the long cold war between the United States and the USSR, and the following break-up of the Soviet Union, dramatically point out the effects of the 9 during the 1990s decade with the double 9s.

OTHER EVENTS:
- President George H. W. Bush, in his short four-year term from 1989 to 1993, signed a treaty with Mikhail Gorbachev implementing the destruction of chemical weapons production.
- Apartheid and white rule ended in South Africa after 342 years when on May 10, 1994, Nelson Mandela became the first black president of South Africa.
- Islamic terrorists made their first attack on the World Trade Center in New York in 1993, where six people died and over 1,000 were injured.
- President Bill Clinton (1993–2001) signed into law the Assault Weapons Ban, banning their use for 10 years. The Brady Handgun Violence Prevention Act became law. Clinton also banned federal funding for human cloning.
- Osama bin Laden announced a fatwa against Jews and Crusaders in 1998, energizing the Islamic fundamentalist plans of terrorism against the West, ending the invulnerability that this nation felt from foreign sources.
- The Euro was introduced into the European nations on January 1, 1999, and the first major anti-globalization movement occurs in Seattle, Washington, in 1999, amidst protests and rioting that caused the cancellation of the World Trade Organization (WTO) opening ceremonies.

The idea of endings (the number 9) was also rampant at the end of the 90s with the Y2K scare that sent some families into the hills to secret hideaways with stores of food, water, medicine, books, and games to await the year 2000 when the computers would turn over from the two digits system (the 19 was implied) at the stroke of midnight on December 31, 1999, into the next century starting the years with the two digits 20 instead of 19. These people believed that society, as they knew it, would be over because all the computer systems would fail.

And . . . on the final days of the "1" thousand millennium, on December 17, 1999, the United Nations General Assembly adopted Resolution 54/134, designating November 25 as the International Day for the Elimination of Violence against Women.

The first celebration of this day began on November 25, 2000! This event figures significantly in the new millennium through the number 2. With this new "2" millennium, we are awakened to an inner understanding that equality of the sexes benefits everyone and that cooperation and negotiation is the only way to resolve conflict.

The letting go energies of the 9 made room for the seeds that were to sprout in the 2000s.

2000s: SEED DECADE FOR THE NEW MILLENNIUM

The 2 in the year 2000 not only introduces the new decade, but the "2" in 2000 also introduces the new millennium. For the next 1,000 years, every date begins with a "2."

The zeroes in the year 2000 are the cosmic eggs that contain the seeds of the 2 potential for the 2,000 years, the next millennium, as well as the 2000 to 2009 decade.

The 2 requires a gentler touch: cooperation, negotiation, working in partnerships for mutual benefit, using sensitivity and intuition to bring about balance and peaceful solutions, understanding the other side. 2 indicates activity behind the scenes, which reminds me of a pregnant woman's T-shirt printed with the words "Under Construction" in bold letters with a large arrow pointing down.

The 2 also suggests the seesaw effect when one side outweighs the other. Because of this imbalance, conflicts arise; the Yin and Yang are out of balance.

We are also in the midst of the shifting of the Ages, a once in 2,160 years event. Welcome the Age of Aquarius, a time of booming technology, invention, global communication, and space travel. We are being made aware of the need for social justice and the need to accept people from all races, religions, and ethnic backgrounds. The humanitarian impulse is rising. Friendships matter; by joining with friends and groups and organizations we are meant to give back to society some of the expertise and knowledge we have gained in our personal lives.

These changes will take a long time and most likely be a painful birthing process because these new energies are changing attitudes that have been ingrained in humanity for the last 1,000-plus years where the "1" said, "me first" and trampled on anyone in its path.

On the positive side, the 1 gave us the courage to go beyond conventional thinking, to explore, be innovative, and daring. However, when cycles end, they run out of steam and the negative side arises perhaps to compel us to make the transition into the next phase.

From the Big Bang, the 1 burst forth from the Cosmic Egg in a release of creative energy. The 2 pulled in that energy to create balance, the Yin and Yang.

2000-2009: AGE OF AQUARIUS, AGE OF THE WOMAN, SPACE EXPLORATION, AND THE INTERNET

As mentioned, the 2000 decade opened with the 2. We entered a period of time that held the seeds of cooperation, the resolution of conflicts through negotiation, respect for each other, equality, harmonious relationships, and working behind the scenes for peace.

Some of the leftover seeds of the aggressive male-oriented 1 millennium (all those dates began with a "1") remain within the cosmic eggs, within the 0s of the 2000 millennium. The old ideas battle the new; change becomes a battlefield as many refuse to leave their ingrained beliefs behind.

The theme of the 2000 decade was the incubating of seeds—the three zeroes—that would grow in the decades to follow.

The booming growth of the internet in the 2000 decade opened lines of instant global communication around the world.

The seeds of the "selfie" phenomenon ("look at me", number 1) first appeared in 2002, when it was used in an Australian online forum. Flickr used it as a hashtag in 2004. Selfie became widely adopted around 2012, when it became a common term used in mainstream media.

George W. Bush was elected president of the United States on November 7, 2000, after a virtual dead-heat with Al Gore for the presidency. A disputed Florida vote terminated with the Supreme Court of the United States voting in favor of Bush who won in the Electoral College but lost the popular vote. The seeds of conflict in the USA began with this presidential election.

Then . . . on September 11, 2001, nineteen Islamic terrorists from the group al-Qaeda hijacked four commercial planes. Two planes attacked NYC's World Trade Center and brought it down; a third plane crashed into the Pentagon; the fourth plane headed toward Washington, DC, but was brought down prematurely outside of Shanksville, Pennsylvania, by hero passengers on board who attacked the terrorists on the plane.

2,996 people died and 6,000 were injured. It was the worst terrorist attack in United States history. This was an attack on the most powerful nation in the world by a handful of extremists. This event changed the consciousness of the world—and the American people. In response, on October 7, 2001, the United States began the first attack in the war on terrorism in Afghanistan.

In March, 2003, the war in Iraq began with the bombing of Baghdad, and on December 13 of that year, the former leader of Iraq, Saddam Hussein, was captured in a bunker in Tikrit.

On February 3, 2004, the CIA admits that the imminent threat of weapons of mass destruction (WMD) from Iraq that prompted the war was not true.

The seeds for the religious battles were cast. Religious fervor mounted; the world was preparing for fierce battles over ideologies that will rage until we fully embrace the Aquarian Age and realize that we are all one, regardless of our belief systems.

The groundbreaking ceremony for the Freedom Tower at the site of the world Trade Center began on July 4, 2004. And in November, George W. Bush became president for another term defeating John Kerry.

This decade witnessed the first celebration on November 25, 2000, of the International Day for the Elimination of Violence against Women, setting the stage for the 2000 millennium battle of the sexes! And the battle for equality!

January 4, 2007, the first female speaker of the US House of Representatives, Representative Nancy Pelosi of San Francisco, California, is sworn into office.

August 29, 2008, Senator John McCain chose Sarah Palin, governor of Alaska, as his running mate for president of the United States. Another first, this presidential election for the first time included both an African American candidate, Barack Obama, and a woman amongst the presidential and vice presidential nominees for president by the Democratic and Republican Parties.

In 2009, the United States, with its short history of a mere 239 years and with a history of black slavery, elected its first black president. Barack Obama was sworn in as the 44th president.

During this decade, the space age was in full swing. Are we preparing for a literal "Star Wars"?

Tragically, on February 1, 2003, the space shuttle *Columbia* exploded upon reentry over Texas. All seven astronauts inside were killed.

Shenzhou 5 launched on October 15, 2003, was the first human spaceflight mission of the Chinese space program.

NASA's Mars Exploration Rover mission began in 2003 with the launch of two rovers—*MER-A Spirit* and *MER-B Opportunity*—

to explore the Martian surface and geology. Both far outlived their planned missions of 90 Martian solar days.

Deep Impact, a NASA space probe, was launched from Cape Canaveral on January 12, 2005, to study the interior composition of the comet Tempel 1. On July 4, 2005, the Impact successfully collided with the comet's nucleus. Photographs showed the comet was made of more dust and less ice than expected.

NASA's *LCROSS* probe discovered significant amounts of water on the Moon. From accumulated data, *Hubble Ultra-Deep Field* (HUDF) imaged a portion of the constellation Formax to search for galaxies 400 to 800 years after the Big Bang.

On August 24, 2006, on the last day of the International Astronomical Union conference in Prague, a handful of the remaining astronomers voted to demote Pluto to a dwarf planet. "I'm embarrassed for astronomy," said Alan Stern, leader of NASA's New Horizon's mission to Pluto. "Less that 5 percent of the world's astronomers voted."

Astrologers beg to differ: They will tell you about Pluto's life-changing effects on planet Earth through events that occurred around its discovery, as well as Pluto's effects on their own lives and on the lives of their clients.

On April 12, 2009, the Tea Party rose as a result of the increased deficits due to actions such as the bailouts of the banking industry and the car industry.

During the 2000 decade, the internet boomed, highlighting the futuristic technological aspects and global reach of the Age of Aquarius. Personal home computers broke the 1 GHz barrier, increasing the speed billions of cycles per second. USB flash drives replaced floppy disks.

We were introduced to handheld devices such as iPods, iPads, Kindle, and the Nook. On February 22, 2006, the one-billionth song was downloaded from the internet music store Apple iTunes.

In this decade, Facebook was launched, followed by YouTube, then Twitter.

The technological Aquarian Age of global communication and space exploration had begun.

In the 2000 decade, the stage was set for the conflict between the fading number 1 millennium and the future number 2 millennium. The feminine themes of equality and cooperation, negotiations, connections, and harmony were incubating.

With the assertive 1 preceding the dates in this decade (2010–2019), the impetus was action and marching into battle against those resistant forces that were hanging on to the oppressive past. The 1, in this decade of the teens, birthed the need for independence, a time to stand up and be counted, to take action and forge ahead, setting up the drive for a new future. Voices needed to be heard.

On the negative side, these energies resulted in a "me first" attitude. It was a time of "get-out-of-my-way," full steam ahead with no thought of the consequences, all of which resulted in acts of angry violence and destruction.

The major themes that defined the 2010 decade, motivated by the 1 digit are:

1. The courage of women (and men) who stood up against their sexual abusers; their demand for equal rights; the courage of those who fought gender discrimination.
2. The courage of the masses who rose up against their oppressive governments.
3. Terrorism in the name of god; lone wolf violence against the innocent.
4. The battle over health care.
5. The ongoing space and global communications theme.
6. The battle over climate change.

WOMEN REBEL

On October 5, 2017, the *New York Times* published the article "Harvey Weinstein Paid off Sexual Harassment Accusers for Decades." And so began the #MeToo movement. Women weren't going to take it anymore.

It started when a few female actors claimed that Hollywood's most powerful movie mogul, Harvey Weinstein, had sexually abused and coerced them. They claimed that many actors' careers were destroyed by Weinstein when they wouldn't succumb to his sexual demands. His behavior had been overlooked in the industry.

The #MeToo hashtag was used 200,000 times on Twitter in the first day of Weinstein's expose. Within days of this article, more than half a million had the courage to speak out under the #MeToo movement. All over the world, women, and men as well, described what happened to them. "Women wrote about grandfathers, stepfathers, bosses, and neighbors. And pain —pain that would not go away even as the years went by." The MeToo movement moved through Twitter in more than eighty-five countries, spurring offshoots in other languages.

Victims spoke out from the music industry, politics, and the business world. Accusations were also leveled against presidents and high-ranking politicians in supposedly civilized countries.

Another stand for women's rights arose when, in 2015, film star Meryl Streep sent a letter to each member of Congress asking that they finally ratify the Equal Rights Amendment of 1923, which states that no one should be discriminated against because of their sex.

The complete text of the Equal Rights Amendment reads:

Section 1: Equality of rights under the law shall not be denied or abridged by the United States or by any state on account of sex.

Section 2: The Congress shall have the power to enforce, by appropriate legislation, the provisions of this article.

Section 3: This amendment shall take effect two years after the date of ratification.

In order to be added to the Constitution, three-quarters of the states (38) must ratify the amendment. As of May 2018, 37 have ratified the Equal Rights Amendment. The 13 states that have not yet ratified the Amendment are Alabama, Arizona, Arkansas, Florida, Georgia, Louisiana, Mississippi, Missouri, North Carolina, Oklahoma, South Carolina, Utah, and Virginia.

To repeat: Equality of rights under the law shall not be denied or abridged by the United States or by any state on account of sex.

I have to ask: What is the controversy over this simple inclusive statement? This issue is and will continue to boil through 2021.

In January 2019, people across the country fighting for women's rights held marches that focused on the 2020 election. They are also working to make sure everyone qualified has the right to vote.

MAJOR REVELATIONS AND STRIDES IN GENDER CHANGES WERE ALSO IN THE NEWS:

A *Time Magazine* article (November 10, 2011) by Jonathan Berr titled: "Sex Change Surgery Is Now Tax Deductible" highlighted the fact that the Internal Revenue Service wasn't going to fight people who wanted to deduct the cost of surgery for changing their gender.

In 2010, there was a 4-part YouTube Documentary: *Sex Change: A Revealing Journey.*

POPULATIONS REBEL AGAINST OPPRESSIVE GOVERNMENTS

The so-called Arab Spring, a series of anti-government uprisings in various countries in North Africa and the Middle East that began in Tunisia in December 2010 shouted the 2010 decade message loud and clear. Social media was the driving force behind the spread of revolution through the world in response to oppressive regimes. Many countries shut down certain sites such as Facebook or blocked internet services.

The dominoes began to fall in Tunisia where President Zine El Abidine Ben Ali and his government were overthrown; then to Egypt where President Hosni Mubarak and his government were overthrown; then on to Libya where Muammar Gaddafi was killed and his government fell, and then to Yemen where President Ali Abdullah Saleh was ousted; from there to Syria where President Bashar al-Assad faced civil war; to a crushed uprising in Bahrain, and to governmental changes in Kuwait, Lebanon, and Oman, and reforms in Morocco and Jordan, along with protests in Saudi Arabia, Sudan, and other Arab countries.

May 2, 2011, Osama Bin Laden was killed at his hideout in Pakistan after a 10-year pursuit by US Navy Seals. As the leader of the terrorist group Al-Queda, he was the mastermind of the 9/11 attacks in 2011 on the World Trade Center and the Pentagon.

VIOLENCE BY RELIGIOUS FACTIONS AND LONE WOLVES

We saw the rise of ISIS, the blood-thirsty terror group attempting to create an Islamic state, using murder and the spectacle of public beheadings. Former British Prime Minister David Cameron said ISIS must be destroyed at its core, because they are out to destroy the west "because of who we are and not what we do."

The violence in the Middle East caused a refugee crisis of enormous proportions.

A wave of bombings and violence (the number 1) increased during this decade: from the terrorist bombing of the 2013 Boston Marathon to an Islamic terrorist shooting at a holiday celebration in San Bernadino to brutal attacks against citizens in Paris to attacks in Orlando, Florida, with 50 killed and 53 injured, to lone gunmen shooting up grade schools, malls, universities, markets, places of worship, theaters, and celebrations, and in mosques and synagogues. These attacks are fueled by the continual rise of ISIS in Syria, Iraq, and other countries around the world and by one or two crazed or racist individuals.

In the United States, cell phone videos appear almost weekly revealing police brutality, which causes even more violence. The majority of the police force carry out their duties admirably every day protecting their communities, but because of a few bad apples, they have to face the backlash from this scrutiny.

HEALTH CARE BATTLE

On March 25, 2010, the US Affordable Care Act, coined Obamacare, passed in the House of Representatives, which finalized the legislation approved by the Senate, extending health benefits and insurance to most Americans.

The Affordable Care Act set up a long-term fight in Congress, with Republicans attempting to repeal or modify the act over seventy times.

On January 1, 2014, the Affordable Care Act, Obamacare, went into affect for millions of Americans. Over 7.3 million joined the system.

On November 6, 2012, Barack Obama wins a second term as president of the United States.

SPACE AND GLOBAL COMMUNICATIONS EXPANSION

Curiously, the movie *Star Wars*, which debuted in 1977, released its 6th episode titled *Star Wars: The Force Awakens*, in December 2015. Number 1 is a number of "force." At that point, the film grossed over 936 million, beating the film *Avatar* whose gross sales were 760 million. The consciousness of the world is tuned into the Age of Aquarius.

Under Note in *The Week* magazine, May 11, 2019: "The US Navy is drafting new, formal guidelines for its pilots to report unidentified flying objects. The move comes in response to a number of such sightings by pilots, including one in 2004 . . . in which Navy jets were outmaneuvered by extremely fast UFOs."

On March 28, 2019, Walt Disney Co. announced that starting May 1, all parks will ban smoking, vaping, and large strollers. The restriction is more in preparation for the crowds that are expected at the new *Star Wars* exhibit.

The internet, although wonderful in some respects, carries seeds of discontent. In April 2018, Facebook founder Mark Zuckerberg answered a congressional inquiry into why 87 million customers had their private information breached by an outside British political consulting firm. By July 2018, Facebook had dropped 20 percent, losing $109 billion.

CLIMATE CHANGE BATTLE

Reported on June 11, 2019, 8,600 square miles of dead zone off the Louisiana coastline are the result of the flooding of farm lands loaded with chemical fertilizers. The dead zone is devoid of oxygen and kills all marine life.

200 counties met at the United Nations Climate Change Conference in Paris from November 30 to December 12, 2015, their objective to achieve a universal agreement from all nations to reduce the toxic emissions that are suffocating our planet. Donald Trump is elected president of the United States in November 2016. On June 1, 2017, the United States withdraws from the Paris Climate Agreement.

"Melting small glaciers could add 10 inches to sea levels."[21]

A recent news report warned that a dangerous flesh-eating bacterium was on the rise at some popular East Coast beaches in the United States due to warmer water temperatures.

The war rages over the health of this planet as more and more scientists warn of cataclysmic events on planet Earth from unusual weather patterns, floods, fire, heat waves, and more if the environment isn't cleaned up.

OTHER 2010 DECADE EVENTS OF NOTE

- After a ten-year-long mission, the *Rosetta* space probe landed on a comet (67P/Churyumov-Gerasimenko), prompting European Union science chief Anne Glover to tweet: "I think Europe just boldly went where no one else has gone before."
- The devastating 8.9 earthquake in Japan on March 13, 2011, near the Fukushima Daiichi Nuclear Power Plant, caused the largest nuclear disaster since Chernobyl in 1986.
- Unheard of in the history of the Catholic Church, Pope Benedict XVI retired. The humble Pope Francis took his place and has initiated surprising changes regarding the laws of the church. Exposes of sex abuses in the clergy continue.
- Julian Assange and Edward Snowden leaked sensitive information into the public domain.
- The new age money exchange, bitcoin, entered the news.
- Yahoo bought the blogging service Tumblr for 1 billion in cash, the largest acquisition of a social networking company, surpassing Facebook's purchase of Instagram the previous year.
- Apple CEO, Steve Jobs, died.
- In 2015, the United States and Cuba announced openings of their embassies after fifty-four years.

EVENTS UP TO JUNE 2019

It is the spring of 2019 as I update this section and prepare to submit this to my publisher. As the last year in this decade, the 9 of 2019 indicates a cycle of endings in preparation for the 2020 decade. The events of this year so far:

- On December 22, 2018, there was a partial government shutdown after President Trump refused to sign any spending package for Homeland Security that does not include border barrier funding to prevent illegal immigration and to boost border security. This thirty-five-day shutdown was the longest in US history.
- Abortion has become a major issue as abortion clinics begin to shut down across the United States. In the 2020 decade, women will begin to rise up to support Roe vs. Wade. Women's rights on all fronts will be a big issue. In the last century, the 1920 decade, women's rights were also an issue with the ratification of the 19th Amendment, granting women the right to vote.
- Immigration becomes a major issue in the 2020 decade as it was in the 1920 decade.
- On March 22, Robert Mueller delivered his report regarding investigations into the allegations about the Trump-Russia collusion.

***

It may be that now, on the brink of the 2020 decade, we've had enough of the negative side of the testosterone fueled, aggressive, stomp-on-the-enemy, win-at-all-costs, narcissistic number 1 energy of these past ten years.

The Middle East still boils with the unreleased sexual energy of young men who have no jobs, no future, no sex, and are even denied the visual pleasure of looking at unclad women. This repressed sexual energy erupts into the violence we have seen in these last ten years in that part of the world. No wonder their idea of paradise is virgins, gardens, and plenty to eat, which satisfies the sensual pleasures that they have been denied here on earth.

One commentator quipped that what the Middle East needs is an army of prostitutes. The ancients knew this. They had temple prostitutes who would lend a comforting ear and a warm embrace to those men who had no relationships, thus draining the frustration that would have led to violence in their communities.

The upcoming 2s of the 2020 decade refer to sexual unions, the mating of the Yin and the Yang.

We saw the stirring of the 2 millennium when, in 2011, a news release tells of the women of a Filipino village who withheld sex to end village infighting. Within a week, the women brought peace to their villages.

This is not something new.

In a comedy written by Aristophanes in 411 BCE, Lysistrata persuades the women of Greece to deny sex to their men to force an end to the Peloponnesian War.

Director Spike Lee took up Aristophane's Greek comedy with his 2015 musical crime drama film *Chi-Raq,* starring Nick Cannon, Wesley Snipes, Jennifer Hudson, Angela Bassett, John Cusack, and Samuel L. Jackson. The film is set in Chicago's South Side where the women band together to deny the men sex until they stop fighting and killing each other. Their slogan: No Peace, No Pussy. *Chi-Raq* was called Spike Lee's best film in ten years.

These events foretell some of the themes of the incoming 2020 decade.

***

Harvard cognitive scientist, Steve Pinker, in his 2011 book, *Why Violence Has Declined: The Better Nature of Our Angels*, states that the intelligence IQ is better now than it has ever been and that the world is becoming "one big village." His 800-page book is sprinkled with graphs that prove violence overall is declining.

His view may appear to be seen through rose-colored-glasses, however; with 24-hour news cycles, we see and hear more about violence now than we did fifty years ago, when there was one news program for one-half hour each day. Perhaps he is correct in that we are in a millennium that is ruled by the 2, peace and partnerships.

So, my friends, in the 1979 version of this book I made predictions for the 1980 decade based on what the number 8 had to say. In this 2nd edition, by turning back to pp. 201–208, you can discover whether my predictions made back then—based upon the influence of the 8—were "thumbs-up" or "thumbs-down" or even "thumbs-horizontal."

In this edition, I have analyzed the 2020 decade to discover what these ten years have in store for us through the language of the numbers. I have no crystal ball to see into the future; I rely on messages from the numbers to assess what the future holds.

This manuscript goes to my publisher June 2019, at which time it will be out of my hands, and on its way to the printed page for the world to see.

Yikes! Will my predictions for this time frame be "thumbs-up" or "thumbs-down" or even "thumbs-horizontal"

SECTION 4
2020-2029: A DECADE
OF PRIVACY DUE TO BURNOUT

. . . .

This coming decade brings double 2s to our calendar (2020, 2021, 2022, 2023, etc.), a ten-year period of making connections, mediating, and making peace "or war." The 2 understands that, after the assertive energy of the 1s, it is essential to take that creative seed and put it to use, a time to step back and settle down so that discussions can take place in calm settings in order to support life on all levels. This frame of mind is necessary to achieve a balanced period of peace among the previously "1" single-minded warring elements.

In this decade, the number 2 is doubled every time we write the years' dates: 2020, 2021, 2023, 2022, etc. We should pay special attention to the year 2022 when there are three 2s in the year's date.

A thought popped into my mind while I was contemplating this chapter. I decided to look back at the 1920 decade to see if there was any correlation to what might be happening now. However, that decade had just the single 2 preceding the dates.

1910-1920:

After World War I, which occurred in the 1910–1919 decade, America entered the 1920s decade. As written in the previous section in this book on the 1920s decade (page 183), "America was tired . . . which resulted in the rejection of the aggressive Woodrow Wilson and the election of the gentle, lovable Warren G. Harding who proclaimed . . . 'America's present need is not heroics but healing. . . .'"

That election pitted the "aggressive Woodrow Wilson" (the 1) against the "gentle lovable Warren G. Harding (the 2).

Harding was psychically tuned in when he said that America needed "healing, not heroics." That quote was a perfect description of the change from the heroic aggressive 1 of the 2010–2019 decade to the healing cooperative 2 energy of the 1920s.

PRESENT DAY:

Does this shift from the 2010 decade to the 2020 decade bring about "not heroics but healing"? In the November 2020 presidential election in the USA, will there be a changing of the guard to a gentler more civil atmosphere in the White House and in the world in general?

1920:

As we entered the 1920 decade, the 18th Amendment had just been ratified which prohibited the sale of alcohol anywhere in the United States. This drove people underground (2, behind the scenes) into speakeasies during the twenties. This continued until 1933, when the 21st Amendment to the Constitution ended national Prohibition. (Some states held on to the temperance laws. The last dry state, Mississippi, ended Prohibition in 1966.)

The 19th Amendment is ratified, granting women the right to vote (2, balance, partnerships).

In 1921, Congress passed immigration restrictions, targeted at "undesirables" from southern and eastern Europe (the number 2, "me vs. you").

PRESENT DAY:

I found some correlations between what I see coming up in the 2020s and those activities in the 1920s, especially the public move back then to having fun behind closed doors (2) with the underground speakeasies, and the demand for equality with women's right, and the focus on immigration.

So, women's rights and immigration are themes once again but they are here to stay for the millennium. The question is: Will we be driven to take actions behind the scenes, out of the public eye, and be forced to go underground during this decade?

The 2020 decade comes with warnings and well as welcomes.

ON THE POSITIVE SIDE:

The 2 is the peacemaker who is sensitive and caring, who sees the good that can be, and who is willing to work behind the scenes to create harmonious relationships. The 2 seeks a gentler touch: cooperation, negotiation, working in partnerships for mutual benefit, using intuition and understanding of both sides to bring about balance and peaceful solutions.

Once again, the 2s power behind the throne reminds me of a pregnant woman's T-shirt upon which are printed the words "Under Construction" in bold letters with a large arrow pointing down.

POSITIVE 2 CASE IN POINT:

I believe that one of the books that may help define this decade is the one that will be written by 32-year-old Mary Latham, who began her 50-state journey in her mother's old Subaru on October 29, 2016. Her journey is in honor of her mother's death; her mom taught her there is far more good than tragedy in the world. (See moregood.today.)

During her road trip, she found herself the recipient of kindnesses: gas cards and glasses of wine and delicious meals; once a $550 repair bill on her car was already paid when she went to pick up her car. As of this writing in the spring of 2019, she plans to collect these acts of kindness for a book, which she will donate to hospital waiting rooms. Her actions speak loudly and clearly through the 2 energies that define this decade (and millennium).

This is the decade of the woman. All one has to do is check online for published books and films in these last few years that are finally recognizing women's contributions to history—their bravery and brilliance and determination and guts.

ON THE NEGATIVE SIDE:

The 2 can also raise deeply buried, previously unexpressed, desires, fears, hatreds, and prejudices that need to be addressed, the "me vs. you" scenario.

THE 2020s BURNOUT:
DEEPFAKE, FACEBOOK, RANSOMWARE, ROBOCALLS, POLITICS, SEX, AND A DIS-COVERY THAT CAN CHANGE THE WORLD

Definition of burnout: "a psychological term that refers to long-term exhaustion resulting from sustained pressure causing a loss of interest."

The invasion of privacy and the mining of personal data for public display will drive many away from the internet and social media platforms.

Two of the warning signs in the 2020s involve Deepfake and Facebook. Through the internet, these platforms have swept around the world wherein lies and doctored videos are repeated to the point where no one knows who or what to believe. And then again, some people will only believe their side of the equation thus driving the divisive wedge deeper between groups.

We will get tired of this rhetoric from 24-hour news programs and social media and will want to retreat into our own quiet worlds in order to protect our privacy and possibly save our relationships, careers, reputations, and sanity.

DEEPFAKE:

Deepfake could be the most dangerous sign post on the road into the 2020s. We have entered a decade where "seeing is not believing"!

Deepfake is the name of an anonymous programmer who, in 2017, created an algorithm that allows people to combine images of people (and animals) doing and saying things they have never done or said. This artificial intelligence-based technology alters video content so that it presents something that did not happen.

The Deepfake app allows the user to synthesize human images. For instance, a famous politician's face can be placed on another person's body who is engaged in illegal or sexual activity so that it seems the politician is actually performing the acts. Animals can also be synthesized into the action. Through using unsuspecting people in fake situations, the world can be manipulated into believing news that could ultimately change history, not to say what it could do to personal relationships and reputations and businesses through false postings.

Samsung Deepfake AI could fabricate a video clip of you from a single profile picture.[22]

This has already begun with altered videos that have been posted online showing politicians slurring their words or speaking incoherently or, through slicing words into sentences, saying things they never said.

We may turn off the road of social media and 24-hour news programs, away from the public EYE, from Big Brother, and onto quiet hidden lanes where privacy is our only protection.

I wrote about the number of the beast, 666, in chapter 7, p. 138. You might want to reread that section because the beast in the Bible's chapter of Revelation can be connected to the computer, which is the vehicle that serves as the conduit for information around the world. Has Deepfake, through the computer's internet, become the destroyer of worlds?

Seeing is not believing anymore! Think twice before reacting to or believing what you see on any news programs or on social platforms.

FACEBOOK:

I believe the Facebook generation has become the FaceBound generation.

The 2020 decade is here to loosen this tangled web and free people to interact with one another in person, in face-to-face meetings, because platforms such as Facebook have opened the door to the minutia of our lives and created constant texting. Yet this slavish attachment to Facebook has also created feelings of isolation. Some hide behind the internet and bully others for any number of reasons, driving some younger people to acts of desperation.

We begin to yearn for the personal—the idea of touching another human, a comforting hand on the shoulder, a warm hug when needed, the look in their eyes, the smell of their perfume, the innate understanding of another's emotional state that comes from observing their facial expressions and body language—these personal attributes cannot be replaced with impersonal internet contact.

RANSOMWARE:

Ransomware is "a type of malware that restricts access to the infected computer system in some way and demands that the user pay a ransom to the malware operators to remove the restriction."

For example: On May 7, 2019, the Baltimore Budget Office was hit by ransomware, which took over the city's computer network. The demand was $18 million. Budget director Bob Cenname estimated that cost would not include nearly $5 million that the municipal office had already spent. Some city workers' emails have been restored. Just over a year ago, similar ransomware attack hit Baltimore's 911 dispatch system.[23]

June 21, 2019, the city of Tallahassee agreed to pay $600,000 in ransom to hackers who took over the city's computers, the latest in thousands of attacks worldwide aimed at extorting money from governments.

ROBOCALLS:

Robocalls are telephone calls that are delivered through recorded messages repeatedly day after day.

Messages like "Hello, this is Jason from Be Safe At Home" or "Your iCloud has been breached," to "Because you have paid your electric bill on time, you are eligible . . . " are a constant harassment, occurring every day and sometimes into the early morning hours. And they're dangerous, tying up telephones lines during emergencies.

Americans were assaulted with an astounding 48 billion robocalls in 2018, and this number was expected to be as high as 75 billion in 2019. Robocalls are one of the most complained-about issues in the United States at this time.

On April 30, 2019, California Representative Anna Eschoo and Oregon Senator Jeff Merkley introduced new legislation, H. R. 2355, the Regulatory Oversight Barring Obnoxious (ROBO) Calls and Texts Act, which sets up communication between the government and the communications industry to comply with federal laws regarding public safety to combat robocalls.

Because of Deepfake, Facebook, ransomware, and robocalls, Congress will be called upon to enforce stricter laws against such platforms.

POLITICS:

Politics has become a dirty word in the United States of America. You can't turn on the television or check the news any day without one political party railing against the other in the surety that they are right. Each side is unwilling to listen to the other side. Politics has drawn battle lines, not in the sand, but in the hardening cement.

In this country, politics have devolved into school yard bullying and name calling. The system has become so splintered that people are turning away from the anger, name-calling, and lying that has swept through Twitter and news programs. There are people so set in their beliefs that there is no talking to them. There are also people who no longer know who or what to believe and are frustrated at the lack of moral leadership by their elected leaders.

In May 2019, John Cornyn, Republican senator from Texas, said: "We got into this paradigm or game where it's a zero-sum operation, where somebody has to win and somebody has to lose, and that's not conducive to compromise."

On the other side of the equation, former Democratic Vice-President Joe Biden "believes in working with Republicans. He says on the stump that Trump is an 'aberration' and predicts that if the president is defeated, Republicans will work toward bipartisan reform, which Biden insists is the only way to get anything worthwhile done. 'This nation cannot function without generating consensus,' he recently said in New Hampshire."[24]

Repeating the mood of the country prior to the 1920 decade: "America was tired . . . which resulted in the rejection of the aggressive Woodrow Wilson and the election of the gentle, lovable Warren G. Harding who proclaimed . . . 'America's present need is not heroics but healing. . . .'"

If this coming presidential election has any parallel to that 1920 decade where the voters rejected an aggressive candidate for the gentler candidate because they desired a healing, will the voters in this upcoming 2020 election reject the present aggressive president in favor of a gentler candidate who wants to heal the divisive wounds of the country?

All those 2s in the 2020 decade suggest a need for compromise and a pulling back for the aggressive 1s.

For every action, there is an equal and opposite reaction. To maintain balance in life, the law of nature dictates this eternal swing from active to the reactive. The language of numbers supports this law. The active 1 is balanced by the reactive 2; the reactive 2 is balanced by the active 3. And so it goes.

I believe that we will elect a new president in 2020 who will reflect the reactive 2, a person whose goal is to heal the nation.

SEX:

Sex comes under the influence of the 2 because this number encourages people to join together, to reach out to one another in search of comfort and loving relationships; it's nature seeking balance. However, when one side is out of balance, battles ensue.

The fierce debate over abortion will increase with one side citing their religious views of the sanctity of life while, in some cases, ironically approving the death penalty, while the other side demands that women have control over their own bodies. This is an issue for the 2020 decade; however, the year 2022 may bring this to a head because of the three 2s in that year. Will restrictions cause women to go underground (2) to find those who will perform abortions?

Will stricter laws in the 2020s affect Roe vs. Wade? Will stricter laws affect the rights of the LGBT communities? Will these issues bring out the "me vs. you" downside of the 2?

Another major issue is equality in the workplace where each individual is paid for the work they do and not for the sexual organs they possess.

And, of course, there is the need to ratify the Equal Rights Amendment after 100 years!

***

2025-2033

A NEW DISCOVERY THAT CAN CHANGE THE WORLD: THREE MAJOR EVENTS

Recently, I discovered an eighty-four-year repeating cycle that could change the world!

This section should be read and seriously pondered. It is said that history repeats itself. However, if we know history, then we have choices over how it will evolve.

I would like to introduce you to a vital seven-year period that occurs once every eighty-four years.

In 2017, I discovered there are three major events that occur once every eighty-four years. These three events occur within a seven-year time span and they have global effects.

Astrologers are aware of the eighty-four-year cycle which began with the discovery of the planet Uranus in 1781 in the sign Gemini. This planet of revolution, freedom, and invention takes eighty-four years to circle the solar system once.

What is not known is that: Every time Uranus returns to the sign Gemini, in which it was discovered, three major events have occurred that changed the world.

The three events are:

1. A major clash between ideologies
2. A major document
3. A life-changing invention involving communication

I bring this up now because the next such cycle will occur from July 2025 to May 2033.

I gave this lecture to our local astrological group in 2017. I remember one member of the audience coming up to me after the lecture and expressing his amazement at the information presented. He said he had never heard anyone mention this cycle before, and he recognized the importance of preparing for the next one which begins in 2025.

As he said, and as we have all heard and read over the years, "If we don't know history, we are doomed to repeat it."

So, let's start with the first in this cycle's series. Uranus was in Gemini from 1774–1781.

THE FIRST SEVEN-YEAR CYCLE: 1774-1781

1. CLASH BETWEEN IDEOLOGIES
1775–1783: The American Revolution
A small band of ill-equipped colonists in the American colonies rose up against Great Britain and the might of King George III of England and won their independence from the absolute rule of the monarchy to create a new nation based upon personal liberties.

2. MAJOR DOCUMENT
1776: The Declaration of Independence
On July 2, 1776, independence was declared, and on July 4, 1776,

Congress approved this unique document, which created a republic based upon the rule of law. John Adams declared it "the most memorable epoch in the history of America."

3. LIFE-CHANGING INVENTION INVOLVING COMMUNICATION

1773–1775: The steam engine created the Industrial Revolution
James Watt invented a steam engine with efficiency greater than that of the other steam engines then in use. This new steam engine helped to power the Industrial Revolution, changing the world from agrarian and handcrafted work to city work and work dominated by machines. Transportation was one of the beneficiaries of steam-powered locomotives and eventually steam-powered ships. Goods were transported over land, and eventually sea, by something other than man or animal power. Communication over land and sea expanded globally.

THE SECOND SEVEN-YEAR CYCLE: 1858–1866

1. CLASH BETWEEN IDEOLOGIES

1861–1865: The Civil War
The Civil War was fought in the United States between the North and the South over issues of slavery and states versus federal rights. This bloody battle pitted the Union Army against the Confederate States of America, killing more than 600,000 Americans and leaving the South in ruins.

2. MAJOR DOCUMENT

1863: Emancipation Proclamation
Lincoln's 1863 Emancipation Proclamation freed about 20,000 slaves in Confederate-held territory, and established emancipation as the goal of the Union War. In 1865, Lincoln helped pass the Thirteenth Amendment, which made slavery unconstitutional.

3. LIFE-CHANGING INVENTION INVOLVING COMMUNICATION

1860: The telephone
History has credited Alexander Graham Bell with the invention of the telephone in 1876. However, in 1860, Antonio Meucci, an Italian inventor, developed a voice-communication apparatus that sources credit as the first telephone, a device through which your voice could travel around the world in seconds.

THE THIRD SEVEN-YEAR CYCLE: 1941-1949

1. CLASH BETWEEN IDEOLOGIES
1939–1945: The Second World War

On December 8, 1941, the United States declared war on Japan, thus entering WWII. Adolph Hitler, with his ideology of the superiority of the white Aryan race, carried out mass executions of the Jewish people. This group also included gypsies and "undesirables."

2. MAJOR DOCUMENT
There were two documents:

1947: The United Nations Partition Resolution
This resolution divided Palestine into a Jewish and an Arab state, the two-state solution.

This resolution hasn't resolved the problem between the Jews and the Arabs. Arabs, who are a race of people, mostly Muslims; Muslims are followers of the religion of Islam. Obviously there is a major conflict simmering here between ideologies.

1949: The Council of Europe

In 1946, Winston Churchill, Prime Minister of England, said that Europe needed to create a sort of United States of Europe. In 1949, the Council of Europe united many European counties that had endured centuries of fighting. This council brought peace amongst these nations and was the precursor of the European Union.

3. LIFE-CHANGING INVENTION INVOLVING COMMUNICATION

There were two inventions:

1946: The ENIAC

In the late thirties, mathematician and cryptologist Alan Turing solved the Enigma code that the Germans used during WWII. He called his invention the "universal machine." His machine evolved into the ENIAC, the electronic and numerical integrator and calculator, a computer built by J. Presper Eckert and John Mauchly between 1943 and 1946. This computer took up a room 20 feet by 40 feet!

You hold this machine in your hand today. It's your digital cell phone!

1945: The Atomic Bomb

On July, 16, 1945, as scientists, Army personnel, and technicians wearing special goggles watched the beginning of the Atomic Age, the first atomic bomb was dropped at the trinity site near Alamogordo, New Mexico. There was a forceful flash, a wave of heat, a huge shock, and a mushroom cloud that extended 40,000 feet into the sky. This invention sent a warning message to the people around the world that humans now had the capacity to destroy each other.

THE FOURTH SEVEN-YEAR CYCLE: 2025–2033

1. CLASH BETWEEN IDEOLOGIES

In the last three cycles, we saw: the American Revolution, where the colonists rebelled against the most powerful nation on earth at that time, ruled by King George, and created a new nation based on the individual's rights; the American Civil War, which pitted the industrial North against the agrarian South and slavery; and the horrors of World War II, where mass eliminations of the Jews, the Gypsies (of Egyptian origin, "gypsy" means traveler), and "undesirables" were carried out by Hitler's pure Aryan race ideology and the establishment of a two-state solution, which to this day holds the seeds of discontent between two religious factions.

First, the USA should tread lightly in internal struggles. With the political situation in the United States so divisive today, where there seems to be no way to bring the two sides together, and hateful rhetoric fuels troublemakers, are we in for another internal revolution? There are those who feel the republic of the United States is in danger.

Secondly, we should step lightly into foreign affairs as well.

Globally, with people fleeing their war-torn homelands, the world has witnessed immigration problems of massive proportions. As cultures merge and are not assimilated, resentments arise. We are witnessing daily violence from terrorists from one ideological group against those with differing views.

Religion plays a large part in this dangerous situation. Will religious differences and fundamentalist attacks on sacred spaces spark a massive confrontation?

Religion is meant to connect people with their spiritual source; government is meant to protect all members of the society through a set of fair and just rules. They are two different "governing" bodies.

As the maxim goes: "never the twain shall meet." This maxim suggests that two things are too different to coexist. Certainly, religion and government can coexist as long as people respect the religious beliefs of others and as long as those religious beliefs don't involve violence against or dominance over others.

We also have to be aware of power-hungry dictators who can never get enough power and land over which to dominate.

Cultural differences, including religion, can escalate into war. The last three cycles have shown us major wars.

With the internet able to spread news instantly around this world and to gather people under one cause, we should take heed from George Santayana who wrote: "Those who cannot remember the past are condemned to repeat it."

We should set about to change our current direction toward conflict and turn our eyes and efforts toward more civil discourse and open the lines of communication between countries and groups so we can listen to both sides with respect. This requires each side to do so.

2: MAJOR DOCUMENT

In the past three cycles, we have seen the Declaration of Independence that gave each individual the right to vote, the Emancipation Proclamation that freed a race from slavery, and the United Nations Partition Resolution that gave a people a country.

These were life changing documents to say the least.

With the clashes between religions today on the global front, will a document arise that will truly broker a peace and understanding between religions and/or cultural differences? Will a document be written that will help solve the problems of world wide immigration?

If indeed we are to experience a massive confrontation over ideologies, a major document will address those beliefs.

3. LIFE-CHANGING INVENTION INVOLVING COMMUNICATION

In the past three cycles, we witnessed the invention of the steam engine and the Industrial Revolution, which changed travel and communication from foot, horseback, and wagon, and the invention of the telephone, and finally the birth of the digital phone you hold in your hand today.

What life-changing invention will we see in this decade? From past inventions, the theme seems to be the evolution of increasing global communication. One wonders how much more global communication can expand.

Perhaps this decade we will witness interstellar communication.

The June 14, 2019, issue of *The Week* magazine arrived at my home, and on the cover, the blurb in bold letters reads: "Taking UFOs Seriously." Depicted is an airborne Navy pilot flying in the foreground while hovering above and a bit behind is a circular craft with pulsing colored lights "piloted" by two little green figures, one of whom is waving.

The inside article says, "UFOs: Why the military isn't scoffing anymore. After decades of blaming weather balloons, bird clusters, and odd cloud formations, the U.S. military is finally taking UFOs seriously . . . In December [2018], the Pentagon acknowledged it has been studying them through the 'shadowy, little-known Advanced Aerospace Threat Identification Program (AATIP) that was formed in 2007.'" They now want their pilots to report encounters. Already pilots are doing just that. The Advanced Aerospace Threat Identification Program (AATIP) was formed in 2007, a group who has been seriously studying encounters that professional pilots have had with unidentified flying objects (UFOs).

Historical religious literature writes of flying objects with spinning wheels and lights, and carvings of what looks like human-type figures clad in space suits adorn ancient buildings.

In this decade, will more come to light about communication between us and "someone" out there?

Perhaps SETI will be taking calls.

Interstellar Communications: SETI

SETI is the Search for Extraterrestrial Intelligence.

Is interstellar communication on the radar, to use a pun?

Interstellar communication will involve the universal language of numbers!

There are those who persist in believing there is intelligent life in the universe, a universe which is composed of billions of stars in billions of galaxies. Given that number, the odds are astronomical that there are other intelligent life forms out there.

The search has been going on for many years. For instance, on November 16, 1974, SETI in Arecebo, Puerto Rico, sent a message from the largest radio telescope at that time toward the globular star cluster M13 some 25,000 light years away.

The first line of the message in binary code was the number 1 through 10!

This was followed by the atomic number of the elements that make up the human body; then the makeup of our DNA. Also, depicted was as simplistic figure of a human along with the layout of our solar system. This was all done in the binary code of zeroes and ones.

Now, how about another idea that would revolutionize communication on our planet?

Teleportation

Teleportation is described as "the theoretical transfer of matter or energy from one point to another without traversing the physical space between them." It's a common theme in science fiction literature and film.

Surely we all remember the TV series *Star Trek* from 1966, starring Captain James T. Kirk and his crew aboard the USS *Enterprise*, a series that takes place in the twenty-third century, and the phrase, "Beam me up, Scotty." The ship carried a "transporter," a translucent tube into which a crew member stepped whereupon his body was dematerialized and reassembled in a given distant destination.

You might want to read the May 29, 2014, article: "Scientists Achieve Reliable Quantum Teleportation for the First Time," by Nick Statt.[25]

More expanded communication possibilities here on Earth.

The Internet

The internet got its start more than fifty years ago and was subsequently used for government purposes such as a Cold War weapon. Prior to that, scientists and researchers used it to communicate and share data with one another. Today, it would be impossible to imagine life without it.

In 1989, computer scientist Tim Berners-Lee, while at the European Organization for Nuclear Research (CERN), invented the worldwide web (www) which was designed as an internet-based platform for sharing global information. Recently (2019), he warned that the end of the internet may be near because it has been "hijacked by crooks."[26]

The following items describe areas that can see tremendous growth, but will they be life changing to the extent that the steam engine, telephone, and the digital phone changed the world? And can they match communication with "little green aliens"?

5G Network

5G, or 5th generation, greatly increases the speed and responses of wireless networks; it's the latest cellular technology, 1000x faster than the 4G network currently in use. It uses the troposphere whereas 4G waves use the stratosphere. It allows for faster speed and data capacity that opens up endless possibilities.

A recent link on the web read: "7 Possibilities of 5G Network That Will Change the World." See the link to read this story.[27]

Artificial Intelligence

Artificial intelligence (AI), or machine intelligence, is in contrast to human or animal intelligence. It describes machines that mimic human minds by learning and problem solving.

Robots

Can AI evolve into shades of *The Terminator* as depicted in the film starring Arnold Schwarzenegger?

Today robots are used for many purposes: marine and space missions, welding, handling chemicals, mowing lawns, and vacuuming floors. Recently, Robot Ducks are seen as the future of rice farming. This little device called a "roomba for grains" keeps Japanese rice paddy fields clear of weeds. Robots are found in the manufacturing and automobile industry. Some are used in hazardous environments. ASIMO (Advanced Step in Innovative Mobility) designed by Honda helps the elderly and disabled. ASIMO also helps in combating fire and disarming bombs.

Can or will robots eventually become more intelligent by taking on human thought processes? We might look to science fiction literature to delve into the futuristic writers' minds.

As an extension of robots, check out robotics at https://phys.org/technology-news/robotics/.

***

Who could have thought back in 1860 that the invention of the telephone would morph into what it is today? That in 2019 we could hold in our hand a device that transmits moving pictures and our words and voices and our faces around this planet instantaneously?

And who would have thought that the fantastical subjects of films and books over the centuries might come true when we communicate with beings beyond our planet.

And before you scoff at the idea of alien life in outer space, let me share an exchange that took place between John Daly, a friend of the family, and his mother. She asked him if he thought there was life in outer space.

His response was, "What do you think we are?"

[Pause—are you thinking?]

I think this was the greatest comeback ever! No more needs to be said.

What else could possibly be on the horizon in this decade that will change the way we communicate? We will have to wait and see. How exciting!

PART V·
ENCYCLOPEDIA
OF KNOWLEDGE

CHAPTER 12

THE MEANING OF THE NUMBERS 1 THROUGH 9 AND THE MASTER NUMBERS 11 THROUGH 99

THIS CHAPTER EXPLAINS THE MEANING OF THE numbers 1 though 9, and the master numbers 11, 22, 33, and 44. Plus, here you will also find descriptions of the master numbers 55 through 99, which I mentioned in passing in the original version of this book.

Because this is a book on the predictive power of numbers, the meanings in this section have been written as temporary and changing experiences. You can apply them to your personal year cycles and period numbers and personal months, and any cycle you experience.

When applying these descriptions to your birth pattern numbers, simply translate them into permanent vibrations in your life.

Back when dinosaurs ruled the earth . . . well, not *that* far back . . . I was taught that there were three master numbers: 11, 22, and 33, and possibly a fourth number, the 44.

Back when the rules about numbers were stricter . . . late at night, when the house was quiet and the kids were tucked in their beds, I snuggled in my bed with a notebook and pen, under a small circle of light from the goose-neck lamp on my bedside, with my husband snoring softly beside me. Sounds like the beginning of a Christmas story, but for me, in a way it was, because it was a magical time under the shadows of night when the world was my own, when I could wander the circuitous paths of my mind.

So, I began thinking about the master numbers. Here's how I wrote them out:

11	22	33	44					
1	2	3	4	5	6	7	8	9

I asked myself why there were only three, maybe four. It was obvious every number can be written twice, thus making it a master number. Then the layout would look like this:

55/10/1	11/2	66/12/3	22/4	77/14/5	33/6	88/16/7	44/8	99/18/9
1	2	3	4	5	6	7	8	9

This would give every one of the nine numbers a master number.

You can't ignore the numbers. If you find a number that is repeated—44, 55, 66, etc.—it will work twice as hard as the single number. Its energy is doubled and intensified. This makes it a master number.

When you encounter identical twins, you take notice. Something inside you stirs at the wonder of two human beings who look so much alike that you can't tell them apart. It awakens the mystery of the birth process and of life itself. You wonder what it would be like to have another "you" staring back at you; what it would be like to see a reflection of yourself moving and acting independently of you.

The master numbers are neither positive nor negative; they just are. But they will be noticed. They require more of you because you have double the resources to produce and double the resources to make an impact than if the number were single. You are given the opportunity to control the use of these energies, to make sure you provide a service to others through their particular meanings. It is not wise to use them for your own gain.

We are on the brink of this Aquarian Age, which will last 2,160 years, an age that demands freedom of thought, new ideas and inventions, and new forms of communication. Obviously this has already started.

We've gone from walking on the ground to walking on the Moon; from pony express to e-mail; from talking over the fence with a neighbor to speaking to someone half way around the world; from horse and carriage to rockets into space; all within the span of about 100 years.

We build upon the past and those who came before us. The practice of numerology is no exception. Master numbers are already being used; they are agents of change. The double energy urges the individual to intensify the expression of those specific qualities.

I have included definitions of the master numbers 44 though 99 here. As I wrote earlier . . . double the energy, double the fun.

Think about the master numbers 44 through 99, and add your analyses to these numbers. Perhaps you will discover new ways of thinking that will open your world. Do keep in mind that the master numbers belong to the family number to which they reduce, and those single numbers are the basis and support of the Master Numbers.

I have included the first nine keys from the Rider-Waite Tarot Deck. Meditation upon these keys can unlock deeper insight into the meaning of the numbers.

Because this is a book on the predictive power of numbers, each of the following numbers is written as if you are experiencing them in the present, whether for a day or a month or an extended period of time.

Again: If the number you are examining is a permanent fixture in your life, for instance from your birth pattern, then translate that definition from a temporary experience into a lifetime experience.

***

TAROT KEY 1: THE MAGICIAN

1 THE MAGICIAN consciously fixes his attention on a specific goal and through sheer will, using his body as a channel, directs the divine life force into the material world where the goal becomes a reality.

Cycle Number 1: new beginnings, independence, self-centering, change, decisions, new goals, courage to act, make a stand

THE MAGICIAN.

Here you stand, alone in the world, born anew as it were. This is the beginning of a brand-new cycle in your life, and you wonder what in the world you are going to do . . . how you are going to make it on your own. You feel alone, but this doesn't necessarily mean lonely. Though you can be surrounded by family and other people, you still feel a sense of isolation and aloneness. This is a necessary attitude on your part because it is time to center your energies, concentrate your will, and think very hard about yourself and your place in the world and what you are going to do in the coming cycles.

Decisions must be made, decisions that will determine your course for some time to come. That is why you are feeling alone. You must be free from outside distractions, cares, requirements, and demands so that you can focus on making those decisions wisely and without interference from others. Therefore, the Higher Forces see to it that you feel removed from the activity around you, however or whatever it takes to accomplish that condition.

This is a new beginning for you, and you feel a strange surge of energy and determination. You know you have to do things yourself because no one will do them for you. And right now you probably don't want anyone to do things for you. You would rather do them yourself.

Tape a sign on your bathroom mirror that says: I come first this year. This will be the first thing you see in the morning and the last thing you see at night. All things being equal . . . are they ever? . . .you do need to come first unless there is an overwhelming need from others.

Defeat is not a word you will accept now. You shut yourself off from outside advice because you feel your own instincts are more accurate. You become centered, concentrating on your own needs and desires and self-expression. You come first now; it is time for number one. You recognize that you are an individual with special needs and, although at other times, you can put your needs last, now they must come first. This is your time.

You are unafraid; at least you will attempt those things now that you might have shuddered at in the past. You become focused, your "eye is single," and you reach out to life in new ways. You try things, pioneer new methods, and examine fresh courses. You begin to exercise your initiative. You find you can draw upon a higher source of power to energize your activities and bring about your desires. There's a sense of unity here as the evolutionary process begins once again.

One important person may come into your life now who acts as a guide, an example, a teacher. You may develop meaningful friendships during this period but you must select your friends carefully because they will be with you for some time to come.

This is an assertive time in your life when you must use your will to accomplish your goals, make yourself heard, speak out, be decisive and unafraid to take a stand, even though it may seem unpopular with those around you. If you feel you are right, then "stand up and be counted." The stand you make now determines the course and perhaps the outcome of your future at least for the next five years and possibly nine years.

You should avoid partnerships and go it alone. This is a time for independence. Be careful that you are not overly aggressive, trampling those around you. Be aware of impulsive moves that you might regret later. You are teeming with energy. Use it wisely.

The number 1 represents the spinal column through which the spinal fluid flows. The kundalini is a coil of energy that rests at the bottom of the spine. According to Hindu philosophy, this energy can be awakened through spiritual development and then moved up the spine activating energy centers in the body. Under the 1, the creative life spark is awakened; the sleeping serpent strikes out on the beginning of its journey.

Geometrically, 1 is the point. Have you got the point? It's time to focus on yourself and your new journey.

MASTER NUMBER CYCLE 55

AN INTENSIFIED 5, A MEMBER OF THE 1 FAMILY: 55/10/1

With the base number one, you stand out in whatever situation in which you are involved when you are under this number. You do this through some form of communication, whether it's through teaching, writing, selling, or just plain pontificating from the mountain top, but always with the assistance of a versatile mind filled with ideas. It is your job to see to it that the "freedom of the press" prevails and endures in this time period. Truth is separated from fiction; the "pen is mightier than the sword." Your mind is your weapon, and ideas are the striking blow.

The 55 practically vibrates with energy; constant motion is the outlet for the changes that you need to announce to the world. You find yourself going in all directions, so it's important to focus on one point at a time so that your fertile mind can explore an idea long enough to give it the energetic push it needs to make an appearance in the world.

Do not scatter your mental energies over so wide an area that they fall on fallow fields. Be a sort of "Johnny Appleseed" who, as the legend goes, scattered apple seeds far and wide but did it with a focused plan. (John Chapman, the late 18th-century pioneer nurseryman, was a leader in conservation. He introduced apples and their importance to a number of states.)

You are a mental gardener during this period, constantly gathering ideas from every quarter, packaging them up as seeds to be distributed to others who will then plant, nurture, and see them into full bloom. You are not in the mood to weed and water, rather you leave that to others. Your job is to gather and distribute, and make sure others are following your lead. This way you implant new ideas that can have major impact.

You are capable of taking multiple courses now because information feeds your desire to know. Your synapses are snapping. You know synapses: those junctions between your nerve cells across which impulses pass in your brain. Well, traffic is heavy and needs a traffic controller, who is you, to avoid traffic jams and to keep the ideas flowing. You know how to scoop up ideas and point them in the right direction.

For instance, you could take a beginners course in marketing, another in cake decorating, and top it off with a gathering of women in your home to discuss money and business, bringing it all together with discussions on how to create a home business from the kitchen with the right marketing tools.

Or you're the new lawyer in a firm layered with established counselors and you're wondering how you're going to fit in when you sight the 55 mph traffic sign ahead (the cycle you're starting) and you step on the gas and your energizing and flexible ideas breeze you past those who are stuck in the break down lane.

Certainly, the 55 shows how you can handle more than one thing at a time. You pull ideas from multiple sources and focus them in one direction, using your mental prowess to make a point. You become the spokesperson for those who may be lost and wondering what they should do with their lives. The 55 opens the door to an entirely new and exciting path way filled with unlimited possibilities.

TAROT KEY 2: THE HIGH PRIESTESS

THE HIGH PRIESTESS.

2 THE HIGH PRIESTESS represents the subconscious mind where all memory is recorded. The curtain behind The High Priestess connects the two columns of light and darkness, and as such indicates pairs of opposites which must be kept in balance.

Cycle Number 2: connections, cooperation, diplomacy, partnerships, sex, reactions, hidden growth, creativity.

As a reaction to the 1's direct, ego-centric action, 2 requires a reactive, calm, waiting attitude. In the 2, you become aware of the needs and desires of others and are concerned with working in unison to bring about harmonious conditions. Situations arise in which you see the duality, the yin and the yang, the negative and the positive. This awareness stimulates discrimination on your part, the need to define and balance. You are the diplomat, sensitive to both sides of the discussion.

Often, being able to see both sides so clearly, you find it hard to make a decision. You may vacillate, preferring to remain in the background, the silent shadows, while others take the lead. However, because you have the ability to discern during this time period, you are the peacemaker, the mediator, or the diplomat who can settle disputes and bring about peaceful settlements. This is a good time for partnerships because you are concerned about the other person's welfare as much as your own.

Where 1 is the will to create, the 2 is the power to nurture that creation. Here artists can find moments of inspiration. The hidden works of the subconscious are active, the energies flow through creative works as well as through telepathic experiences. You are tuned in to the polarities, that delicate sense of balance, the equilibrium of the cosmos. The seeds dropped by number 1 are now stirring beneath the surface and, although hidden at the moment, will soon burst forth. In the meantime, you are the caretaker of those seeds.

You should not make major decisions now because this is a waiting period, while the seeds of number 1 establish themselves firmly in the ground. If affairs seem unstable, fluctuating, and uncertain, it is only because you are meant to wait while nature takes its course. There is a time for action and a time for reaction; this is the period of reaction. You have already sown; now you await the results. Take action only upon those affairs that are absolutely necessary. When you have investigated all the nooks and crannies, then you will find you are able to make informed decisions.

A love affair and sexual connections under a 2 may be unstable with hidden elements involved. Or the relationship can be deeply satisfying if each person is open and attuned to the other's needs. Certainly the 2 implies a coming together, pairs, when two entities seek harmony and balance; therefore, a wonderfully satisfying relationship is possible.

There can be secret energies at work that you are unaware of. Be alert to those who would deceive you. Approach life confidently and with faith, but expect the unexpected. For goodness, return goodness; for "badness," return justice.

Also, be aware that these secret energies activate your instincts and the magical forces that work beneath the surface in preparation for the blossoming of life. Which brings to mind the T-shirt a pregnant woman wore: the arrow pointed down to the message "Under Construction."

2 is the law of polarity. Whenever one force arises, another opposite and equal force arises to meet it. In sacred geometry, 1 is the seed, the point; 2 is an extension of the 1, represented by the extension of that point into a straight line. With the 1 and the 2, the world is preparing to create.

AN INTENSIFIED 1, A MEMBER OF THE 2 FAMILY: 11/2

MASTER NUMBER CYCLE 11

Under this master number, you can expect sudden events, inspiration, unusual circumstances, and legal matters that may arise without warning. Circumstances, arising from out of nowhere, may require decisive action on your part. You may have to make important decisions overnight or on the spot. This is a testing period during which you must balance any inharmonious situations that arise or that already exist.

Under the 11, you relinquish wrong ideas and the negative circumstances in your life, and set about to bring the correct combination of attitudes within yourself that will ensure desirable results in the future. The need for a balanced mind may urge you towards some form of education during this time.

Justice is important so you may feel required to involve yourself in legal situations in order to balance the scales. You could engage in some kind of legal dealings involving the courts or legal counseling. Financial settlements, legacies, wills, accident claims, and sales agreements that occur during the 11 period are bringing to an end unbalanced circumstances that are unsettling your life.

Because the energy of the 11 is tuned into a higher vibration, through the intensity of the doubling of the 1, you may have flashes of intuition, insight, and understanding that will aid you in solving difficult situations. These illuminating flashes may also bring moments of inspiration in which exquisitely beautiful works of art are produced. Wolfgang Mozart was born under an 11 (January 27, 1756).

Avoid being too centered on yourself through the double 1s, but do take a stand. Use your charisma, your electric personality, to inspire others. Be the diplomat.

Lightning, an illuminating flash from the heavens, casts light on the darkened world beneath. Just so, the lightning flashes of your 11 period can cast light, awareness, on you. This comes in the form of an "aha" moment, or public recognition for some act or work long forgotten or a project you are working on at the moment for which you never expected recognition.

This 11 period is quick, exciting, and totally unexpected. Your entire body may feel highly electrified. You are the magician, reaching on high, and channeling the highly charged energy from above.

The 11 stands as two upright columns found traditionally representing the female and male principles of equality in the temples of old. It represents the perfect equilibrium you should strive for within yourself, balancing the yin and yang. Through the 11, you are presented with imbalance so that through testing you can find that perfect equilibrium.

TAROT KEY 3: THE EMPRESS

3 THE EMPRESS is that part of the subconscious mind that responds to the memory of The High Priestess and produces growth through imagination. She is pictured as pregnant; the landscape around her is blooming as well. She is the activity behind all manifestation.

THE EMPRESS.

Cycle Number 3: expansion, growth, freedom, creativity, activity, long distance travel, luck

You need room to move and express yourself freely now, experiencing life and freedom and the joy of living. All the experiences you encounter during a 3 have one purpose . . . to help you grow and expand your horizons. If a long trip to another part of this land or another country will do the job, then the opportunity for such a trip will present itself.

You will meet people who will enlarge your idea of the world and your role in it. Positive feedback will encourage you to speak out and express yourself as never before. Since this cycle is social, you may be invited to parties, engagements, and various pubic functions where you suddenly become the center of attention. People will notice you. Because of this new exposure, you become more aware of your appearance, and may decide to indulge in a new wardrobe, hairstyle, and consider other body-enhancing treatments, even though this is not your usual habit.

Now is the time that you need to look well because your appearance will make a difference with those you contact. You have a new image and those around you will take notice. You may take elocution or acting lessons, or get involved in other activities that will help you express yourself more eloquently.

This could be a lucky period in your life. If you feel that it is, buy that sweepstakes ticket—you just need one to win—or try for the big bingo pot. Enter every free contest and buy those one-dollar tickets from your local organizations. Money as well as material winnings can start flowing in now. Because you feel "lucky," you send out positive energies which, following the law of cause and effect, draw positive results back to you.

As an expansive period, 3 brings growth and fertility in all areas of your life. If you are in the child-bearing years, the birth of a child is certainly possible. Or the baby could be a creation of your mind through an artistic pursuit. Everything is growing now; the life force is bursting forth.

Enthusiasm and optimism and joy are attitudes you express freely; they help you mix business with pleasure. Some of the people you meet socially can turn out to be important business contacts in the future.

Be careful that the optimism and expansion of this period does not lead you towards extravagance, overindulgence, and wastefulness. Then, loss of money and material possessions can result. The danger of this period is spreading your creative energies in too many directions, thus depleting their effectiveness. Indulgence in food and drink can cause obesity, so be careful that your body does not expand along with your bank account. Also, don't be so overly confident that you stretch yourself and your resources beyond their elasticity.

3 is a fundamental creative force in nature—"things happen in 3s." For example, length, breadth, and width; the 3-dimensional world; the primary colors of red, yellow, and blue; the head, trunk, and limbs of the human body; the past, present, and future; and so on.

The concept of the trinity is universally recognized: Mother-Father-Child.

In geometry, the triangle is the first perfect form that can be created with the straight line which emanates from the number 2. The first three numbers—1, 2, and 3—the point, the straight line, and the triangle—are the geometry behind the creative pattern of the material world. "Things happen in threes."

MASTER NUMBER CYCLE 66

AN INTENSIFIED 6, A MEMBER OF THE 3 FAMILY: 66/12/3

Love is intensified; it's in the air, everywhere. The love, devotion to family and justice, and the need for beauty in all its forms is intensified under the 66. While under this influence, the purpose here is to dedicate yourself to these issues so that you can uplift those you touch in positive ways.

During this period, beautify your home environment in ways that bring out the creative nature of life. This does not require spending money necessarily, just requires that you spend emotion, expressing the love you feel for those in your life. Set the mood with flowers on the table and lighted candles in the evening, soft music, and a gentle touch on the shoulder. Let those you love know you love them. A gesture, a smile, can reach inside someone's heart as they go out the door and change their whole day, and perhaps that ripple will change their entire life.

Spend your 66 time period doing kind deeds. One kind act or gesture can multiply . . . pay it forward. Paying the toll for someone in the car behind you can change her day; smiling at a harried wait person in a restaurant can lift her spirits. Kind words can set up effects that you may never know but they will bloom. Mother Teresa said: "If you can't feed a hundred people, then just feed one."

Justice issues touch you more deeply during this period, to the point where you feel you have to stand up and be counted. Stretched out in an easy chair with the remote in one hand, a beer in the other hand, and complaining about the injustices in the world doesn't cut it now. You see what is happening and you feel the urge to be a voice of change. It could be posting your opinion on a blog, writing letters to or emailing your representatives, or joining with others in a groundswell of demands for positive change.

Your sense of beauty and proportion is heightened now. Everyone has some talent; find yours. Go back to your easel, pick up the brush, and let the paint flow over the canvas; plant yourself at your desk and let your "fingers doing the walking" on the keyboard; pull out the pans and spices, and reinvigorate that recipe you were working on; rework the plans for your summer garden; dig into those crafts you stuffed in the closet. Or involve yourself in beautifying your neighborhood or town.

Now is the time you can find the inspiration that seemed to be lacking in the past. This process can bring you great joy.

If your profession is in the field of beauty, you could use your talents to give facials, new hair styles, and tips on body care to underprivileged women in your state or even in third-world countries. There is nothing like a beauty makeover to make a woman feel like she matters, like someone cares. 66 is all about caring.

When you feel joyful, you spread that joy to others. It's contagious. Never underestimate the power of love as a moving force that grows and expands exponentially. Master number 66 gives you the opportunity to learn that, indeed, love conquers all.

TAROT KEY 4: THE EMPEROR

4 THE EMPEROR symbolizes reason, which is a function of the conscious mind. He brings cohesion of the first three keys of will, balance, and growth. He produces concrete results. In his wisdom, he handles the affairs of the material world in a systematic and orderly manner.

Cycle Number 4: work, organization, foundations, money, budgeting, health and healing, enjoyment of the physical, "work is love made visible."

THE EMPEROR.

This is a period of work on the material plane. You have such an urge to organize your life that you may begin by cleaning the attic, the cellar, the closets, your desk drawers and office, the garage, and the shed. No corner is safe from your organizing energy. The overriding need to build strong secure foundations in your life drives you to clean up your environment and put it in order.

Your subconscious takes in suggestions from what it hears you say and what it sees every day. If you live in a mess, your subconscious thinks that's the way you want things to be, so it sets about to create a "mess" in other areas of your life as well. Under the 4, you sense this truth and are driven to clean your thoughts and your physical living area. Once your subconscious sees order and is convinced that this is what you really want, it sets about to bring order to all levels of your life.

Emphasis under the 4 is on material things. You desire money and possessions now because they add to your sense of security and satisfy your heightened physical desires and needs. You may purchase good and services and then realize you need to set up a budget to make payments.

Land and property and building and remodeling come under this vibration, so you may seek to purchase and/or beautify these areas. But you should be economical and practical now; organizing your funds carefully and wisely. Take care of your money and it will take care of you.

Your body is your home as well and, after that potentially disastrous expansive 3 cycle, you body may have expanded along with your mind and income. So out come the sweats, the diet book, and the bathroom scales, or you choose to go to the gym or join a weight loss program to tone up, flatten, and lose.

Since all your physical senses are heightened, your sexual relationships can be rewarding and physically stimulating. You are aware of sensations now that are often muted under other cycles.

The sense of touch is highlighted under the physical 4. Recent studies show that naked skin-to-skin contact of new born babies with their mothers helps the transition from the womb into the outside world, and affords babies at risk a higher percentage of survival. So, use your sense of touch to stimulate your contact with the physical world.

This can be a money cycle—money that comes to you in direct proportion to the effort you have expended. Some might call this lucky money although I don't believe there is such a thing as luck. Somewhere along the line, you earned it, even if you have forgotten those past deeds. I recall a line that goes something like: If you go back far enough, coincidence becomes inevitable. There is cause and effect, so when you see the effect, it came from a cause. 4 money is earned money; you work, you get paid.

4 is also law and order. I know of one case where a woman was called to jury duty in a 4 cycle. 4 is also a doorway to worldly success and the acquisition of material possessions, or a window to heaven where insight, perception, and finely tuned senses reveal the essence of life, the beauty of life in all its forms.

Avoid putting yourself into too much debt to satisfy your desire for material possessions. You can be stubborn, tenacious, and overly sensitive about these issues in this cycle. Do not become a prisoner bound to your earthly needs. Enjoy them, own them, but do not let them own you.

In geometry, 4 is the square, the second perfect form that can be created with straight lines. 4 is the foundation stone upon which the temple not made with human hands (which is the human body) is built. We say, the four corners of the Earth even though the Earth has no corners. Each year has four seasons. The Christian Bible states that the Earth was created on the 4th day. Wherever we find the 4, we are connecting with the material world.

AN INTENSIFIED 2, A MEMBER OF THE 4 FAMILY: 22/4

22 is the master builder. With a base number of 4 representing the physical plane, you are now in a position of power and strength through the ability to negotiate peaceful solutions to problems through the 22. The 22 brings things full circle. Power can be placed in your hands to control an enterprise, business, or organization. This is influence on the physical plane; your energies can manifest in supreme accomplishments. You have already put in the necessary work, gaining the experience to handle whatever rewards will come your way. The training and testing is over; the exercise of leadership begins now, if you have earned it.

Travel may be part of this cycle but not for pure enjoyment as much as for business reasons. Of course, business for some is pure enjoyment.

You may find yourself removed from friends and the people you usually associate with because of your newly acquired position. Often a period of isolation, silence, and solitude accompany this vibration. It's as if you need the quiet time to discover how well you can handle the power that has been handed to you.

This is a time to think big, plan big, and dare great deeds, always with both feet planted firmly on the ground and one eye on the bank account. Be practical, but dare to dream and use your dreams efficiently.

It's as if you are now finely tuned, with your finger on the material pulse of society. You have a sort of x-ray vision, a depth of insight that might frighten others if they knew because it is almost a supernatural awareness. Use your reason and intuition hand-in-hand to build your empire. Rely on your past experiences as guides because you are ready for the job. Listen to the advice of those you respect and who are "in the know," then carefully screen the results.

When the pressure becomes too much, avoid retreating and going within to hide where it feels safe. This action will waste your ability to build something important now. Use your inner strength and awareness to overcome any obstacles.

An uncanny supply of physical endurance and strength is supplied when the going gets tough and, as a great coach once said, that's when the tough get going. And right now, that is you. You will not allow obstacles to defeat you. You have a goal in mind and you pursue it intensely, without a sideways glance. You now have a one-track mind and a full-powered locomotive to direct you toward your destination.

22 holds a unique position in metaphysical literature. The ancients used it as the symbol for the circle. Pi, a mathematical constant

often expressed as 22/7, is used to determine the ratio of a circle to its diameter. Beyond mathematics, it is found in number theory, statistics, fractals, electromagnetism, and much more. Because it is widely known inside and outside the scientific community, the number is celebrated on Pi Day, which is March 14. The first three numbers of Pi are 314.

22 is indeed a magical number.

TAROT KEY 5: THE HIEROPHANT

THE HIEROPHANT.

5 THE HIEROPHANT represents true intuition based on inner hearing and reason. The triple crown symbolizes the conscious, subconscious, and superconscious minds. The Hierophant is the teacher and seeker of facts which are then assimilated, sorted, and sent back for correct analysis as conventional knowledge.

Cycle Number 5: communication, activity, decisions, change, sexual magnetism

You are so busy now that you don't know which end is up. You are totally involved in the activities of life—meetings, errands, answering mail and phone calls, texting, making arrangements, attending parties and public functions. All of a sudden everyone needs you; you feel as if you are on a merry-go-round.

You are in the midst of a flurry of communication. You meet many people and become involved in various activities because you are in a changing cycle. You need these experiences so that you have enough information available to make the decisions that eventually have to be made. A variety of experiences are important now, and change will be the end result.

This period is a turning point in your life when the revolving doors in your life allow you to look at your life up to this point and to decide if you like the direction in which you are heading. If you are dissatisfied with the status quo, then this is the time to do something about it. Find a way by reaching out to people, listening to the conversations around you, joining a group that interest you; even a news item may click and send you on the path to a new experience that can clarify your direction.

The 5 indicates a time to rethink all your options by first examining how you got to this point, and now it's time to decide how to continue on your path.

Paths will open through the many encounters you experience now; therein, you will find solutions. You might call this a "tweaking" cycle when you can think back to the decisions you made about four years ago, and, if you desire, you can nudge them in a different direction.

You feel restless, which keeps you on the move. You want to get into the mainstream of life and be doing and living. You don't want to miss anything. Staying home night after night is not an option.

Your curiosity is heightened so you may decide to take courses in order to satisfy your need for more experience and education. New interests continually pop up, enticingly.

Under this 5 vibration, you are sexually magnetic. Others in your life suddenly "discover" you, and your calendar is filled. You are the life of the party, surrounded by admirers. All this activity may require traveling, certainly locally. Your wheels will be rolling in an endless stream of places to go and things to do. Be careful you do not deplete not only your gas tank but your own fuel reserves.

Your nervous system is highly activated so you should avoid alcohol and drugs; be careful of accidents when you feel stressed. Do not waste these wonderful energies through superficial activities and in meaningless relationships. Resist temptations that are forbidden, whatever that means in your philosophy.

The pentagram, or 5-pointed star, is the symbol for the number 5. The pentagram represents the human body, standing erect, with feet apart and arms stretched out to either side. 5 also represents the five senses. 5 is the central digit in the 1 though 9 series. As such, it has been called "the keystone in the arch of the structure of life."

AN INTENSIFIED 7, A MEMBER OF THE 5 FAMILY: 77/14/5

MASTER NUMBER CYCLE 77

Your mind is calling and you'd better make time for it. Even though you have other things to attend to, you must slow down and smell the roses. You have gathered so much information and experience at this point that you have to allot periods of time when you can sort things out. Remember the 7-year itch?

Claude Debussy said: "Music is the space between the notes." Sting paraphrased this by stating: "Music is the silence between the notes."

It is said that some of the best musicians leave enough space between the notes for your mind to fill in the melody you think you hear. That which is not drawn by an artist makes a statement by its empty space. Comedians know that "timing is everything," and that pauses, that empty time between words, is necessary for the desired effect.

This period of time is calling for large blocks of "pause time" when you retreat from the demands of the outside world when you can curl up in a quiet corner with books that feed your intellectual curiosity or camp alone deep amongst "the murmuring pines and hemlocks" or shelter in a cove by the shores of a lagoon. Keep a journal and plenty of pens at hand because your mind is working overtime, wondering about this and that, making lists them crossing them out, drawing illustrations, doodling, meditating, and generally giving your mind the "space" to think, the silence between the notes, while your body rests.

Post a "Do Not Enter" sign on your private space . . . even if it's the furnace room. Stephen King wrote *Carrie* on an old typewriter while wedged in the furnace room of his small trailer.

Find your spot; make it your own during this thought provoking period. Hang garlic over the door if necessary in order to keep the vampires out, those who would drain your energy. You might as well because your mind won't let you rest until you give it "pause." It's better than tossing and turning in bed all night.

The purpose of this intensified period is to formulate your thoughts so that you can eventually articulate them through your ability to speak, write, make decisions, and generally deal with the changes that are happening in your life . . . all from an informed state of mind.

These periods of quiet time provide you with the opportunity to examine your skills and how you should best use them. Reflect on those things you always wanted to do or become. Take courses that can bring those dreams into reality. And listen to your dreams; write them down. You have an enormous creative playground waiting there for you during this period. Your dreams will guide you toward perfecting your skills.

The goal of this period is to spend large periods of time thinking, contemplating, and perfecting what you already know so that it can be shared through your inborn ability to communicate: writing, teaching, lecturing, and perhaps even in general daily conversations that affect other people's lives in ways you may never know.

6THE LOVERS represent the union of opposite but complementary elements, the active and reactive forces of nature. The Lovers have the ability to discriminate by separating the true from the false. The male looks to the female who looks to the angel for higher guidance to unity and wholeness.

TAROT KEY 6:
THE LOVERS

THE LOVERS.

Cycle Number 6: love, beauty, justice, home, family, community, peace, and war

During this cycle, the emphasis is usually on the home and family. There will be changes on the domestic front. Family members may enter or leave the home. Children go off to school or get married. Babies are born. Relatives need financial assistance; they may move in with you temporarily. Responsibilities at home increase when family may need your emotional support.

You are so tuned in now to treating most everything in your life in a fair and balanced manner that others, sensing this, come to you for help in settling their differences. Others seek your advice; it seems everyone from family members to neighbors to the clerk at the check-out counter is crying on your shoulder, telling you their problems. You become Mother Confessor. Keep a thick towel handy.

You may also find that your sense of responsibility extends beyond the family into your community through beautification of the town, joining the school board, or involvement in town or state politics where you can bring justice and unity to those structures, all because of your love and desire to make things better for everyone. You may engage in your local social services providing for those less fortunate, all because of your need to restore your inner need for balance and harmony.

6 is the number of advantageous partnerships with the opposite sex and therefore rules unions. After the number 5 cycle of sexual magnetism, in which you had an opportunity to experience relationships with a variety of individuals, you may have selected a mate and now decide to settle down and establish your own home. 6 seeks balance at the very roots of your being, manifesting in establishing your home and an important relationship, and finding that peace within yourself.

Beauty becomes important. Your sense of artistic proportion is sensitized therefore you recognize the symmetry and beauty in art. You may remodel or redecorate your home because you need to bring harmony into your environment. Feng Shui could interest you as you seek to create a positive flow through your home. Then you turn to your personal home, your body, and decide it needs attention: perhaps a new wardrobe, with attention paid to facials, makeup, hairstyle . . . and even thoughts of a tuck here and a tuck there.

If balance is not restored, then separations occur. On a personal level, the home and close relationships may suffer because differences are irreconcilable. On a national level, this can result in war. A man engaged in war games as a hobby told me that during the Middle Ages, most wars occurred under 6s. I haven't checked this out but certainly the 1960s decade was one of love and war.

Metaphysically, 6 is associated with two interlaced equilateral triangles, one pointing up and the other pointing down. This symbol is also known as the Great Yantra, the blending of the female and male energies in perfect balance. It's also called the Philosopher's Stone, and the Star of David, amongst other designations.

MASTER NUMBER CYCLE 33

AN INTENSIFIED 3, A MEMBER OF THE 6 FAMILY: 33/6

The master number 33 often requires sacrifice, compassion, and martyrdom on some level. Since it is the higher side of 6, it elevates those qualities of love, mercy, and sacrifice. There is an intensification of understanding, love, compassion, forgiveness, tolerance, and service through positive uplifting expressions.

Home and family members may need services beyond what you believe you are physically and emotionally capable of giving, but you find the strength through a positive mind set knowing that the future will be better. Like Annie, the sun will come out tomorrow becomes your mantra.

That demand could also come from a world-wide humanitarian group or organization that needs your time, effort, and total dedication, which you feel compelled to offer. This may require sacrifices by leaving home to travel to Third-World countries, where the need is so desperate.

You gather your deep faith to give freely and willingly if the request is truly for the overall good, trusting that it is not a wasteful act on your part. Only the most urgent causes should be attended to because you need to be selective if your energies are not to fall on fallow earth and wither.

The double 3s give you the optimism, enthusiasm, and energy to get the job done in the most creative manner possible because, surely, you are brimming with ideas that will burst forth into bloom and delight those around you: a beautifully crafted hummingbird snow globe beside a hospital bed; a flower bed resembling a golden retriever puppy planted on the town green to the delight of children and adults; or the single mom who, in her struggle to support her three children, carves a cupcake empire with the recipe handed down from her great-grandmother, and then donates ten percent of her profits to children in need in honor of her great-grandma.

Look to your inner courage for help in accepting responsibilities that may be heaped upon you, and for the enthusiasm and good will to keep you going. Once you have selected the proper cause, be steadfast in the face of opposition because, surely under this number, cause and effect will reward you in great measure.

The master number 33 may also be associated with the two interlaced triangles, the Great Yantra, which draws energy from above through the upper triangle and from below through the lower triangle, uniting heaven and earth into a compassionate mindset that knows no fuel shortage.

7 **THE CHARIOTEER** is the soul directing the Chariot, the body. It is through a quiet and receptive state that the mind within is activated. Mind controls matter. Without the use of reins, The Charioteer mentally controls the black and white sphinxes who are half-man and half-beast.

TAROT KEY 7: THE CHARIOT

THE CHARIOT.

Cycle Number 7: rest, perfection, health, analysis, thinking, "7-year itch"

Take a nap.

You may feel more tired than usual and may not want to socialize. You do need time to be alone, to think, meditate, and reflect, so these moments by yourself will set the mood. It's the perfect time for a vacation, a weekend at the mountains or by the sea, or just being left alone in your home. You would rather be alone, or at least with just a few people who are in tune with your contemplative nature. 7 is a time to rest.

Outer activity and interests will cease, or at least slow down considerably. Maintain these outside duties at minimal levels because the energy is now being transferred to the inner realms of the mind. You will do a lot of necessary thinking now as gathered experiences are analyzed. This is a pause in you life cycles during which you need to think and become conscious of your spiritual side, the inner stirrings of your soul. You have done enough outside work for the time being. Now let nature take her course.

Set material worries aside. The things you have been worrying about will mysteriously take care of themselves. You are not to push your affairs or assert your energies in order to accomplish worldly goals. If you persist in these attempts, you can become ill. The Higher Forces say stop, look, and listen. If you do not heed them, they will place you where you have to listen—perhaps in a sick bed. So slow your pace and take care of your health.

This introspective period is the time to perfect the skills you already have. Take a course to polish your talents. Or enroll in a philosophical or metaphysical course, such as yoga, astrology, or numerology, amongst others. Your intuition is in high gear. Dreams, visions, and telepathic experiences are all possible as you delve into the mystical side of life.

7 brings attainment and completion on the physical level. The efforts you have expended in past cycles can bring rewards now that may not be material, although they can be. 7 is the number of perfection, and it is here that you need to feel some sense of accomplishment through your personal efforts.

This is the "7-year itch." You analyze your past cycles, think about your present conditions, and look forward to learn how you can change things for the better in the future. Your mind is your strength now. Use it to overcome any negative conditions in your life by concentrating on the power of positive thinking.

But do avoid becoming so reclusive that you shut yourself off from everyone. Watch your health. Rest, pace yourself, eat well, and sleep wisely. If signing any legal documents, check the fine print: cross the "t"s and dot the "i"s. Again, 7 demands perfection.

7 has always been considered the spiritual number. Hepta, the Greek word for 7, means holy, divine, and motherless. 7 is perfection (a combination of 3, the triangle, + 4, the square) and is reflected through the seven colors in the rainbow. We associate 7 with the seven original planets, the seven holes in the human head, the seven white keys on the musical scale, the seven days of the week, the seven days of creation, and so on. As I write in the chapter "Thoughts From My Notebook," "7 and 9 seem to defy geometrical definition, expect in figures that are difficult to construct: e.g., the 7- or 9-pointed stars." The 7 represents the pattern of creation; the 9 is the completion of the cycle preparing for a change.

AN INTENSIFIED 8, A MEMBER OF THE 7 FAMILY: 88/16/7

Double up on the power, sex, and money now, but do keep it a secret. Do I have your attention? Along with power, sex, and money comes the key word: responsibility. This master number reflects the power behind the throne. The last few paragraphs of the single number 8 (which follows) reveal the metaphysical power of 8. Double that power and you are in the driver's seat, but it isn't a Volkswagen; you're being chauffeured in the presidential limo with smoky, black privacy windows. Well, maybe not the presidential limo, but something close to it.

The double 8 means double responsibility to take charge of any enterprise in which you are involved in any field—home, work, or business.

The efforts of past planning, organization, along with the confidence you exuded, brings you now to a point where success is almost in your hands. You can get the job done, a job that influences others on a large scale through a big project or undertaking. However, as stated, this is a contemplative period, which requires just a bit more planning to perfect that which you already know. With preparation, you can be the master entrepreneur, builder of companies and cities.

The 7 demands you think your brilliant plans through to their conclusion. The key word is *think* the plans through. Because this cycle is about how your thoughts create reality, your thoughts create the pattern that precedes the architectural structures that will result.

You don't want recognition. You prefer to be ensconced in the limo's back seat surrounded by darkened windows, like the fictional attorney in the *Lincoln Lawyer*, comfortably continuing to study, plan, and put the finishing touches on the final product or idea that will soon be introduced to the public through the brilliance of your mind.

That's the power and money angle. What about the sex? With power and money, so many other aspects of life are available for the taking. Powerful people are sexual magnets regardless of their physical appearance, with few exceptions. Along with the power that comes off them in waves, they exude sexual pheromones, the chemical factors that trigger responses in others. It's the mating response.

Smell is said to be the most powerful of our five senses. Smell can bring back a memory from childhood, thought long forgotten; it can stimulate sexual responses. Think of the perfume industry whose advertisements, featuring sultry women and bedroom-eyed men, who promise the fulfillment of sexual fantasies.

Yes, power, sex, and money, the triumvirate of the material world, can be yours if you work diligently. There is a caveat, however. You must express your power with love and concern for justice; you must stand up for what's right and then use the powers of your mental creativity to processes and then formulate a plan from which the world can benefit.

8 is the keen sense of balance between the material (8) and spiritual (7) worlds. The figure 8 drawn horizontally is the lemniscates, a mathematical symbol for infinity, the "signature of the universe," the life current that sweeps through the universe, over the Earth and through our bodies, endlessly. 8 is the dragon, the serpent, the kundalini, and the promise of life eternal, which is reincarnation for some. 8 can be drawn over and over without lifting the pen from the paper.

This is the time to put pen to paper and design your architectural dreams.

TAROT KEY 8: STRENGTH

8 STRENGTH is the woman, the subconscious mind, who has control over the lion, the physical body and its functions. Her power over the lion is gentle and mental. The chain of roses uniting the woman and lion show that cultivation (roses need care) of our desires sets up a chain reaction, which eventually produces tangible results.

STRENGTH.

Cycle Number 8: karma, recognition, responsibility, business, finances, sex, strength

8 is the number of material domination. The world of business and finance is governed by the 8. (In 1967, 800 was the first free telephone prefix for consumers to call businesses.)

First of all, if you've ever been in doubt about how effective you are as a moving force in this material world, under the 8 you need doubt no longer. The 8 clearly defines responsibility; karma reigns. This is the law of cause and effect, and you will receive exactly what you deserve.

If you have worked well in the past cycles, this is the time for recognition, rewards, job advancements, raises, and honors. If you have not put the time in or did not recognize opportunities and take them as they came along, you may experience financial loss. This does not mean you are a "failure" but it does indicate that you have not handled your time wisely, and you did not pursue the proper goals towards achievement. Remedy this situation by taking stock of how you can handle your life with more awareness in the future.

But then again, those losses may be the impetus for your advancement into a better and more secure situation. Examine any opportunities that come your way.

You may first feel the effects of this cycle at your job when pressures and responsibilities begin to mount. Your "job" could be the head of a company, a teacher, a salesperson, or a parent raising children. Regardless, more work seems to pile up. Attending to this increased workload, you will eventually be rewarded because your character will shine through. Additional monies may result from your efforts.

Since 8 is a karmic number, you could receive an inheritance or win a lottery—all ultimately the result of positive efforts on your part in the past. You could be a waiter who greeted an old woman every morning with a smile, a friendly conversation, and a cup of hot water while she pulled out her own tea bag. She orders nothing, sitting by herself at the end of the counter. A few years later, you wonder why she hasn't been in. Then you receive a substantial inheritance from this woman whom you never realized was quite wealthy. Your kindness has been rewarded. What goes around, comes around, as they say.

You may desire intense sexual relationships now. Imagine the 8th sign of the zodiac, Scorpio, and its deep sexual needs and its loyalty to its partner. The way the 8 is drawn suggests a need for balance and equality, as both equally sized circles join in the center indicating a coming together, a union of equality.

Because 8 represents the three-dimensional physical world, sex is one outlet. The pure physical enjoyment of the relationships must be experienced. The union must be spiritually fulfilling as well (the circles in the drawing of the 8 represent the joining of the body and the soul, spirit and matter). This relationship can be heaven on Earth because you and your partner feel a responsibility to love and support each other on all levels.

As mentioned, the 8 can bring a loss of material possessions and resources. Base materialism can overcome an individual who then launches a power drive that crushes all who get in the way. There can be deliberate blindness to the suffering of others, and displays of cruelty because the individual is driven by the fear of poverty and loss.

The dense mineral, salt, crystallizes in cubes. We say we are "the salt of the earth." The geometrical symbol for the 8 is the cube, and metaphysically, the cube represents the Earth and all things that have blossomed from the 4 pattern into the three-dimensional world of material form. The Christian cross folds into a cube; symbolically being crucified on the cross is a metaphor for living in the material world, within the limits of the physical body, with all that entails.

With the 8, you are strong and you have the power!

MASTER NUMBER CYCLE 44

AN INTENSIFIED 4, A MEMBER OF THE 8 FAMILY: 44/8

The master number 44 requires dedicated service to the Earth, productivity, and material progress. It presents opportunities on a large scale. Karma rules here big time. You are given the opportunity to re-evaluate your present conditions and the events that brought you to this point. You begin to think about the processes that brought you the rewards you may now be receiving. Opportunities come out of nowhere and your stores can increase. You may be tempted to sit back and relax. This attitude would be a mistake because you now have the opportunity to accomplish so much on the material plane. Friends can be a big help in you work.

If you feel your progress is blocked you should examine your methods of operation, your attitude, and your philosophy about your efforts to get ahead in the world. By doing so, you may find the missing link, the one thing that seems to hinder your progress. You begin to question your values and goals, and you look for answers that can put your world together more effectively. Your intuitions are especially keen as you search for the link between the material and the spiritual worlds.

You find the answers during this period through offering yourself in service to others through practical means. Advice and counseling are one way to heal but this must come through common sense and a "let's work this out now" attitude, not some intellectual fantasy that says in your next lifetime you will be happy. Your practical, no-nonsense advice could have widespread influence.

Khalil Gibran wrote: "Work is love made visible. And if you cannot work with love but only with distaste, it is better that you should leave your work and sit at the gates of the temple and take alms of those who work with joy." This is the master number 44!

The 44 requires you to strengthen your body along with your ethics and purpose.

This strong physically healing number must be approached one step at a time. Slow and easy does win this race. Slow your pace, and be aware of all bodily sensations: Let your body speak to you. You need a strong body to fulfill the work you must perform.

Master number 44 is the number that requires you approach your service to others with joy, and in ways that ease their physical burdens. Through practical, down-to-earth methods and types of work, you reveal the goodness that the physical world has to offer others. You might raise a group of volunteers to work with the sick or the mentally challenged; help build houses for the poor; or teach a family to grow gardens whose vegetables feed not only them but others along the way; or organize groups to build an animal shelter. You are now tapped into organizational skills that need to be exercised in order to help others fulfill their earthly destinies.

The key to a successful use of this master number 44 is to approach all matters with a calm, patient determination, and then work to produce material results that have healing effects upon others. In this way, you offer others the opportunity to live healthy happy lives.

TAROT KEY 9: THE HERMIT

9 THE HERMIT represents the achievement of wisdom as he stands on the mountain of attainment. He has made the arduous climb to the top where he has gained mastery of himself, and he now turns to shine his light of wisdom for those who would follow.

Cycle Number 9: endings, transition, charity, wisdom

THE HERMIT.

It's time to let go. This is a cleansing period in which those things that are no longer necessary in your life must be relinquished. Situations that are used up, worn out, useless in relation to your growth at this moment must be released in order to make room for the new starts in your life. Since you don't always know what you need and what you do not need, higher forces step in and remove any blocks to your future growth.

People may leave your life, children grow and move on, some relationships have completed their cycle, job changes require relocation, and things to which you are attached may have to be given up. The status quo is upset.

This can be an emotionally trying experience if change and transition are difficult for you. You may need time alone to sort out the pieces, to converse with your inner self. Do some serious house-cleaning—physically and emotionally. If endings occur under a 9, it's because there is something new just around the bend. When one door closes, another opens.

Use some of your time to perform charity work. You have gathered much from the past cycles, and in this final phase, you should give back to the universe some part of what you have gained. This is tithing time. Your giving is a demonstration of your faith in the unending flow from the cornucopia of life. When you give, you physically demonstrate that you do not fear not having, because you are wiling to give, knowing that life will supply you abundantly. You should not work alone now but rather with others for a common good.

Be sympathetic, compassionate, understanding, and loving to those you encounter in this cycle. Old friendships are especially meaningful and heartwarming, and new relationships can develop. Gifts and favors my come your way. You should observe this cycle closely. Many of your goals have been accomplished, and you should finish any that are still in process. Much wisdom can gained through observation.

Some people become overly emotional, refusing to listen, reason, or understand. They cling to those things that they can no longer have thereby prolonging a transitional period that could have passed more smoothly.

The Greeks compared 9 to the ocean, constantly flowing around the other 8 numbers. Pythagoras said it was the symbol of constantly changing matter. The Christian Bible expresses the 9 in Revelations as the number of the beast (666/18/9) as well as the number of the saved (144,000/9), both manifestations of the human condition in flux.

9, as the final digit in the series 1 through 9, is boundless, eternally reproducing itself. Multiplied by another number, it returns to itself: 2 x 9 = 18/9; 4 x 9 = 36/9, 256 x 9 = 2,034/9. The 360 degrees in a circle reduces to a 9, and the circle returns to itself.

When 9 is added to a number, that number returns to itself:
9 + 7 = 16/7; 9 + 24 = 33/6 (24 = 6); 9 + 320 = 329/14/5 (320 = 5).

9 is the "whole nine yards." It is evidence of eternal recycling and the promise that the ending is the beginning. 9 is The Hermit standing on the mountain top, holding the light of wisdom to show the way but only for those with eyes to see.

MASTER NUMBER CYCLE 99

AN INTENSIFIED 9, A MEMBER OF THE 9 FAMILY: 99/18/9

This is the master number par-excellence. Just as The Hermit in the Tarot stands on the mountain top shining the light of knowledge for those who would follow, this number gathers accumulated knowledge into a sea of wisdom.

99 knows the difference between knowledge and wisdom. Knowledge indicates a gathering of facts that the mind sorts into pockets from which those facts can be drawn at the appropriate time. The individual with a good memory can draw upon these separate pockets of facts when necessary. We often think someone is smart because they have a good memory. That may or may not be true. An intelligent person can use those facts in a sensible manner. Intellect is of the mind.

Wisdom, on the other hand, is to go beneath the surface of the facts to learn the deeper meaning of those separate facts, and then understand how to apply these meanings in ways that embrace humanity with understanding and compassion. The individual who digs beneath the surface to find meanings becomes the Light Bearer for those who are searching for meaning beyond the obvious material world.

Master number 99 must learn that the light cannot be forced upon others. Those others must be ready and have the eyes to see. Only then, can the master number 99 lead others towards the light of wisdom.

In one of D. W. Buffa's novels (writing as Lawrence Alexander), a character says: ". . . the problem is that people make the mistake of believing that the aim of intelligence is the expansion of knowledge rather than the depth of understanding."

When I read that line, I felt a chill go up my spine. That one line, spoken by a fictional character in a novel, is the clearest definition of wisdom that I have ever heard. I communicated with the author to tell him how profoundly that definition affected me.

As mentioned earlier, the number 9, multiplied by another number, always returns to itself. $9 \times 2 = 18/9$; $9 \times 4 = 36/9$; and so on. The number 9 means that you have to live your beliefs; you have to be an example for others. Just as the 9 multiplied returns to itself, what you do and say comes back to you. This is not a time when you can preach one thing and privately do the opposite because you will be "outed." Live your words; be an example of your philosophy in life. This message is doubly important under the master number 99.

Master number 99 embodies the "depth of understanding." 99 may be those experiences in your life that "passeth all understanding."

Years ago, I took a badly needed nap before my children came home from school. I settled down on the bed, nestled into the pillow, and closed my eyes. A few moments later, I found myself floating high above the Earth. I looked down and saw that I had no physical body; my body was made of pure light. The feeling of ecstasy was so overwhelming and fulfilling that I knew there was nothing else; I was whole. This was all that mattered. Words are a poor substitute for what I felt.

For me, that was a 99 moment. And perhaps that's what the 99 means, moments of pure light.

AND IN CONCLUSION . . .

EACH INDIVIDUAL LANGUAGE EXPRESSES THE TRUTH of any "word" through its numerical vibrations for the people who speak that language. The Hebrews and Greeks used their language and number codes to express truths just as we use the English language, and Italians use Italian, and Russians use an east Slavic language.

The given number vibrations in each language express how that culture views any words they use. The word "table" in English has a different number vibration from the word "tavola" in Italian because the two cultures see the table in different ways. In the United States, the table is something you pound on at a meeting or drop your school books on as you rush to change your clothes for practice. In Italy, the table traditionally is the focus of the family meal where a few leisurely hours are spent in family communion and discussion of the day's activities.

Each culture expresses its own traditions through its language which is revealed through the numerical vibrations of its language.

Look around you. Observe the message written in nature, in your personal life, in the business world, in your religions, through the symbols and the words. We are unconsciously urged to express the truth in all we think, say, and do. Study the language of geometry and the language of numbers, and you will hear.

Thank you for joining me on this numerological journey. I hope that our combined efforts in this book—my writing it and your reading it—have provided some food for thought. I have had my moments of awareness in its writing and, if you have had your moments of awareness in its reading, then our experience is doubly fruitful. I wish you many 99 moments.

I'D LOVE TO HEAR FROM YOU.

You can reach me at
WWW.DUSTYBUNKER.COM

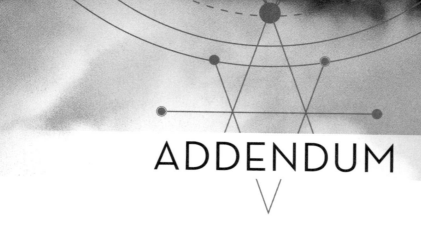

ADDENDUM

V

WHAT FOLLOWS IS THE TRANSLATION OF THE verses from I Corinthians 12: verses 7–11 from the Lamsa Bible by George Lamsa who spoke Aramaic, the original language of the New Testament. These verses are compared to the translations of those same verses by scholars who did not speak the original Aramaic.

THE LAMSA BIBLE

George Lamsa, an Assyrian author, lived 1892–1975. He was brought up in the biblical lands where, up until World War I, Lamsa's homeland was isolated from the outside world. Therefore, he and his people retained the customs, culture, and language of their ancestors. They all spoke the same Aramaic language as Jesus. His translation of the Bible from the original Aramaic is more accurate than the translations of other scholars from different nationalities who had to learn Aramaic before they could translate the Bible from the original manuscripts. Many nuances and subtleties can be lost to a "foreigner" trying to interpret another language. You've heard the expression "lost in translation." See Lamsa's Bible, 1957.

Saint Jerome (340?–420), when publishing the Latin Vulgate version of the Bible, wrote: "When we translate the Hebrew into Latin, we are sometimes guided by conjecture." The Swiss Protestant theologian and scholar, Jean Le Clerc (1657–1736), admitted that "the learned merely guess at the sense of the Old Testament in an infinity of places."

Let's compare Lamsa's translation of these verses with that of two other editions.

The New King James Bible (1982): *The New King James Bible* was translated by a 130-person team, including Greek, Hebrew, and English scholars, editors, church leaders, and Christian laity. One wonders how many of them, if any, spoke the original Aramaic language of Jesus.

The second translation, *The New International Version* (2011): One of the original founders of the movement to translate this version was Howard Long who worked as an engineer at General Electric in Seattle, Washington. I haven't found any proof that anyone connected with this original translation spoke the original Aramaic language of Jesus.

For accuracy in translation, my bet is on George Lamsa!

I CORINTHIANS, CHAPTER 12, V. 7–11

7. But the manifestation of the Spirit is given to every man as help to him.

8. For to one is given by the Spirit the word of wisdom; to another the word of knowledge by the same Spirit.

9. To another faith by the same Spirit; to another gifts of healing by the same Spirit.

10. To another the working of miracles; to another prophecy; to another the means to distinguish the true Spirit; to another different languages; to another interpretation of languages.

11. But all of these gifts are wrought by that one and the same Spirit, dividing to every one severally as he will.

Below is a look at the translations of the passages about gifts of the spirit beginning with the Lamsa Bible (LB) and comparing it with the translations of the New King James Bible (NKJ) and the New International Version (NIV).

VERSE 7:

LB: But the manifestation of the Spirit is given to every man as help to him.

NKJ: But the manifestation of the Spirit is given to each one for the profit of all.

NIV: Now to each one the manifestation of the Spirit is given for the common good.

LB says that Spirit is given to every man to help "him."

NKJ says for the "profit of all."

NIV says for the "common good."

There is a distinction here. LB says specifically *for the individual*; NKJ says f*or the profit of all;* NIV says *for the common good.* The Lamsa Bible states that the manifestation of the Spirit is given specially to each man, individually.

VERSE 8:

LB: For to one is given by the Spirit the word of wisdom; to another the word of knowledge by the same Spirit.

NKJ: For to one is given the word of wisdom through the Spirit, to another the word of knowledge through the same Spirit.

NIV: To one there is given through the Spirit a message of wisdom, to another a message of knowledge by means of the same Spirit.

LB and NKJ are quite close. NIV however changes "word" to "message." There is a big difference.

One definition of "message" is "a verbal, written, or recorded communication sent to or left for a recipient who cannot be contacted directly." One definition of "word" is "a single distinct meaningful element of speech or writing."

"The word of God" has a distinctly different meaning from "the message of God." "Word" has a specific intent that implies importance, depth, intensity, and you'd better listen! Much like when you were a teenager and you were told your mother had left a message for you taped on the refrigerator door. Not too alarming . . . maybe to pick up your clothes and clean your room, or to do your homework. But if your mother wanted a word with you, your ears pricked up, your heart palpitated a little. Now we're talking serious! You see the difference between "message of God" and "word of God."

VERSE 9:

LB: To another faith by the same Spirit; to another gifts of healing by the same Spirit.

NKJ: to another faith by the same Spirit, to another gifts of healings by the same Spirit.

NIV: to another faith by the same Spirit, to another gifts of healing by that one Spirit.

All three versions are the same with the exception of NKJ word "healings," plural.

VERSE 10:

LB: To another the working of miracles; to another prophecy; to another the means to distinguish the true Spirit; to another different languages; to another interpretation of languages.

NKJ: To another the working of miracles, to another prophecy, to another discerning of spirits, to another different kinds of tongues, to another the interpretation of tongues.

NIV: To another miraculous powers, to another prophecy, to another distinguishing between spirits, to another speaking in different kinds of tongues, and still to another the interpretation of tongues.

LB reads "the working of miracles," whereas NIV reads "miraculous powers." To "work" miracles . . . there is the word "work". . . instructs the taking of action whereas having miraculous powers does not imply action, merely the possession of those powers.

LB writes "to another the means to distinguish the true Spirit." Capital "S." The other two versions speak of discerning of spirits and distinguishing between spirits, with a small "s," implying more than one spirit . . . not the true Spirit as spoken of in Lamsa's translation. Big difference there.

VERSE 11:

LB: But all of these gifts are wrought by that one and the same Spirit, dividing to every one severally as he will.

NKJ: But one and the same spirit works all these things, distributing to each one individually as He wills.

NIV: Al these are the work of one and the same Spirit, and he distributes them to each one, just as he determines.

Lamsa's interpretation is that the dividing is done by the person, the individual "he." The NKJ version capitalizes "He," implying that God is male and a figure symbolized in human form in religious paintings. This image does not reflect each individual person.

***

Some of my analyses of the interpretations above may seem subtle, but they can change the context and that of the passages for those who read them, and can change dramatically as each future interpretation by non-Aramaic speakers is built upon its predecessor.

Remember the game of gossip where one person in the circle whispers a message to the person on the left, then that person whispers the same message to the next person on the left, and so on around the circle. When the final person repeats the message out loud, it is entirely different than the one that started.

ENDNOTES

1. DeLubicz, Schwaller, R. A., *The Temple in Man* (New York: Inner Traditions International, 1977), translated by Robert and Deborah Lawlor, translator's foreword, p. 10.

2. *A Brief History of Sound Healing in Ancient Times* . . . templeofsoundandlight.com/soundlightdna/a-brief-history-of-sound-healing-in-ancient-times/.

3. blackbiretta.blogspot.com.

4. Cooper, J. C., *An Illustrated Encyclopedia of Traditional Symbols* (London: Thames and Hudson, 1980), p. 6.

5. Walker, Barbara, *Women's Encyclopedia of Myths and Secrets* (New York: Harper and Row, 1983), pps. 1097–1098.

6. *Color, Psychology and Color Therapy* (Citadel Press, 1950).

7. Ross Wallace, William, (1819–1881), "The Hand That Rocks the Cradle Rules the World."

8. www.artisanpublishers.com/holy-bible-aramaic-translation-george-lamsa-p-25818.html.

9. Utah officers say mysterious voice called them to rescue . . . www.aol.com/article/2015/03/09/how-toddler-survived-14-hours.

10. Abraxas—Gnostic Teachings. gnosticteachings.org/glossary/a/1850-abraxas.html.

11. Bunker, Dusty, *Numerology, Astrology's Hidden Aspects, 2018* (Atglen, PA: Schiffer), p. 31.

12. Higgins, Frank C., *Hermetic Masonry* (Pyramid, 1916). p. 43

13. Ibid., p. 41.

14. Bunker, Dusty, *Numerology, Astrology and Dreams* (Atglen, PA: Schiffer), p. 11.

15. www.leaf.tv/articles/carbon-based-foods-that-humans-eat/.

16. Crockett, James Underwood, *Crockett's Victory Garden*, from PBS television show, 1977.

17. www.crazyfads.com/80s.htm.

18. http://social.rollins.edu/wpsites/filmsofthe80s/2014/05/28/hivaids-in-the-1980s/.

19. https: allthatsinteresting.com/1980s-mafia.

20. www.history.com.

21. Phys.org 5/23/2019.

22. techzooms.com.

23. *Tribune News Service*, May 26, 2019.

24. Thiessen, Marc, *Washington Post*, May 30, 2019.

25. www.cnet.com/news/scientists-achieve-reliable-quantum-teleportation-for-the-first-time/.

26. www.newsbreak.ng/internet-hijacked, March 4, 2019.

27. www.techtechnik.com/possibilities -of-5g/.

BIBLIOGRAPHY

Birren, Faber. *Color Psychology and Color Therapy*. Kessinger Publishing, 1961.

Bunker, Dusty. *Astrology's Hidden Aspects: Quintile and Sesquiquintiles*. Atglen, PA: Red Feather, 2017.

_____. *The Beginner's Guide to Astrology: Class Is in Session*. 2018. Atglen, PA: Red Feather. 2017.

_____. *Dream Cycles*. Atglen, PA: Schiffer, 1981.

_____. *Numerology, Astrology, and Dreams*. Atglen, PA: Schiffer, 1987.

Case, Paul Foster. *The Tarot: A Key to the Wisdom of the Ages*. Richmond, VA: Macoy, 1947.

Crockett, Janes. *Crockett's Victory Garden*. Toronto: Little, Brown, 1977.

De Lubicz, R. A. Schwaller. *The Temple in Man*, Translated by Robert Lawlor. New York: Inner Traditions, 1977.

Encyclopedia Americana. New York: Americana Corporation, 1966.

Ferguson, Marilyn. *The Brain Revolution*. New York: Bantam Books, 1973.

Field, Paul. *50,000 Birthdays*. Richmond, VA: Macoy, 1964.

Golden Home and High School Encyclopedia. New York: Golden Press, 1961.

Gray, Eden. *A Complete Guide to the Tarot*. New York: Bantam Books, 1972.

Gribbin, John R., and Stephen H. Plagemann. *The Jupiter Effect*. New York: Random House, 1976.

1980 Hammond Almanac. Maplewood, NJ: Hammond, 1979.

Heline, Corrine. *Sacred Science of Numbers*. LaCanada, CA: New Age Press, 1971.

Higgins, Frank C. *Hermetic Masonry*. Ferndale, MI: Trismegistus, 1980.

Javane, Faith, and Dusty Bunker. *Numerology and the Divine Triangle*. Rockport, MA: Para Research, 1979.

King James Bible. New York: World Publishing.

L'Amour, Louis. *Education of a Wandering Man*. New York: Bantam Books, 1989.

Lamsa Bible, I Cor. 12:7–11; 13. Philadelphia, PA: A. J. Holman, 1968.

Lesmerurier, Peter. *The Great Pyramid Decoded*. New York: St. Martin's, 1977.

Lucas, Jerry, and Del Washburn. *Theomatics*. New York: Stein and Day, 1986.

Luxton, Leonora. *Astrology, Key to Self-Understanding*. St. Paul, MN: Llewellyn, 1978.

Ogg, Oscar. *The 26 Letters*. New York. Thomas Y. Cromwell, 1948.

Pinker, Steven. *Why Violence Has Declined*. New York: Penguin Random House, 2011.

Random House Dictionary of the English Language. New York: Random House, 1969.

Schmalz, John Barnes. *Nuggets from King Solomon's Mine*. Ferndale, MI: Trismegistus, 1980.

Schneider, Michael S. *A Beginner's Guide to Constructing the Universe: The Mathematical Archetypes of Nature, Art, and Science, A Voyage from 1 to 10*. New York: Harper Perennial, 1951.

Spangler, David. *Revelation: The Birth of a New Age*. Findhorn, Scotland: Findhorn, 1976.

Walker, Barbara. *The Woman's Dictionary of Myths and Secrets*. San Francisco: Harper & Row, 1983.